Anne Boleyn Collection II

Copyright © 2013
MadeGlobal Publishing

ISBN: 978-84-944574-5-6

First Edition: September 2013
Second Edition: October 2015

M
MadeGlobal Publishing

For more information on
MadeGlobal Publishing, visit our website:
www.madeglobal.com

The
Anne Boleyn
Collection II

Dedication

In memory of Eric Ives (1931-2012) whose passion for Anne Boleyn was contagious.

To Tim, Christian, Verity and Joel,
Always and forever.
Xxxx

"If any person will meddle with my cause, I require them to judge the best."

Queen Anne Boleyn, 19th May 1536

Acknowledgements

This book is the result of over four years of research and hard work, but it would never have been published had I not received the ongoing support and encouragement of the following people:

Tim Ridgway, Clare Cherry, Leanda de Lisle, Dawn Hatswell, Roland Hui. Thanks also to Teri Fitzgerald, Olivia Peyton and Gareth Russell.

I would also like to thank the online Tudor community, the historians, bloggers, Facebook pages and Anne Boleyn Files visitors who debate with me, encourage me, give me feedback and who prove that I'm not alone in my Tudor fascination.

ANNE
BOLEYN.

Wide delin.   Walker sculp.

Figure 1 - Anne Boleyn Engraving

Contents

Introduction

My journey into the world of the Boleyns began in January 2009 when I started researching the life of Anne Boleyn. I decided to blog about my research, never dreaming that anyone would read my ramblings, but by summer 2009 I had built up a regular following. I took the step to give up my freelance-writing business and, instead, work full-time on my history research and writing; I've never regretted it. I spend my days, and most weekends, surrounded by books and documents, but history is my passion and I feel blessed to be able to dedicate myself to its study.

I published my first book, *The Anne Boleyn Collection*, in February 2012 (second edition 2015) and was thrilled with the response. It was an unusual book in that it was a collection of articles, rather than a normal history book, and it was also written in a chatty style. I wasn't sure how it would be received, but emails and reviews that said that reading my book was like having a coffee with me and chatting about history proved that readers 'got' what I was trying to do. My aims have always been to get to the truth (or as near to it as possible), to debunk the myths and 'accepted truths' by using primary sources, to challenge perceptions based on fiction, and to share my findings in an understandable way. Much of what I find is open to interpretation and up for debate, but that is what is exciting about history; it's not dead, it's living and breathing. I learn so much by sharing my research and my opinions, and then entering into a debate with visitors to The Anne Boleyn Files. There's nothing better than bouncing ideas off each other.

The Anne Boleyn Collection II is a second volume of articles, but this time they're not just off the website, many of them are previously unpublished pieces based on talks I've done and research I've carried out on Anne Boleyn and the Boleyn family. I've included full references and a bibliography so that you can check the sources for yourself and come to your own conclusion. I am always happy to discuss my research, so please feel free to contact me at claire@theanneboleynfiles.com, or to comment at www.theanneboleynfiles.com or on The Anne Boleyn Files Facebook page – https://www.facebook.com/theanneboleynfiles.

1. The Origins of the Boleyn Family

Genealogists, historians and researchers have been discussing Anne Boleyn's roots for centuries and today there still does not seem to be a complete agreement over the origins of the Boleyn family. I am no genealogy expert, but I've been researching the Boleyns full time since early 2009. This chapter is a presentation of my findings and a discussion of the various theories.

A Fabricated Family Tree?

In his 19th century biography of Anne Boleyn, Paul Friedmann accused Anne Boleyn of fabricating her family tree in December 1530:

"Anne became daily more overbearing. The latest Anne's exploit in her honour had been the fabrication of the wonderful pedigree, in which good Sir William Bullen the mercer was represented as the descendant of a Norman knight. Though these pretensions were laughed at, and though Anne's aunt the duchess freely told her what they were worth, she was nowise abashed."[1]

This accusation was based on a letter written by Eustace

Chapuys, the imperial ambassador, in which he reported the Duchess of Norfolk scoffing at Anne Boleyn's family tree.[2] However, no details of this family tree were given, and Chapuys is the only source for this claim. We also know that Elizabeth Howard, Duchess of Norfolk, was no friend of Anne's at this time so she may well have made fun of anything that her niece did. There were plenty of reasons for the Duchess to dislike Anne and her rise at court:

- Anne's relationship with Elizabeth (Bess) Holland, the Duke of Norfolk's mistress. When Anne became Marquis of Pembroke in 1532, two years later, Bess was appointed as one of her ladies.

- The Duchess was "hypersensitive about her status"[3],[4] and Eric Ives writes of how she had previously "clashed with Queen Katherine by claiming she took precedence over the duke's step-mother, the dowager duchess" and yet "now her niece went ahead of both of them!"[5] The Duchess was the eldest daughter of the late Edward Stafford, 3rd Duke of Buckingham, a man who'd been the premier peer in England.

- Anne Boleyn and the Duchess had clashed over the marriage of the Duchess's daughter, Mary Howard. The King and Anne felt that Mary should marry Henry Fitzroy, Henry VIII's illegitimate son,[6] but the Duchess disagreed. An argument between Anne and her aunt nearly led to the Duchess being banished from court.

- The Duchess supported Catherine of Aragon and even sent Catherine a secret message hidden in an orange.[7]

It is little wonder that "by Christmas 1530 the duchess's Stafford blood could not resist some acid comments on the upstart Boleyns."[8]

But perhaps we should take Chapuys' words with a healthy pinch of salt. Chapuys saw Anne as the King's "concubine" and did not like her; his loyalty lay with Catherine of Aragon. Also, in his report, Chapuys says "Lon ma dict que la duchesse…", i.e. "Someone told me that the duchess…", so this was second hand information.

The French Connection

We don't know exactly what was on the family tree mentioned by Chapuys, nor who was responsible for it, but many believe that the Boleyns did in fact originate in France. Joanna Denny wrote of the Boleyns as "an upwardly mobile family originating from the English-held territories in France",[9] noting that "Baldwin de Bolon came from Boulogne, which in the Chronicles of Calais is spelt 'Boleyn.'" In the 17th century, Julien Brodeau wrote:

"Si l'on remonte plus haut, on trouuera que la famille des Boulens vient de France, & est bien plus ancienne. L'ay un tiltre du Samedi apres la S. Martin 1344, de Baudonin de Biaunoir, Sire d'Avesnes proebe de Peronne, qui nomme entre ses hommes de fief Vautier de Boulen."[10]

Here, Brodeau is saying that the Boleyns were an ancient family from France and that there was a Walter de Boulen who held land in Peronne, in the Picardie region of northern France, in 1344. He went on to say that the family were linked, by marriage, to the family of "Moulin, Seigneurs de Fontenay en Brie". Hence the links with Brie, or Briis-sous-Forges, where a tower called the Tour d'Anne Boleyn still stands today.

Friedmann, however, was sceptical of the Boleyns' links to France, calling the idea "fantastic" and writing that "all that is really known of Anne's origin is that her great-grandfather, Geoffrey Boleyn, was a wealthy London merchant. He was elected alderman, and in due time arrived at knighthood and the dignity of Lord Mayor." But in my reading and research on the Boleyns, I have found that most historians and genealogists *do* believe that the Boleyns had their origins in France, with some believing that they were descended from the Norman Counts of Boulogne and others believing that they came over later as merchants.

The Counts of Bolougne

Those who believe that the Boleyns descended from the Counts of Boulogne say that the Counts came over in the 11th century with the Norman invasion and settled in Martock, Somerset, and parts of Surrey.[11] It is alleged that Simon de Boleyne (or de Boulogne) then moved to Norfolk: records show that he held lands in the Salle area in the mid 13th century. Salle is, of course, just a few miles from Blickling, where it is thought that Anne Boleyn was born. Furthermore, St Peter and St Paul Church, in Salle, is the resting place of Geoffrey Boleyn (d.1440) and his wife, Alice, Anne's great-great grandparents.

In "The Battle Abbey Roll",[12] the Duchess of Cleveland describes how the lineage of the Counts of Bolougne (Eustace I, II and III) continued in England after the Norman invasion. She explains that Pharamus de Boulogne "held lands in England of the Honour of Boulogne, which then consisted of 112 knight's fees" and that "in the Liber Niger we find Herebert de Buliun holding half a knight's fee of Roger Bigod, Earl of Norfolk; and William de Bolein holding one fee in York and one in Lincoln". The Duchess goes on to say that the name Boleyn, with its various spellings, came from 'de Boulogne' and that the authors of the *Recherches sur le Domesday* concluded that this English branch of the Counts of Bolougne "may possibly have been an illegitimate one."[13] I looked up this information in the *Recherches sur le Domesday* and it said that a daughter of the last descendant of Ernulf d'Ardes (or Ardres) married an illegitimate son of the Counts of Boulogne and that the resulting family in England took the name of "Bouloigne", or, "by corruption, 'de Bouleyn.'"[14]

The Norman People and their Existing Descendants in the British Dominions and the United States of America,[15] under "Boleyn – Queen Anna Boleyn", records how Anne was "lineally descended from John de Boleyne of Sall, living 1283, whose father Simon purchased lands in Norfolk by fine 1252" and also records that "In 1165 Herebert de Buliun held half a knight's fee from Roger

Bigod, E. of Norfolk (Lib. Niger). At the same time William de Bolein held 1 fee in York and 1 in Lincoln; which shows that there were then two branches of the family in England. Accordingly, in the preceding generation, Eustace and Simon de Bologne, brothers of Pharamus de B., are mentioned in a charter of the latter (Mon. Ang. i. 583)." It goes on to say that the Counts of Boulogne were "descended from Angilbert, a Frank noble, who m. Bertha, dau. of the Emperor Charlemagne, and before 790 was created Duke of the maritime territory afterwards styled Ponthieu" and that Eustace I of Boulogne was the ancestor of the Boleyn family.

There are many efforts in online ancestry groups and websites to establish the connection between the Boleyns of Salle and the Counts of Bolougne. The general consensus is that Pharamus de Bolougne was the father of William de Bolein/Boleyne, who, in turn, was the father of the Simon de Boleyne who held lands in Norfolk ca.1253. His son, John de Boleyne of Salle, is mentioned in 1283.

The Research of Reverend Canon Parsons

In 1935, the Norfolk and Norwich Archaeological Society's journal published an article entitled "Some Notes on the Boleyn Family," written by the Rev. Canon W. L. E. Parsons, Rector of Salle.[16] Parsons used a variety of primary sources to try and establish the roots of the Boleyn family, including contemporary wills and the Court Rolls of the manors of Salle and Stinton.

The earliest evidence he could find for Boleyns having lived in the Salle area was regarding John Boleyn and William Boleyn in the 13th century. In the Register of Walsingham Abbey, a "John Boleyn" was mentioned in 1283. There is also a record of the Prior of Walsingham suing William Boleyn of Thurning, who was Prior's Bailiff in Salle, for an account. In this record, John Boleyn was acting as a surety.

The next Boleyn that Parsons could find was Nicolas Boleyn

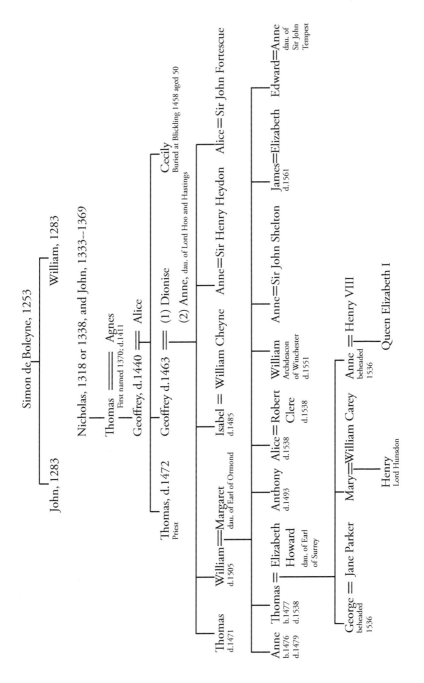

Figure 2 - Boleyn Family Tree, Parsons

of Salle, who was accused of theft in either 1318 or 1338. A Court of Rolls entry mentions him in 1333: "Nicolas Boleyn for damage done to pastures and trees of the Lord: he is ordered to repair the bank between the Lord and Nicolas." Another John Boleyn then comes up in the records, firstly in 1333 and then regularly after the Black Death, which he fortunately survived. The mentions include John paying "the Lord" fines and rent, serving on the jury of a coroner's inquest in 1363 and being fined for trespass in 1369. It appears that he died sometime shortly after 1369 and that his lands were passed to a "Thomas Bulleyn of Salle", who is thought to be his son. Thomas is mentioned at various time in the records. Examples include Thomas and his wife, Agnes, appearing on a list of indulgences granted by Pope Boniface IX, and the following record in the Court of Rolls in 1399: "Thomas gave to Geoffrey his son one messuage in Salle without leave." It is believed that he died in or around 1411.

Then, we have the first Geoffrey Boleyn of Salle, son of Thomas. His first mention after 1399 is in 1408, with regard to timber for the building of the church at Salle. It appears that he had some involvement in the building of the church and we know that his father left money for the glazing of a south aisle window. Geoffrey frequently crops up in the records; there are mentions of his landholdings, of him trespassing, of fines paid and of the selling of barley and oat straw for thatching. According to the Survey of Stinton Manor 1430-40, Geoffrey held twenty-three parcels of land, but it appears that he was a tenant farmer, rather than the lord of the manor. He died in 1440 and was laid to rest in Salle Church. His brass has the inscription "Here lie Geoffrey Boleyn, who died 25th March, 1440, and Alice his wife and their children: on whose souls may God have mercy. Amen." His children included Cecily, who was buried at Blickling; Geoffrey, Lord Mayor of London, and Thomas, a priest and Master of Gonville Hall, Cambridge, from 1454-72. Thomas also served the King, by attending the Council of Basle. Interestingly, Parsons found a piece of evidence from the

1463 de Banco Rolls which linked Thomas the priest with Nicolas Boleyn and established the family tree:

"Thomas Boleyn, clerk, seeks against William Doreward and others, the Manor of Calthorpe, called Hookhall, as his right and inheritance in which William, etc. have no entry, except after the disseisin which Bartholomew Calthorpe, Kt., made to Nicolas Boleyn, kinsman of the said Thomas, who is his heir. Thomas says that Nicolas was seized of the Manor as of fee and right in the reign of Edward III. And took the explees, and from the same Nicolas descended the right to Thomas as son and heir, and from Thomas to Geoffrey as son and heir, and from Geoffrey to this Thomas, who now seeks as son and heir."

This piece of evidence shows that this line of the Boleyns was descended from Nicholas Boleyn, not from the John Boleyn who also appears in the records in the 1330s, and that they weren't just holders of land under the Lord but they owned the manor of Calthorpe "as of fee and right". The manor of Calthorpe later belonged to William Boleyn (d.1505) so it appears that the Boleyns did have rights to it.

The next Boleyn is the man who is credited as bringing the family to prominence: Sir Geoffrey Boleyn, a successful merchant and Lord Mayor of London. Geoffrey was favoured by Sir John Fastolf and travelled with him to London. There, he became a wealthy merchant and important subject of King Henry VI. He married into the nobility, by taking as his second wife Anne, daughter of Lord Hoo and Hastings (his first wife was called Dionise). He served as Sheriff of London and also of Middlesex; and he bought Blickling manor from Fastolf, although it took him a while to pay for it because he also lent the King £1246 to pay for the expedition to France. He became Lord Mayor in 1457, died in 1463, and was buried in the Chapel of St. John in the Church of St. Laurence, Jewry, London. Unfortunately, the church was destroyed in the 1666 Great Fire. His children included Alice, who married Sir John Fortescue; Isabel, who married William Cheyney; Anne, who married Sir Henry Heydon of Baconsthorpe; Thomas, who died in 1471; and William, who married Margaret Butler, daughter of the Earl of Ormond. William was made a Knight of the Bath during Richard III's coronation celebrations and served as Sheriff of Norfolk from 1500 to 1501. He died in 1505 and was buried in Norwich Cathedral.

According to Parsons, William and Margaret Boleyn had a large family:

- Anne, who died in 1479, shortly before her fourth birthday.
- Anthony, who died in 1493.
- Thomas (born ca. 1477), who married Elizabeth Howard, daughter of the Earl of Surrey.
- William, who became a priest.
- James, who married Elizabeth Wood.
- Edward, who married Anne Tempest.
- Alice, who married Robert Clere.
- Margaret, who married Sir John Sackville.
- Anne, who married Sir John Shelton.

Blomefield[17] adds a "John," who died in 1484, and a "Jane," who married Sir Phillip Calthorp of Norwich.

On his father's death, Thomas Boleyn inherited the manors of Blickling, Calthorpe, Wikmere, Mekylberton, Fylby, West Lexham, Possewick and Stiffkey as well, of course, as Hever Castle. Thomas Boleyn was the father of Anne Boleyn, so we finally arrive at Anne in the family tree.

Parsons concluded that the Boleyns, like the famous Pastons, were "of somewhat humble origin" and that it was the second Geoffrey, a "Dick Whittington", who had "established the position of the family financially by successful trade, and socially by marriage with the nobility." This view is disputed by others, though. Sylvanus Urban wrote:

"The family of Boleyn was of Norman extraction. They were possessed of manors and lands at Salle and the adjacent villages in the 12th century. Among the Blickling evidences there is a deed, 1280, with the Boleyn seal attached, retaining enough to show that they bore then the same arms as were afterwards used by this family.

I presume that this will settle the question as to the 'gentility' of the Boleyns."[18]

In *"Annals & Antiquities of the Counties & County Families of Wales"*, Thomas Nicholas, in writing of the lineage of Williams of Abercamlais, records:

"Among the companion knights of Bernard [Norman knight Bernard de Neuf Marché] was one who had probably come from the neighbourhood of Boulogne, for he went by the name de Boulogne, or Bullen, but it is uncertain whether his Christian name was Richard or Thomas. Opinion seems to be in favour of the latter.

"Sir Thomas de Boulogne, or Bullen (from one branch of whose descendants Anne Boleyn, mother of Queen Elizabeth, derived), was rewarded for his services with a lordship in Talgarth."[19]

Furthermore, Frederick Lewis Weis et al.[20] believe that Anne's name "came into England much later with merchants from the Boullonnais."

Ralph Boleyn

Some genealogists add a "Ralph Boleyn" to the Boleyn family tree. Sylwia Thrupp writes "The records of the skinners' company fraternity of Corpus Christi show the entrance of a Raulyn (Ralph) Boleyn in 1402 and of a Bennid de Boleyn, Lombard, in 1436".[21] It is hard to see how he fits in to Anne's family tree, though, so perhaps he was from one of the other branches.

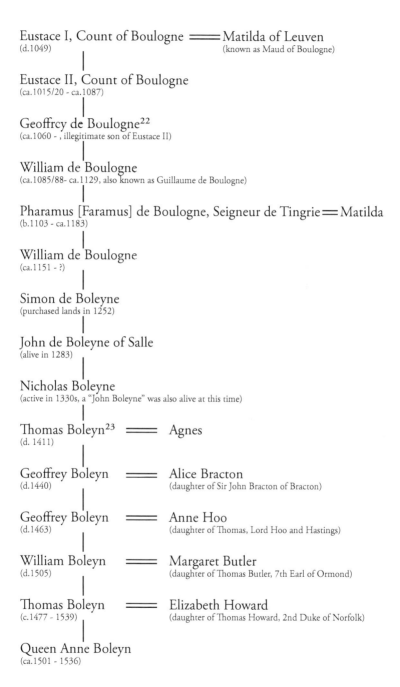

Eustace I, Count of Boulogne ══ Matilda of Leuven
(d.1049)   (known as Maud of Boulogne)

Eustace II, Count of Boulogne
(ca.1015/20 - ca.1087)

Geoffrcy de Boulogne[22]
(ca.1060 - , illegitimate son of Eustace II)

William de Boulogne
(ca.1085/88- ca.1129, also known as Guillaume de Boulogne)

Pharamus [Faramus] de Boulogne, Seigneur de Tingrie ══ Matilda
(b.1103 - ca.1183)

William de Boulogne
(ca.1151 - ?)

Simon de Boleyne
(purchased lands in 1252)

John de Boleyne of Salle
(alive in 1283)

Nicholas Boleyne
(active in 1330s, a "John Boleyne" was also alive at this time)

Thomas Boleyn[23]   ══   Agnes
(d. 1411)

Geoffrey Boleyn   ══   Alice Bracton
(d.1440)   (daughter of Sir John Bracton of Bracton)

Geoffrey Boleyn   ══   Anne Hoo
(d.1463)   (daughter of Thomas, Lord Hoo and Hastings)

William Boleyn   ══   Margaret Butler
(d.1505)   (daughter of Thomas Butler, 7th Earl of Ormond)

Thomas Boleyn   ══   Elizabeth Howard
(c.1477 - 1539)   (daughter of Thomas Howard, 2nd Duke of Norfolk)

Queen Anne Boleyn
(ca.1501 - 1536)

Figure 3 - Family Tree

A Provisional Boleyn Family Tree

Figure 3 shows a provisional family tree based on the sources already mentioned, but simplified so that it shows the direct line from Anne Boleyn back to the Counts of Boulogne. There is no way, however, that we can prove that this tree is wholly accurate since concrete evidence is lacking.

Boleyn – The Name

It has been claimed, on various occasions, that Anne Boleyn 'frenchified' her name by changing it from 'Bullen' to 'Boleyn', making it less common - "Anne Boleyn" versus "Nan Bullen". This is a myth, however. In his research of records going back to the 13th century, Rev. Canon Parsons found it "spelt variously – Boleyn, Buleyn, Bolen, Bulleyne, Boleyne, Bolleyne, Boyleyn, Bowleyne, Bulloigne, and the modern form Bullen" and concluded that "Boleyn was the most common of the mediaeval forms." It is also spelled various ways in documents from Henry VIII's reign, in reference to Thomas Boleyn and Anne Boleyn. We also know that the city of Boulogne in France was written as "Boleyn" in the Chronicles of Calais, suggesting that the family name may well have had its origins there. There does not seem to be any record of any variations of the name before the Norman conquest.

Final Thoughts

We cannot know for certain where the Boleyns came from, so it is impossible to accuse Anne of fabricating a family tree, especially when we don't even know who was on that tree. As for the idea that Anne fabricated her family tree because she was ashamed of the Boleyns and their merchant roots; there is no evidence that Anne was ashamed of the Boleyns. It is thought that she wore a necklace consisting of the letter "B" for Boleyn; and why should she be ashamed of a family who had risen to such wealth and favour? Her family may not have been ancient nobles (we just don't know), but they weren't alone in that fact; the de la Pole family (the Earls and Dukes of Suffolk) descended from a merchant from Hull.

∞∞

Notes and Sources

1   Friedmann, Anne Boleyn, A Chapter of English History, 1527-1536, 128.
2   Chapuys, "Letter to Charles V, 31 December 1530."
3   Ives, The Life and Death of Anne Boleyn, 141.
4   "Calendar of State Papers, Spain, Volume 4: Part 1, Henry VIII, 1529-1530," 368.
5   Ives, "The Fall of Anne Boleyn Reconsidered," 141.
6   "Calendar of State Papers, Spain, Volume 4: Part 1, Henry VIII, 1529-1530," 762.
7   Ibid., 819.
8   Ives, The Life and Death of Anne Boleyn, 141.
9   Denny, Anne Boleyn: A New Life of England's Tragic Queen, 26.
10   Brodeau, La Vie de Maistre Charles Du-Moulin Advocat Au Parlement de Paris, 6.
11   Bullen, "Anne Boleyn A Norfolk Girl?".
12   Duchess of Cleveland, The Battle Abbey Roll with Some Account of the Norman Lineages in Three Volumes, 1:27–29.
13   Ibid., 1:29.
14   Léchaudé-d'Anisy and marquis de Sainte-Marie, Recherches Sur Le Domesday, Ou Liber Censualis d'Angleterre, Tome Premier:207.
15   The Norman People and Their Existing Descendants in the British Dominions and the United States of America, 164.
16   W. L. E. Parsons, Rev. Canon, "Some Notes on the Boleyn Family."
17   Blomefield, An Essay Towards a Topographical History of the County of Norfolk, 3:626.
18   Urban, "The Family of Boleyn," 155.
19   Nicholas, Annals & Antiquities of the Counties & County Families of Wales, 2:121.
20   Weis et al., Ancestral Roots Of Certain American Colonists Who Came To America Before 1700 Lineages from Alfred the Great Charlemagne Malcolm of Scotland Robert the Strong and Other Historical Individuals.
21   Thrupp, The Merchant Class of Medieval London 1300-1500, 325.
22   Amt, The Accession of Henry II in England: Royal Government Restored, 1149-1159, 85.
23   Norton, The Boleyn Women, chap. 1. Elizabeth Norton believes that Thomas was the grandson of Nicholas Boleyn and that his father was another John Boleyn.

2. Anne Boleyn's Birth Date

Nobody knows for sure when Anne Boleyn was born; all we can say is that it was in the first decade of the sixteenth century. There are two main dates given for Anne Boleyn's birth – 1501 and 1507 – and there are valid arguments for each year. Her place of birth is dependent on the year of her birth – if you take 1501 as her birth date then it is likely that Anne was born at Blicking Hall in Norfolk, if you take 1507 as her birth date then it is likely that she was born at Hever Castle in the Kent countryside. In addition, the date of her birth affects the way we view her life and her fall. As author Gareth Russell points out:

"If she was 28, as one of her stepdaughter's ladies-in-waiting claimed, then the reasons behind her execution become infinitely more sinister – at 28, Anne Boleyn was still undeniably in her childbearing years. Yes, she would have been at the tail-end of them by Tudor standards, but she would have had at least four or five more years before she was considered infertile, and so the idea that it was just her "failure" to produce a son which led to her death in 1536 suddenly becomes a good deal less convincing and the idea that it was her husband who orchestrated her monstrously unfair death becomes infinitely more likely. However, if she was 35, then she was already practically middle-aged by Tudor standards and it becomes far more likely that the entire reason for her destruction was politics pure and

simple, with Anne – and to some extent, perhaps, maybe even her husband – being victims of a savagely brilliant process of character assassination, lies, manufactured hysteria and a ruthless palace coup organised by the King's chief adviser, Thomas Cromwell."[1]

So, what's the evidence for each suggested birth date?

1501

Those who believe that Anne Boleyn was born in 1501 put forward the following arguments and pieces of evidence:

- **Anne Boleyn's father's letter to Cromwell, dated July 1536.**[2] In this letter, Thomas Boleyn refers to the financial hardship of the early years of his marriage, writing that his wife "brought me every year a child." If we consider that the Boleyns married ca.1498/1499, then surely all five Boleyn children (Mary, Anne, George, Thomas and Henry) were born before 1505? Also, Thomas Boleyn became a wealthy man on the death of his father in 1505, so he must have been referring to Elizabeth's pregnancies pre-1505.

- **Anne Boleyn's letter to her father in 1513.** Art historian Hugh Paget[3] examined an early letter from Anne Boleyn to her father, Thomas, and concluded that it was written in 1513 and sent from La Vure, the royal park in Brussels (the location of Margaret of Austria's summer palace and hunting lodge). Paget also wrote of how we know from correspondence between the Emperor and Margaret that the appropriate age for a "demoiselle d'honneur" at Margaret's court was around thirteen or fourteen. A 1507 birth date would make Anne six years of age in 1513, so Paget concluded that Anne was born in 1501, making her a year younger than the usual age. Historians such as Eric Ives note that the "formed hand"[4] of the letter belongs to a twelve year-old, rather than a six year-old.

- **Anne Boleyn's fall.** A birth date of 1501 would make Anne around thirty-five years of age at her execution and it may explain why Henry VIII was worried that Anne could not give him a male heir and why he was so ready to replace her with the younger Jane Seymour. At thirty-five, Anne was past her prime in Tudor terms. Jane Seymour is thought to have been born in around 1508, so if Anne was born in 1507, why would Henry replace her with someone just a year or so younger?

- **Going into the service of Catherine of Aragon.** Lord Herbert of Cherbury writes that Anne Boleyn was "about the twentieth year of her age"[5] when she became one of Catherine of Aragon's ladies. We know that Anne returned from France around Christmas 1521, so that would give a birth date of 1501. Interestingly, though, Lord Herbert concludes that Anne was born around 1498. He arrives at this conclusion because he believes her to have been around fifteen when she was appointed to serve Mary Tudor in 1514.[6]

- **Going into the service of Mary Tudor.** Nicholas Sander, author of *Rise and Growth of the Anglican Schism* (1585), writes, "It is hardly credible that Anne Boleyn - supposing her to have been born, as Camden says, in 1507 - was one of the ladies in attendance on queen Mary of France in 1514, and to have been the only one allowed to remain when the king dismissed the Englishwomen in attendance on Mary."[7] Later in the book, Sander describes how Anne was sent to France at the age of fifteen, putting her date of birth around 1499.[8] Although Sander's book has many inaccuracies, we know for a fact that in 1514 Thomas Boleyn asked Margaret of Austria to release Anne from her care so that Anne could return to England to accompany Henry VIII's sister on her journey to France to marry Louis XII.[9] We don't know whether Anne did travel to England or whether she ended up going directly to France, but we do know that she was one of the ladies that

Louis allowed Mary to keep with her in France and not one of the ones sent back to England. A seven year-old would surely not be chosen to serve a Queen of France.

1507

The arguments for a 1507 birth date include:

- **W. Camden's marginal note in his *Annales*.**[10] This says "Anne Bolena nata M.D. VII.", i.e. 1507. Gareth Russell[11] states that Camden started writing his account of Anne Boleyn's life in the late 16th century, in the reign of Anne's daughter Elizabeth I, "with the backing of the English government"; and that he had access to William Cecil's personal papers and state archives. Russell believes, therefore, that Camden would have got Anne's year of birth right.

- **Thomas Boleyn's reference to Anne as "la petite Boulaine" in his letter to Margaret of Austria in 1514.** Historian Retha Warnicke argues that Thomas would not refer to a thirteen year-old girl in this way.[12]

- **Margaret of Austria's comment in a letter to Thomas Boleyn.** Margaret wrote that Anne was "so pleasant for her young age that I am more beholden to you for sending her, than you are to me."[13]

- **John Weever's *Ancient funerall monuments*, published in 1631.** Warnicke writes of how Weever recorded that Anne Boleyn and Henry VIII had fallen in love when she was twenty-eight and he was thirty-eight. Henry VIII was thirty-eight in 1529, so for Anne to be twenty-two 1529, she must have been born in 1507.

- **The birth of Elizabeth I in 1533.** Retha Warnicke comments that if we take 1501 as Anne's date of birth, then it would make her thirty-two when Elizabeth was born, which would have been rather old by Tudor standards. Warnicke believes that 17th century historians would have picked up on this detail.

- **The evidence of Jane Dormer, Duchess of Feria.** In his biography of Jane Dormer, her chaplain Henry Clifford wrote that when Anne Boleyn was executed in May 1536, she "was not twenty-nine years of age,"[14] meaning that she hadn't yet turned twenty-nine. Jane Dormer was one of Mary I's ladies, so some historians argue that although Jane was not born until 1538 she would have known from Mary how old Anne was.

- **Anne being a resident at Margaret of Austria's palace, not a maid-of-honour.** Retha Warnicke[15] argues that Anne was sent to Margaret of Austria not to serve her, but to be educated together with Margaret's nephews and nieces. Warnicke backs this up with Anne's words in the letter to her father when she refers to the teaching techniques of of her tutor: "Semmonet dictates the letter to me and leaves me to write it myself".

- **Anne's chaperone.** Gareth Russell[16] points out that Anne was escorted from Hever to Brussels by a man, Claude Bouton, and not a female chaperone which would surely have been more appropriate if Anne was only twelve years of age.

- **The fact that Anne was still unmarried in 1526.** Gareth Russell points out that a birth date of 1501 would have made Anne twenty-five in 1526, close to an "unmarriageable age" by Tudor standards.

- **Anne's suitability as queen.** Gareth Russell comments that in all of the objections cited during Henry's struggle for divorce and his quest to marry Anne, nobody mentioned that Anne might possibly be too old to give Henry a son and heir. If she had been in her late twenties or early thirties, this would surely have arisen.

Although the arguments of Retha Warnicke and Gareth Russell did sway me for a while towards 1507, I have come to believe that

Anne was born in 1501. Even if Margaret of Austria had done Thomas Boleyn a favour by allowing his daughter to come to Mechelen at the age of six to be educated, I cannot imagine a seven year-old being appointed to serve Mary Tudor in France or being chosen to stay on in France and serve Queen Claude. Both queens would have been in need of a lady to serve them, not a child to keep an eye on, and why would Thomas Boleyn's daughter have been chosen to join the French royal nursery? Besides, the imperial ambassadors who reported Anne's return to England wrote of her being "in the service of the French queen",[17] and Renée of France, Duchess of Ferrara and sister of Queen Claude, referred to Anne as a maid-of-honour to her sister, not as a fellow member of the schoolroom or nursery.[18]

I realise that one of the main arguments for 1507 is the evidence of Jane Dormer, who may have heard of Anne's age from Mary I, but then Mary I also stated on a few occasions that Mark Smeaton fathered Elizabeth I. As far as Thomas Boleyn's "la petite Boulain" comment, that could just have been his pet name for his youngest daughter and nothing more. Unfortunately, unless more evidence comes to light, Anne's birth date will always be a puzzle and a bone of contention between authors and historians.

Notes and Sources

1   Russell, "The Age of Anne Boleyn."
2   "Letters and Papers, Foreign and Domestic, Henry VIII, Volume 11: July-December 1536," n. 17.
3   Paget, "The Youth of Anne Boleyn."
4   Ives, The Life and Death of Anne Boleyn, 15.
5   Herbert, The Life and Raigne of King Henry the Eighth., 257.
6   Ibid., 259.
7   Sander, Rise and Growth of the Anglican Schism, xlvi.
8   Ibid., 25.
9   The Manuscripts of J. Eliot Hodgkin, Fifteenth Report: Appendix, Part II:30.
10   Camden, Annales Rerum Anglicarum et Hibernicarum, Regnante Elizabetha Ad Annum Salutis M.D. LXXXIX.

11   Russell, "The Age of Anne Boleyn."

12   Warnicke, "Anne Boleyn's Childhood and Adolescence."

13   Ives, The Life and Death of Anne Boleyn, 19.

14   Clifford, The Life of Jane Dormer, Duchess of Feria, 80.

15   Warnicke, "Anne Boleyn's Childhood and Adolescence."

16   Russell, "The Age of Anne Boleyn."

17   "Calendar of State Papers, Spain: Further Supplement to Volumes 1 and 2," 30.

18   "Calendar of State Papers Foreign, Elizabeth, Volume 3: 1560-1561," 489–90.

3. Anne Boleyn's Royal Blood

Many people talk of the Boleyns as upstarts or commoners but, just like Henry VIII's other five wives and, indeed, Henry himself, Anne Boleyn was a descendant of Edward I and had royal blood. Both of Anne's parents were descended from ancient and noble families - Thomas Boleyn from the Butlers (as well as the Boleyns) and Elizabeth Boleyn from the Howards; and both had royal blood.

The Howard Family's Ancestry

Burke's Peerage says of the Howard family, "The Ducal and illustrious Howards stand, next to the Blood Royal, at the head of the Peerage of England"[1] and it is true that they have always been one of the most important families in the history of England. The family traces its ancestry back to William Howard of East Wynch, Norfolk, who was knighted by Edward I and who served the King as Chief Justice of the Common Pleas. William's son, Sir John Howard, served Edward I as a gentleman of the bedchamber and his grandson, another Sir John, served Edward III as Admiral and Captain of the King's Navy in the North.

The family carried on faithfully serving English monarchs for generations. However, the family did not win the title of Duke of Norfolk until 1483. In this year, Richard III conferred the titles of Duke of Norfolk and Earl of Marshall of England upon Yorkist John Howard. Howard was subsequently made Lord Admiral of England.[2] His son, Thomas, Anne Boleyn's grandfather, was created Earl of Surrey. Unfortunately, John was killed just two years later at the Battle of Bosworth Field. In November 1485, both the dead Duke and his son, Surrey, were attainted by Henry VII's Parliament for their support of Richard III. The dukedom and earldom were forfeited, and Thomas Howard was stripped of his lands and imprisoned in the Tower of London for three years. He was restored to the earldom in May 1499 and went on to serve Henry VII as a lieutenant in the North and as Lord High Treasurer. He acted as an executor of the King's will in 1509 and as Earl Marshal at Henry VIII's coronation. Surrey was created Duke of Norfolk in 1514 after his victory leading the English troops at the Battle of Flodden. Surrey's daughter, Elizabeth Howard, is thought to have married Thomas Boleyn around 1498/1499,[3] i.e., before her father had been restored to his titles and lands.

The Howard family could also trace their roots back to Edward I by two lines of descent:

1st Line[4]

Anne Boleyn's mother was Lady Elizabeth Howard (c.1480 – 1538), daughter of **Thomas Howard (1443 – 1524), Earl of Surrey and the 2nd Duke of Norfolk** from 1514, and of his first wife, Elizabeth Tilney.

Thomas Howard, 2nd Duke of Norfolk was the son of **John Howard, 1st Duke of Norfolk (1421 – 1485)** and of Katherine Moleyns.

John Howard was the son of Sir Robert Howard (1385 – 1436) and of **Lady Margaret de Mowbray** (1388 – 1459).

\\

Margaret de Mowbray was the daughter of **Thomas de Mowbray, 1st Duke of Norfolk** (1366 – 1399), of the first creation, and of Elizabeth Fitzalan.

\\

Thomas de Mowbray was the son of John de Mowbray, 4th Baron Mowbray (1340 – 1368), and of **Elizabeth, Baroness Segrave** (d.1375).

\\

Elizabeth was the daughter of John de Segrave, 4th Baron Segrave, and of **Margaret Plantagenet, Duchess of Norfolk** (c. 1320 – 1399).

\\

Margaret was the eldest daughter of **Thomas of Brotherton, 1st Earl of Norfolk** (1300 – 1338), and of Alice Halys.

\\

Thomas was a son of **Edward I** (1239 – 1307) and of his second wife, Margaret of France (c.1279 – 1318).

\\

2nd Line[5]

Anne Boleyn's mother was Lady Elizabeth Howard (c.1480 – 1538), the daughter of **Thomas Howard (1443 – 1524), Earl of Surrey and the 2nd Duke of Norfolk** from 1514, and of his first wife, Elizabeth Tilney.

\\

Thomas Howard, 2nd Duke of Norfolk was the son of **John Howard, 1st Duke of Norfolk** (1421 – 1485) and of Katherine Moleyns.

\\

John Howard was the son of Sir Robert Howard (1385 – 1436) and of **Lady Margaret de Mowbray** (1388 – 1459).

\\

Margaret de Mowbray was the daughter of Thomas de Mowbray, 1st Duke of Norfolk (of the first creation), (1366 – 1399), and of **Elizabeth Fitzalan.**

\\\\

Elizabeth Fitzalan was the daughter and co-heir of **Elizabeth de Bohun** and of Richard Fitzalan, Earl of Arundel and Surrey.

\\\\

Elizabeth de Bohun was the daughter of **William de Bohun, 1st Earl of Northampton** (d. 1360), and of Elizabeth de Badlesmere (1313 – 1356).

\\\\

William de Bohun was the son of **Elizabeth Plantagenet**, also known as Elizabeth of Rhuddlan (1282 – 1316), and of Humphrey de Bohun, 4th Earl of Hereford (1276 – 1322).

\\\\

Elizabeth Plantagenet was the daughter of **Edward I** (1239 – 1307) and of his first wife, Eleanor of Castile (1241 – 1290).

\\\\

The Butler Family's Ancestry

The Butlers, Thomas Boleyn's maternal family, were descended from Theobald Walter, 1st Baron Butler (d. 1205), who was of Norman origin. Theobald was the eldest son of Hervey (or Herveius) Walter and his wife Maud de Valoignes. Maud, also known as Matilda, was one of the daughters (and co-heiresses) of Theobald de Valoignes, who was Lord of Parham in Suffolk. Theobald and his brother, Hubert, were raised in the household of Ranulf de Glanville, Justiciar of England in the 1180s, and knew Prince John (the future King John) who also spent time there. In 1185, Theobald accompanied Prince John to Ireland when the Prince visited as Lord of Ireland and Theobald established religious houses in Wicklow, Limerick and Tipperary.

The family surname changed from Walter to Butler during the reign of Henry II. The name came from the fact that Theobald

Walter was made the first Chief Butler of Ireland in 1177. This meant that he was the ceremonial cup-bearer to Prince John, the *boteillier* (Norman French) or "butler". He became known as Theobald Walter le Boteler (le Botiller), or as Theobald Butler, after his title and the Butler family were "born". As Butler of Ireland, he and his successors "were to attend the kings of England at their coronation, and that day present them with the first cup of wine, for which they were to have certain pieces of the king's plate".[6] By the time he died in 1205, he had built up extensive landholdings in Ireland, in Munster and south Leinster.

The title of Ormond, the earldom granted to Anne Boleyn's father in 1529, also traces back to Theobald, who was granted Irish lands (including East Munster, or Ormond) by Prince John. James Butler (c.1305-1338), a descendant of Theobald and the eldest surviving son of Edmund Butler, Earl of Carrick (d. 1321), and of Joan Fitzgerald, was the first Earl of Ormond; the title was created especially for him. He served as a yeoman or *valettus* in Edward II's household in the early 1320s, but trouble in Ireland led to him returning there in the mid-1320s. His father died in 1321; although James did not inherit the title of Earl of Carrick, he did inherit the title of Chief Butler, becoming 7th Chief Butler of Ireland. James's father had served as a justiciar when Roger Mortimer was Lieutenant of Ireland 1317-18. This relationship, along with James's loyalty to the Crown, led to Edward III making James Earl of Ormond by patent in 1328, when Mortimer became Earl of March. James was also granted a life-grant of the liberty of the county of Tipperary, which was held by the family until 1716. James was loyal to Edward III and married the King's cousin, Eleanor de Bohun. According to his biographer, Robin Frame, "inquisitions at his death show that, besides his Irish lordships, he had property in ten English counties, all held jointly with his wife",[7] so we can see that he was rewarded well for his service. His son, James, was granted his lands in 1347.

The Ormond title is still with the Butler family today. In 1997,

James Butler, 7th Marquess of Ormond, died childless. Thus, the marquessate became extinct and the earldom dormant, although it is likely that Piers James Richard Butler, 18th Viscount Mountgarret, will be able to claim it. The Butler family shield displays cups, symbolising the office of the Chief Butler of Ireland, and the motto is "Comme Je Trouve", meaning "As I Find". The cups and motto are used today by Kilkenny College private school because it was founded in 1538 by Piers Butler, 8th Earl of Ormond.

The seat of the Butler family in Ireland was Kilkenny Castle. The castle is in the city of Kilkenny in the province of Leinster, south-east Ireland. It was built at the beginning of the 13th century for William Marshal, 4th Earl of Pembroke, and was bought from Sir Hugh le Despencer, Earl of Gloucester, in 1391 by James Butler, 3rd Earl of Ormond. When King Richard II visited Ireland in 1394-95, Butler was made Justiciar of Ireland because the King regarded him as the premier Irish earl. Kilkenny Castle remained the main residence of the Butler family from that point until 1967 when Arthur, 6th Marquess of Ormond, gave it to the residents of Kilkenny for a payment of £50.

As well as being an ancient and noble family, the 16th century Butlers carried royal blood, being descended from Edward I by three lines of descent:

1st Line

Anne Boleyn's father, Thomas Boleyn, was the son of Sir William Boleyn (1451 – 1505) and of **Lady Margaret Butler** (1454 – 1539).

Lady Margaret Butler was the daughter of **Thomas Butler, 7th Earl of Ormond** (1426 – 1515), and of Anne Hankford.

Thomas Butler was the son of **James Butler, 4th Earl of Ormond** (1392 - 1452), and of Joan de Beauchamp.

James Butler was the son of **James Butler, 3rd Earl of Ormond** (d. 1405), and of Anne Welles.

\\

James Butler was the son of **James Butler, 2nd Earl of Ormond** (1331 – 1382) and of Elizabeth Darcy.

\\

James Butler was the son of James Butler, 1st Earl of Ormond (c. 1305 - 1338) and of **Eleanor de Bohun** (1304 - 1363).

\\

Lady Eleanor de Bohun was the daughter of **Elizabeth Plantagenet**, also known as Elizabeth of Rhuddlan (1282 – 1316), and of Humphrey de Bohun, 4th Earl of Hereford (1276 – 1322).

\\

Elizabeth Plantagenet was the daughter of **Edward I** (1239 – 1307) and of his first wife, Eleanor of Castile (1241 – 1290).

\\

2nd Line

Anne Boleyn's father, Thomas Boleyn, was the son of Sir William Boleyn (1451 – 1505) and of **Lady Margaret Butler** (1454 – 1539).

\\

Lady Margaret Butler was the daughter of **Thomas Butler, 7th Earl of Ormond** (1426 – 1515), and of Anne Hankford.

\\

Thomas Butler was the son of James Butler, 4th Earl of Ormond (1392 - 1452), and of **Joan de Beauchamp** (1396 - 1430).

\\

Joan de Beauchamp was the daughter of William de Beauchamp, 1st Baron Bergavenny (c. 1343 - 1411) and of **Lady Joan Fitzalan** (1375 – 1435).

\\

Lady Joan Fitzalan was the daughter of Richard
Fitzalan, 11th Earl of Arundel and 9th Earl of Surrey
(1346 - 1397), and of his first wife **Elizabeth de
Bohun.**

\\\

Elizabeth de Bohun was the daughter of **William de
Bohun, 1st Earl of Northampton** (d. 1360), and of
Elizabeth de Badlesmere (1313 – 1356)

\\\

William de Bohun was son of **Elizabeth Plantagenet**,
also known as Elizabeth of Rhuddlan (1282 – 1316),
and of Humphrey de Bohun, 4th Earl of Hereford
(1276 – 1322)

\\\

Elizabeth Plantagenet was the daughter of **Edward I**
(1239 – 1307) and of his first wife, Eleanor of Castile
(1241 – 1290).

\\\

3rd Line

Anne Boleyn's father, Thomas Boleyn, was the son
of Sir William Boleyn (1451 – 1505) and of **Lady
Margaret Butler** (1454 – 1539).

\\\

Lady Margaret Butler was the daughter of Thomas
Butler, 7th Earl of Ormond (1426 – 1515), and of
Anne Hankford (c. 1431 - 1485).

Anne Hankford was the daughter of Sir Richard
Hankford and of **Anne Montagu, or Montacute,** (d.
1457).

\\\

Anne Montagu was the daughter of **John Montacute,
3rd Earl of Salisbury** (c. 1350 – 1400), and of Maud
Francis.

\\\

John Montacute was the son of Sir John de Montacute,
1st Baron Montacute (d. 1390) and of **Margaret de
Monthermer.**

\\\

Margaret de Monthermer was the daughter of **Thomas de Monthermer, 2nd Baron de Monthermer** (1301 - 1340), and of Margaret Teyes.

Thomas de Monthermer was the son of Ralph de Monthermer, 1st Baron Monthermer (c. 1270 – 1325), and of **Joan of Acre, Countess of Hertford and Countess of Gloucester** (1272 – 1307).

Joan of Acre was a daughter of **Edward I** (1239 – 1307) and of his first wife, Eleanor of Castile (1241 – 1290).

Notes and Sources

1   Burke, A General and Heraldic Dictionary of the Peerage and Baronetage of the British Empire, 2:231.

2   Ibid., 2:232.

3   Ives, The Life and Death of Anne Boleyn, 17.

4   Brenan and Philips Statham, The House of Howard, 73.

5   Ibid.

6   Debrett, Debrett's Peerage of England, Scotland, and Ireland. Revised, Corrected and Continued by G. W. Collen, II, Scotland and Ireland:871.

7   Frame, "Butler, James, First Earl of Ormond (c. 1305 - 1338)."

4. Anne Boleyn, the Court of Margaret of Austria and the French Court

The majority of historians and authors believe that Anne Boleyn spent her formative years on the continent, first at Margaret of Austria's court in Mechelen and then in France serving Queen Claude, wife of Francis I. Thomas Boleyn was an ambitious man who believed in educating his daughters. Through his close relationship with Margaret of Austria, he was able to secure a place for his daughter, Anne, at Margaret's court, known as "the Mecca of aristocratic and princely behaviour".[1] It was the ideal place to send his highly intelligent and precocious daughter; Thomas had plans for Anne to serve Margaret's sister-in-law, Catherine of Aragon, and for that she would require good French and continental manners. Eric Ives describes Margaret's court as "Europe's premier finishing school" and the cultural heart of Europe, a place where Anne Boleyn could finish her education with Margaret's Hapsburg nephews and nieces and the children of "the elite of Europe". If Margaret agreed to accept Anne, then Anne would be mixing with the future rulers of Europe in a true Renaissance Court; an amazing opportunity for a twelve year-old girl.

The Court of Margaret of Austria

Margaret of Austria was born in 1480 and was the daughter of Maximilian of Austria (Maximilian I, Holy Roman Emperor) and of Mary of Burgundy. In 1482, when she was just two, Margaret's father made the Treaty of Arras with France, and Margaret, his only daughter, was promised in marriage to the Dauphin, Louis XI's son Charles. To prepare her for being the Queen Consort of France, Margaret was sent to be educated in France. The marriage never took place, with Charles choosing to marry Anne of Brittany instead. In 1497, Margaret went on to marry John, Prince of Asturias, the only son of Isabella I of Castile and Ferdinand II of Aragon. John died after just six months of marriage and the pregnant Margaret gave birth to a stillborn daughter two months after his death. In 1501, Margaret married Philibert II, Duke of Savoy, but he died three years later. Margaret vowed never to marry again and spent the rest of her life in mourning, wearing black.

In 1507, Margaret's father appointed her as Governor of the Habsburg Netherlands, the regent for her six year-old nephew, Charles, the future Charles V, Holy Roman Emperor. Although Charles did rebel against her when he came of age in 1515, and removed her title of governor for four years, he reappointed her as governor in 1519 when he realised what an asset she was. In this position, Margaret was one of the most powerful women in Europe.

Spending the formative years of her life in France had not only made Margaret fluent in the language but also very French in her ways. She was also highly educated and accomplished at music and poetry. Belgian historian Ghislain de Boom, described her palace at Mechelen ("Malines" in French) as "un école d'éducation princière et un centre de haute civilisation"; "a princely school and a centre of high culture/advanced civilisation", and so it was.[2] Her court was visited by the likes of Erasmus, and other well-known Humanists, and was known for its superb library which contained poetry, missals and historical work. It also held work by authors such as

Figure 4 - Statue of Margaret of Austria in Mechelen

Christine de Pizan, who was known for challenging misogyny and the stereotypical views of women. In addition, the library contained the works of Boccaccio, Aesop, Ovid, Boethius and Aristotle. Margaret was a patron of the arts and her court was also known for her collections of illuminated manuscripts, music books and paintings by masters such as Jan van Eyck. She surrounded herself with men of letters, poets and painters. Margaret also enjoyed the tradition of courtly love, which was "an integral element in chivalry, the complex of attitudes and institutions which was central to the life of the Tudor court and elite".[3]

What better place to send your daughter to finish her education than the court of the most powerful and influential women of Europe, a court known for its culture? Thomas Boleyn took advantage of his close relationship with Margaret and asked if it was possible to send his daughter to her. Although places at Margaret's court were highly sought after, and Anne was no European princess, Margaret agreed, and Anne Boleyn was dispatched to the Low Countries in the summer of 1513. At the time, as Hugh Paget points out, it appeared that Thomas Boleyn would be sent back to the Habsburg Court, but this did not happen. Margaret assigned Anne a tutor, Symonnet, to help her improve her French and Anne would also have learned many other skills, such as deportment, conversation, dance and music. Hugh Paget quotes Jane de Longh (author of Margaret of Austria, *Regent of the Netherlands*), as saying of Margaret's court:

"The nobles and ladies of her court reflected the influence of the taste and preferences of their mistress. They made music, wrote poetry, composed and recited at this little court in the quiet and seclusion of Malines."[4]

Margaret of Austria's Influence on Anne Boleyn

Anne Boleyn's love of fine art, music, poetry and her love of illuminated manuscripts obviously had its beginning at Margaret's court. Margaret had many examples of the new style of Flemish illumination, as well as older masterpieces. She also had a vast collection of chanson, masses and motets by composers who Anne was later known to have loved. In addition, Margaret's palace was full of colourful tapestries and beautiful fabric. Eric Ives writes of how "in later life Anne was excited by fabric and colour";[5] this love surely started in the Netherlands. Furthermore, Anne became the patron of artist Hans Holbein the Younger, just as Margaret was patron to top artists on the continent.

Margaret of Austria's palace at Mechelen also affected Anne Boleyn's taste in architecture. Whitehall Palace, the palace that Anne and Henry rebuilt, was a recreation of what Anne had seen in Mechelen.[6]

Anne Boleyn's time at Margaret of Austria's court had a number of "important consequences":[7]

- It was the foundation of her knowledge in French and "other courtly accomplishments" which influenced Mary Tudor to pick Anne to serve her in 1514.

- The skills she learned in Mechelen, which were then developed in France, probably made her "a not unworthy consort" for Henry VIII.

- Her time in Mechelen may have had an effect on the development of music and art in England. The Flemish style of music became popular and Hugh Paget points out that the Boleyns were patrons of Gerard and Lucas Hornebolt, "to whom we are indebted for the founding of the art of the miniature portrait in this country."

It is clear that this climate of culture rubbed off on Anne Boleyn and it is no wonder that Henry VIII saw Anne as a fitting queen consort and mother of his children. She had been educated with princes and princesses, she had style and culture, she was highly intelligent, and she could talk to him on his level and discuss the things he loved. She was a Renaissance woman and he saw himself as a Renaissance prince. There is no way, however, that Thomas Boleyn had any inkling in 1512 that his daughter would one day be queen, or that Margaret of Austria groomed Anne to be Henry VIII's consort. In 1512, Henry VIII had only been married to Catherine of Aragon for three years and was perfectly happy, anticipating that he would be married to Catherine for the rest of his life and that they would, in time, have a son and heir. But what Thomas Boleyn did do was to give his daughter the best chance of obtaining an appointment as a queen's lady, and in this he was successful. Anne was chosen in 1514 to serve Mary Tudor, Henry VIII's sister and Queen of France, and then in 1515 to serve Queen Claude, Francis I's wife. Anne had spent only a year at Mechelen, but that year had a dramatic impact on her and what she learned at Margaret's court was built on during her time in France.

Anne's Move to the French Court

On the 14th August 1514, Thomas Boleyn wrote to his great friend, Margaret of Austria, asking her to release Anne and return her to England under the care of a chaperone sent by him.[8] It seems that Anne had been chosen to serve the new Queen of France due to her fluency in French and, as Thomas Boleyn wrote to Margaret, it was a request that "I could not, nor did I know how to refuse." Although it is clear from Thomas Boleyn's letter that Anne had been chosen to attend the new Queen of France, the records are not exactly clear as to which Boleyn girl travelled to France with Mary Tudor and where Anne joined her new mistress. The list of ladies paid for the period October to December 1514 shows the name "Marie Boulonne", but not Anne, so it may be that Mary Boleyn attended Mary Tudor on her crossing to France and for the wedding which took place on the 9th October 1514 at Abbeville, and that Anne caught up with the royal party in Paris on 9th November, when Mary was crowned queen. Eric Ives hypothesises that Margaret of Austria, who was visiting the islands of Zeeland at that juncture, may not have got Thomas Boleyn's letter in time to send Anne home to England, so instead Anne travelled directly to France.[9]

We don't know for sure whether the "Madamoyselle Boleyne" mentioned by King Louis XII in his "Names of the gentlemen and ladies retained by the King (Louis XII.) to do service to the Queen"[10] refers to Mary or Anne, but what we do know is that Anne Boleyn did, at some time, arrive in France to serve the new queen.

On 1st January 1515, less than three months after his marriage to his eighteen year-old bride, the fifty-two year-old Louis XII died. It was said that he had been worn out by sexual relations with his younger wife. Louis had no son and Salic law prevented his daughter, Claude, from becoming queen. Therefore, when it was clear that Mary Tudor was not pregnant, Claude's husband, who was also Louis' first cousin's son, inherited the throne and became Francis I of France. Mary Tudor had never wanted to marry the ageing Louis XII as she had already set her heart on Charles Brandon, the Duke of Suffolk. So when her brother, Henry VIII, sent Brandon to France to bring her back home to England, Mary followed her heart and married Brandon in secret on the 3rd March 1515. This was an act of treason and Henry VIII was furious, fining the couple for their disobedience. However, he eventually forgave them and they were officially married on the 13th May 1515 at Greenwich Palace.

Even though Anne Boleyn was one of Mary Tudor's attendants, she did not travel back to England with Mary In 1515, but, instead stayed on in France and served the new queen consort, Queen Claude. Claude and Anne were of a similar age and Anne was fluent in French, so it is possible that Anne had acted as an interpreter between Claude and Mary Tudor, and that Claude and Anne had got to know each other. Anne went on to serve Queen Claude for seven years and this is a period of Anne's life about which we know relatively little.

The French Legends and Traditions Regarding Anne Boleyn

French tradition links Anne Boleyn with Briare, a town on the River Loire, and also with the village of Briis-sous-Forges, where there is even a tower called the Tour d'Anne Boleyn. According to one French website,[11] this tower is the only remaining part of a medieval castle which was once stayed in by Anne, before her marriage to Henry VIII; her parents were friends of Du Moulin, the castle's owner. This story is backed up by the work of seventeenth century French historian, Julien Brodeau,[12] who wrote that Anne Boleyn was educated in the home of nobleman Philippe de Moulin de Brie, a relation of her parents.

Nicholas Sander, writing in the reign of Elizabeth I, wrote that Anne Boleyn was sent to France at the age of fifteen after she had "sinned first with her father's butler, and then with his chaplain" and was placed "under the care of a certain nobleman not far from Brie". Sander also writes that "soon afterwards she appeared at the French court where she was called the English Mare, because of her shameless behaviour; and then the royal mule, when she became acquainted with the king of France."[13] This makes me wonder if he was confusing Anne with her sister, Mary Boleyn, who was, allegedly, the mistress of King Francis I and who was, apparently, referred to by the King as an "English Mare" and "una grandissima ribalda, infame sopra tutte" (a great and infamous whore).

In one of her recent talks on Mary Boleyn, Alison Weir quoted historian Sarah Tytler (1896) as saying that Anne Boleyn went to a convent school at Brie to finish her education. However, Weir wonders if historians have confused the two Boleyn girls and hypothesises that the Boleyns, upset at Mary's bad behaviour at the French court, could have entered her into a French convent for educational purposes.

The link between Anne Boleyn and Briare could have some foundation because "the town was well placed in relation to the movements of the court of Queen Claude, where Anne's duties kept her."[14] Claude was constantly pregnant, giving birth to seven children between 1515 and 1523. Claude tended to spend her pregnancies in the Upper Loire area, at Amboise and her palace in Blois, and Anne would obviously have accompanied her there.

The French Court

When she moved from Mechelen to the French court, Anne Boleyn went from one sophisticated centre of culture to another. Lancelot de Carles wrote that Anne "knew perfectly how to sing and dance... to play the lute and other instruments" and Nicholas Sander said of Anne "She was handsome to look at, with a pretty mouth, amusing in her ways, playing well on the lute, and was a good dancer. She was the model and mirror of those who were at court, for she was always well dressed, and every day made some change in the fashion of her garments."[15] It is clear that Anne had learned music, dance and style during her time in France.

Anne's love of illuminated manuscripts blossomed in France because Queen Claude, like Margaret of Austria, loved illumination, as is clear from her Prayer Book and Book of Hours from 1517. Claude's prayer book, which is now held by the Morgan Library and Museum in New York, is described as "a tiny, jewel-like manuscript" which is "richly illustrated... with 132 scenes from the lives of Christ, the Virgin Mary, and numerous saints."[16] The prayer book and its matching Book of Hours were made by an artist known as Master Claude, who "worked in a style that can be characterized as the pinnacle of elegance." They are beautiful books. Anne Boleyn went on to have her own illuminated manuscripts and books; these were made in the Renaissance style, which had been popular in France and used by Claude, rather than being made in the style she had seen in the Low Countries. Like Margaret of Austria, Claude was also an art lover (she was a patron of the miniature), so Anne was surrounded by art and culture; she couldn't help but be influenced by this amazing experience.

Those seeking to blacken Anne Boleyn's name say that Anne must also have been influenced by the loose morals and sexuality of the French court, but we have to remember that Anne Boleyn was serving Queen Claude, a woman known for her piety and who was often away from court due to her annual pregnancies. Anne was serving in a morally strict household, not one of scandal.

Anne Boleyn would also have probably taken part in the coronation of Queen Claude at St Denis in May 1516, in her triumphant entry into Paris, and also in her entry into Cognac in 1520. Queen Claude was also present at the banquet at the Bastille on 22nd December 1518. This banquet was given in honour of the visit of the English diplomats sent to negotiate a marriage between the Dauphin and Henry VIII's daughter, Mary. She was also present at the Field of Cloth of Gold in June 1520, just outside Calais. At both events, Claude was accompanied by her ladies; it is likely that Anne would have been useful as an interpreter.

The French Influence

It wasn't just the Renaissance culture which influenced the young Anne Boleyn; she was also heavily influenced by the women she saw and spent time with in France.

Claude of France

Claude was the eldest daughter of Louis XII of France and of Anne of Brittany, who Pierre de Bourdeille, seigneur de Brantôme, described as "the most worthy and honourable queen that has ever been since Queen Blanche, mother of the King Saint-Louis, and very sage and virtuous".[17] In his chapter on Anne of Brittany,

Brantôme wrote that "she was the first queen to hold a great Court of ladies", a "noble school for ladies" where "she had them taught and brought up wisely; and all, taking pattern by her, made themselves wise and virtuous".[18]

Claude was the heiress of the Duchy of Brittany and also first in line to the throne. However, as I mentioned earlier, Salic law prevented her becoming the Queen of France when her father died. Instead, she became queen by marrying Francis, Duke of Angoulême, who became Francis I of France.

Millicent Garrett Fawcett writes of how Claude "was from her birth delicate, plain and lame",[19] Antonio de Beatis, secretary to the Cardinal of Aragon, described her as "young and though very small in stature, plain and badly lame in both hips, is said to be very cultivated, generous and pious" and the Austrian ambassador said that "she was a retiring young girl with a pale complexion, thin, a little sickly, slightly hunchbacked, and rather unattractive."[20] As far as her character was concerned, Brantôme described Claude as "very good, very charitable, and very gentle to all, never doing any unkindness or harm to any one either at her Court or in the kingdom" and it is clear that she followed her mother's example by running a virtuous and learned court. The virtuous, pious and kind Claude would have been a role model to Anne. I'm sure that when Anne herself became queen, albeit in England, in 1533, she must have thought back to Claude's behaviour as queen.

Claude's husband, Francis I, was brought up at the Royal Château Amboise and he was often there during his reign (as well as being present at Fontainebleau and the Louvre), living a life full of banquets, balls and tournaments. In 1515, Leonardo da Vinci was invited by Francis I to live and work in Clos Lucé, which was connected to the royal château by an underground passage. Queen Claude preferred nearby Château Blois, which Francis had renovated for her; this is where Anne would have served her royal mistress.

Figure 5 - Engraving of Château Blois

Figure 6 - Marguerite of Angoulême

Claude had seven children, including Henry II, King of France, but died in 1524 at the tender age of twenty-four. Brantôme declared that Claude's husband, Francis I, gave her "a disease that shortened her days", meaning syphilis, but it is not known for certain. It seems that after it lost its pious queen, the French court slid into debauchery.

Louise of Savoy

Louise of Savoy was the mother of Francis I and Marguerite of Angoulême (later Marguerite of Navarre), and the daughter of Philip II, Duke of Savoy, and of Margaret of Bourbon. Louise, an intelligent, ambitious and politically astute woman, ensured that Francis and Marguerite had a Renaissance education. After the death of her husband, Charles of Orléans (cousin of Louis XII), she moved to the French court with her children, a move that was responsible for her son, Francis, becoming one of the King's favourites and ensuring his succession to the throne. Louis XII gave Louise the royal château at Amboise where she brought up Francis and Marguerite.

Louise acted as regent for Francis whenever he was away and, along with his sister Marguerite of Angoulême, was the most powerful woman at court, particularly in the early years of Francis's reign. Between them they ran Francis's court for him. Louise was serving as regent in 1515, when Anne Boleyn was at the French Court, and Anne would have seen this strong, politically active woman run the country.

Marguerite of Angoulême

Louise's daughter, Marguerite of France and Navarre, or Marguerite of Angoulême, is praised by Brantôme for her "perfect beauty" and is described as the "rare princess" and a woman who "was full of majesty and eloquence... full of charming grace in gay and witty speech" and "a queen in all things".[21] She was brought up with her brother, Francis, and given an excellent Renaissance education. However, Marguerite soon outstripped her brother "in her knowledge of Greek, Latin and Hebrew, and in her easy grasp of modern languages."[22] But it wasn't just education that Marguerite was passionate about; she also felt strongly about religious reform. As well as being known for her patronage of the arts, Marguerite is also known for her work *Le miroir l'âme pécheresse*, the same poem which Anne Boleyn's daughter, Elizabeth, later translated as a gift for her stepmother, Catherine Parr. This wonderful literary work is a mystical poem which combines evangelical Protestant ideas with Marguerite's idea of her relationship with God as a very personal and familial one. The editors of *Marguerite (Queen, consort of Henry II, King of Navarre): Selected Writings* say this of *Le Miroir*:

> "In addition to the obvious intimate familiarity with biblical literature, the poem follows closely the reformist views Marguerite learned from her mentor/confessor, Guillaume Briçonnet. Here we find all the essential earmarks of the devotio moderna, with its heavy emphasis on personal piety, exaggerated self-deprecation, preoccupation with death, and total dependence on divine grace for salvation."[23]

Le Miroir is a beautiful piece of writing, very moving and obviously written from the heart, and it shows the depth of Marguerite's faith and her personal relationship with God her Father.

Although Marguerite's work was condemned as heresy, Fawcett writes of how Marguerite never broke with the Church and became Protestant. However, "she never wavered from the position she took up all through the years... of the protector of the new learning and the humble devotee of a religion which was pure and undefiled."[24] Those same words could be used to describe Anne Boleyn, I feel. Both women had a true faith, religious fervour, and were passionate about reform and new ideas, but they did not want to 'throw the baby out with the bath water'. They wanted to reform the Catholic Church from within.

Fawcett goes on to describe German reformer, Philip Melancthon, as "a reformer after Margaret's own heart, gentle and moderate, desiring to reconcile rather than to estrange; earnestly working for the reform of the Church from within so as to prevent the disruption of Christendom";[25] again I think of Anne Boleyn and wonder if she was influenced by Marguerite's views and her faith.

We don't know the extent of Anne's relationship with Marguerite. We know that Marguerite was influential at the French Court, sharing power in the early years of her brother's reign with her mother, Louise of Savoy, so Anne Boleyn would have certainly met her. Some, including Lord Herbert of Cherbury, have wondered whether Anne Boleyn actually served Marguerite as a lady-in-waiting, but there is no evidence of that and Anne's name does not appear in the "Comptes de Louise de Savoie et de Marguerite d'Angouleme" (the accounts), which you would expect if she was employed by Marguerite.[26] Furthermore, in 1522, on her departure from France, Anne was described as one of Queen Claude's ladies. We do, however, have evidence that there was some kind of relationship between the two women: two letters from Anne to Marguerite. In July 1534, instructions were given to Anne's brother, Lord Rochford:

"1. Rochford is to repair to the French king with all speed, and in passing by Paris to make the King's and Queen's hearty recommendations to the queen of Navarre, if she be there, and say that the Queen his mistress much rejoices in the deeply-rooted amity of the two kings, but wishes her to get the interview deferred, as the time would be very inconvenient to her, and the King is so anxious to see his good brother that he will not put it off on her account. Her reasons are, that being so far gone with child, she could not cross the sea with the King, and she would be deprived of his Highness's presence when it was most necessary, unless the interview can be deferred till April next. Rochford is to press this matter very earnestly, and say that the King having at this time appointed another personage to go to his

Figure 7 - Renée of France

good brother, the Queen, with much suit, got leave for Rochford to go in his place, principally on this account.

2. That there was nothing she regretted at the last interview so much as not having an interview with the said queen of Navarre; and she hopes she may be able to come to Calais with her brother in April next, if the interview be deferred till then."[27]

In September 1535, another message was sent to Marguerite saying that, "The Queen[Anne Boleyn] said that her greatest wish, next to having a son, is to see you again."[28]

These words could simply be flattery and good diplomacy, but they sound like Anne was intimate with Marguerite, that they shared a friendship and that Anne was saddened to miss seeing Marguerite in 1534 and was really missing her in 1535.

Renée of France

Renée of France was Queen Claude's younger sister and a woman known for her heretical beliefs. Millicent Garret Fawcett writes that Renée "partly through the influence of her cousin, Margaret of Angoulême, afterwards Queen of Navarre, and partly through that of her friend and governess, Madam de Soubise, was very favourable inclined to the reformed religion"[29] and that when she became the Duchess of Ferrara she gathered around her famous scholars like Bernardo Tasso, Clément Marot, John Calvin, Rabelais, Vittorio Colonna (a friend of Michelangelo), Lavinia della Rovere (great niece of Pope Julius II) the great Capuchin preacher Bernardino Ochino, and many more. Renée also used her power and status to protect Reformers from persecution.

During her time in Ferrara, Renée was actually arrested as a heretic, although she escaped with her life after recanting and receiving the Eucharist at mass. However, after the death of her husband, the Duke of Ferrara, in 1559, Renée was able to return to her home country of France. In December 1560, her nephew,

Francis II, died and the power of the Catholic Francis, Duke of Guise, was broken, enabling Renée to provide Protestant worship at her estate in Montargis. Her castle became a refuge for Protestants and she earned the praise of John Calvin himself for her efforts for the cause. Renée died at her home in Montargis on 12th June 1574, aged sixty-three.

As the sister of Anne Boleyn's mistress, Queen Claude, she is bound to have come into contact with Anne, and Retha Warnicke writes that Claude's constant pregnancies meant that she, and therefore Anne, were "frequently in residence near Renée."[30] Warnicke is also of the opinion that Anne shared Renée's schoolroom lessons, but if we believe that Anne was one of Claude's ladies then she certainly would not have shared lessons with a princess. Notwithstanding, Renée was intimate enough with Anne to refer to their childhood friendship with Sir Nicholas Throckmorton, the English ambassador to France, during the reign of Anne's daughter, Elizabeth I.

Diane de Poitiers

Diane de Poitiers was the daughter of Jean de Poitiers, Seigneur de Saint Vallier and Jeanne de Batarnay, and was an intelligent girl who was given a Renaissance Humanist education. She served Anne de Beaujeu, the eldest sister of Charles VIII of France, and while she was married to Louis de Brézé, seigneur d'Anet, she served Queen Claude and then Louise of Savoy. She was known for her beauty, intellect and wit, and also, later for being Henry II's mistress. It is not known whether she and Anne Boleyn were close, but it is possible; they both shared a love of learning and music, and they both served Queen Claude.

The Effect on Anne

When you look at the education and experiences Anne had on the continent, and the women she mixed with from 1513 to 1522, you can understand why she had strong Reformist views, why she stood out at the English Court, why she caught Henry VIII's eye and why he deemed her a worthy consort and mother of his children. Anne Boleyn had received a princess's education, she had mixed with royalty and met Renaissance men and women, and she was an intelligent and ambitious woman. She was on Henry VIII's wavelength, they understood each other and had shared interests and passions. I don't believe that Anne seduced Henry or that she cast some kind of spell on him. I believe that their relationship was a true meeting of minds and that they fell in love.

Notes and Sources

1   Ives, The Life and Death of Anne Boleyn, 18.
2   Paget, "The Youth of Anne Boleyn," quoting Ghislaine de Boom, "Marguerite d'Autriche–Sauoie et la Pré–Renaissance" (Paris and Brussels).
3   Ives, The Life and Death of Anne Boleyn, 68.
4   Paget, "The Youth of Anne Boleyn."
5   Ives, The Life and Death of Anne Boleyn, 24.
6   Ibid., 23.
7   Paget, "The Youth of Anne Boleyn."
8   The Manuscripts of J. Eliot Hodgkin, Fifteenth Report: Appendix, Part II:30.
9   Ives, The Life and Death of Anne Boleyn, 28.
10   "Letters and Papers, Foreign and Domestic, Henry VIII, Volume 1: 1509-1514," n. 3357.
11   "Tour d'Anne Boleyn."
12   Warnicke, The Rise and Fall of Anne Boleyn: Family Politics at the Court of Henry VIII, 246.
13   Sander, Rise and Growth of the Anglican Schism, 25–26.
14   Ives, The Life and Death of Anne Boleyn, 32.
15   Sander, Rise and Growth of the Anglican Schism, 25.
16   "The Prayer Book of Claude de France."

17 Pierre de Bourdeille, seigneur de Brantôme, Illustrious Dames of the Court of the Valois Kings, 24.

18 Ibid., 30.

19 Garrett Fawcett, Five Famous French Women, 58.

20 Wellman, Queens and Mistresses of Renaissance France, 120.

21 Pierre de Bourdeille, seigneur de Brantôme, Illustrious Dames of the Court of the Valois Kings, 166.

22 Garrett Fawcett, Five Famous French Women, 70.

23 Cholakian and Skemp, Marguerite (Queen, Consort of Henry II, King of Navarre): Selected Writings (Bilingual Edition), 73.

24 Garrett Fawcett, Five Famous French Women, 81.

25 Ibid., 84.

26 Ives, The Life and Death of Anne Boleyn, 32.

27 "Letters and Papers, Foreign and Domestic, Henry VIII, Volume 7," n. 958.

28 "Letters and Papers, Foreign and Domestic, Henry VIII, Volume 9: August-December 1535," n. 378.

29 Garrett Fawcett, Five Famous French Women, 251–252.

30 Warnicke, The Rise and Fall of Anne Boleyn: Family Politics at the Court of Henry VIII, 21.

5. Did Anne Boleyn actually go to Mechelen and France?

That Anne Boleyn spent time at the courts of Margaret of Austria and Queen Claude of France (wife of Francis I) has never before been disputed. Historians argue over how old Anne was when she was sent to Mechelen - whether she was six or twelve years of age – and whether she served as a maid of honour there or whether she was simply being educated in Margaret's household, but the general consensus is that she was in Mechelen (in the Low Countries) from 1513-1514 and in France from late 1514 to late 1521. However, one author, Sylwia Zupanec, has recently challenged this belief, saying "Anne Boleyn simply could not have had [*sic*] served Margaret of Austria [or] the Queen Claude" and that "the assertions about Anne Boleyn's early years are based on rather shaky references."[1]

In this chapter I will share those "shaky references" and the reasons why I am convinced that Anne did serve both women.

Evidence for Anne Boleyn being sent to Margaret of Austria's Court

The first piece of evidence is an extract from Margaret of Austria's letter to Thomas Boleyn in which she thanks him for entrusting her with his daughter:

"J'ai reçeu vostre lettre par l'escuyer Bouton qui m'a présenté vostre fille que m'a esté la très bien-venue, et espère la traicter de sorte que aurez cause vous en contenter; du moings tiens que à vostre retour ne fauldra aultre truchement entre vous et moi que elle; et la treuvc si bien adressée et si plaisante suivant son josne eaige, que je suis plus tenu à vous de la m'avoir envoyée que vous à moi."[2]

Translation from Eric Ives' *The Life and Death of Anne Boleyn*:

"I have received your letter by the Esquire [Claude] Bouton who has presented your daughter to me, who is very welcome, and I am confident of being able to deal with her in a way which will give you satisfaction, so that on your return the two of us will need no intermediary other than she. I find her so bright and pleasant for her young age that I am more beholden to you for sending her to me than you are to me."[3]

This extract appears in the notes section of *Correspondance de l'empereur Maximilien Ier et de Marguerite d'Autriche, sa fille, Gouvernante de Pays-Bas, de 1507 à 1519, Tome Second* and is an extract from a letter written by Margaret of Austria to Thomas Boleyn. Margaret mentions "votre fille" ("your daughter"), so is quite clearly referring to a daughter of Thomas Boleyn. Although, as Hugh Paget[4] points out, the full letter is now not traceable in the Lille Archives, the editor of the 1839 edition of *Correspondance* quite clearly refers to the extract being part of a letter from Margaret to Thomas Boleyn. He does not cast any doubt on to whom the letter was written, so the original letter must have been clearly marked and it must have been obvious from the rest of the content that the letter was from Margaret to Thomas. Zupanec dismisses the letter entirely, believing that it could have been written to any courtier about any daughter.

The editor of *Correspondance* refers to Anne Boleyn's name being mentioned on a list of eighteen "filles d'honneur" who served Margaret. The reference given is *Chronique métrique de Chastellain et de Molinet: avec des notices sur ces auteurs et des remarques sur le texte corrigé*. The name "Bullan" does indeed appear on this list, although there is no first name given:

"Aultre plat pour les filles d'honneur et aultres femmes ordonnés par Madame de manger avec elles que sont XVIII, assavoir:-

Mesdames de Verneul, Waldich, Reynenebourg, Bréderode, d'Aultroy, Hallewyn, Rosimbos, Longueval, Bullan, les II filles Neufville, Saillant, Middelbourg, Cerf, Barbe Lallemand et la mère."[5]

Another piece of evidence to support the theory that Anne Boleyn was sent to Margaret's court is Anne's letter to her father. The original French can be read in the appendix of Philip W. Sergeant's *The Life of Anne Boleyn*;[6] here is Sergeant's translation:

"Sir, – I understand by your letter that you desire that I shall be a worthy woman when I come to the Court and you inform me that the Queen will take the trouble to converse with me, which rejoices me much to think of talking with a person so wise and worthy. This will make me have greater desire to continue to speak French well and also spell, especially because you have so enjoined it on me, and with my own hand I inform you that I will observe it the best I can. Sir, I beg you to excuse me if my letter is badly written, for I assure you that the orthography is from my own understanding alone, while the others were only written by my hand, and Semmonet tells me the letter but waits so that I may do it myself, for fear that it shall not be known unless I acquaint you, and I pray you that the light of [?] may not be allowed to drive away the will which you say you have to help me, for it seems to me that you are sure [??] you can, if you please, make me a declaration of your word, and concerning me be certain that there

shall be neither [??] nor ingratitude which might check or efface my
affection, which is determined to [?] as much unless it shall please you
to order me, and I promise you that my love is based on such great
strength that it will never grow less, and I will make an end to my [?]
after having commended myself right humbly to your good grace.

Written at [?Veure] by

Your very humble and very obedient daughter,

Anna de Boullan."

There have been various theories as to where Anne was writing
the letter from, with some historians arguing that the word "Veure"
was actually Hever, or that it meant the fifth hour (5 o'clock).
However, Hugh Paget argued that it was "the French version of
the name of the royal park at Brussels", the place where Margaret
of Austria visited during the summer months. Sylwia Zupanec
dismisses this idea, saying that there was no residence with that
name. However, Margaret's father, Maximilian I, signed various
letters from "au Château de la Veuren" and referred to "nostre
chasteaul de La Veuren"; "our castle of La Veuren", in a letter written
to Margaret in June 1512. In a time with no standardized spelling,
Anne could well have been referring to "Veuren" when she wrote
"Veure", or may simply have missed the "n" off the end. The letter
was full of such errors and "no intelligible English translation can
give the flavour of the phonetic and idiosyncratic original."[7]

In her letter, Anne also referred to "Semmonet", who was
quite clearly helping her with her French, and a "Symmonet" was
a member of Margaret's household. We know this because there
are various mentions of "Symmonet" in the correspondence of
Emperor Maximilian and Margaret of Austria – for example, a
letter written by Maximilian to Margaret on 25th May 1510.[8] I
can't believe that this is a coincidence.

The final piece of evidence for Anne Boleyn being at the court
of Margaret of Austria is Thomas Boleyn's letter to Margaret of

Austria recalling his daughter, written from Greenwich on 14th August 1514:

"Ma treschiere et tres redoubtee dame dans sy humble cuer quil mest possible a votre bonne grace me recommande. Il vous playra a savoir comment la seur du Roy mon maistre madame marie Reyne fyancee de France ma requyse davoir avecques elle ma fille la petite Boulain laquelle ma tresredoubtee dame est a present avecques vous en votre court a laquelle requeste je nay peult ne sceut refuzer nullement sy est ma tresredoubtee dame que je vous supplie treshumblement quil vous plaise de donner et octroyer congiet a ma fille de povoir retourner pardevers moy avecques mes gens lesquelz jay envoyet devers vous a ceste cause ma tresredoubte dame je me tiens fort obligiet envers votre bonne grace a cause de la grant honneur que fait aves a ma fille et que ne mest possible a desservir devers votre bonne grace non obstant que je ne dezire aultre chose synon queje vous puisse faire auleun service agreable ce que jespere de faire encores cy en apros au plaisir de dieu auquel je prie ma tresredoubtee dame quil vous doinst lentier accomplissement de vos nobles et bon dcsirs escript desoubz mon signe manuel a la court royalle de Grynewiths en engleterre, le xiiii jour daoust anno xv et xiiii.

Votre treshumble serviteur, Sr Thomas Boleyn."[9]

In this letter, Thomas Boleyn is asking Margaret to release his daughter, "la petitte Boulain", into the care of the escort he had sent across, so that Anne could return to England. Anne needed to do this because she had been chosen to accompany Mary Tudor, the sister of Henry VIII, who was due to leave for France to marry Louis XII. I cannot see to whom else Thomas Boleyn could have been referring when he writes of "ma fille la petitte Boulain", "my daughter the little Boleyn". Contrary to Zupanec's claim that the letter is undated, Thomas has written the date at the end: "le xiiii jour daoust anno xv et xiiii", meaning the 14th August 1514. Furthermore, there has never been any doubt cast on the authenticity of the letter, so it cannot be dismissed.

Another thing that suggests that Anne Boleyn knew Margaret of Austria was Anne's use of the motto "Ainsi sera, groigne qui groigne" (Let them grumble, that is how it is going to be). This, as Eric Ives and Joanna Denny point out, was a play on Margaret of Austria's motto "Groigne qui groigne, Vive Bourgogne!" (Grudge who Grudges, Long Live Burgundy!). Why would Anne make use of a motto of a woman she'd never met and whose court she had never attended?

Evidence for Anne Boleyn serving Queen Claude of France

It has been argued that Anne did not serve Queen Claude because the household lists of Queen Claude make no mention of either Boleyn girl, Anne or Mary, and that "the Boleyn sisters were probably confused with "Anne de Boulogne" and "Magdaleine de Boulogne" who were in the Queen Claude's household from 1509". Zupanec even doubts that Anne served Mary Tudor. She believes, instead, that Anne was sent by Thomas Boleyn to relatives in Briis-sous-Forges because "she may have indeed been guilty of some kind of a scandal", as Nicholas Sander, the 16th century Catholic recusant, believed.

Regardless of whether or not Anne's name appears in Queen Claude's household lists and whether or not she has been confused with other women, there is plenty of other evidence to back up the view that Anne served Mary Tudor then Queen Claude:

- A "Madamoyselle Boleyne" is in the list of "gentlemen and ladies retained by the King (Louis XII.) to do service to the Queen":
  "Le conte de Nonshere," Dr. Denton, almoner, Mr. Richard Blounte, "escuyer descuyerie," the sons of Lord Roos, Lord Cobham, and Mr. Seymour, "enfans d'honneur"; Evrard, brother of the Marquis, Arthur Polle, brother of Lord Montague, Le Poulayn, "pannetiers échansons et valetz trenchans"; Francis

Buddis, usher of the chamber, Maistre Guillaume, physician, Henry Calays, "varlet des robes," Rob. Wast. Mesdemoiselles Grey (sister of the Marquis), Mary Finis (daughter of Lord Dacres), Elizabeth (sister of Lord Grey), Madamoyselle Boleyne, Maistres Anne Jenyngham, "femme de chambre," and Jeanne Barnesse, "chamberiere." Signed by Louis XII."[10] This obviously could have been Mary Boleyn, Anne's sister, so is not complete evidence.

- King Francis I reported on 22nd January 1522 that "Mr. Boullan"'s daughter had been recalled from the French court: "I think it very strange that this treaty of Bruges was concealed from me, and also the powder and balls which are going to Antwerp;—that his subjects go and take the Emperor's pay;—that the English scholars at Paris have returned home, and also the daughter of Mr. Boullan, while ships were being made at Dover, and musters taken in England, the rumor being that it was to make war on France."[11] This must have been Anne because Mary was already in England at this time, having married William Carey in 1520.

- The imperial ambassadors reported to Charles V in January 1522 "that Boleyn's daughter, who was in the service of the French queen, had been called home" and that "The cardinal said that he himself was responsible for her recall, because he intended, by her marriage, to pacify certain quarrels and litigation between Boleyn and other English nobles."[12] It is clear that they are referring to Anne being recalled from France to marry James Butler. We know that the Boleyns and St Legers were, at this time, arguing with Sir Piers Butler over the title Earl of Ormonde, and that Cardinal Wolsey was attempting to broker a marriage between Piers's son and Anne to solve the problem.

- Renée of France, Duchess of Ferrara and sister of Queen Claude, told Nicholas Throckmorton in Elizabeth I's reign "There was another cause which worked in her a goodwill towards the Queen; there was an old acquaintance between the Queen's mother and her, when the former was one of the maids-of-honour of the Duchess's sister, Queen Claude."[13]

- Lancelot de Carles, in his poem about Anne Boleyn's execution, "*De la Royne d'Angleterre*", wrote:

> "*Or, Monseigneur, je croy que bien savez*
> *Et des longtemps la congnoissance avez*
> *Que Anne Boullant premierement sortit*
> *De ce pays, quant Marye en partit*
> *Pour s'en aller trouver le Roy en France,*
> *Pour accomplir des deux Roys l'alliance.*"

or

> "My lord, I am well aware that you know and have known for a long time that Anne Boullant first came from this country when Mary [Tudor] left to go to join the king [Louis XII] in France to bring about the alliance of the two sovereigns."

He went on to say:

> "*Apres que fut Marye revenue*
> *En ce pays, elle fut retenue*
> *Par Claude, qui Royne apres succedda.*"[14]

or

> "After Mary returned to her country, she [Anne] was retained by Claude, the Queen who succeeded her".

- Sixteenth century historians and chroniclers cite this as fact. William Camden's *Annales*,[15] his chronicle of Elizabeth I's life and reign, was written during Elizabeth I's reign and Camden was given access to William Cecil, Lord Burghley's private papers and various archives.[16] He wrote that Elizabeth's mother, Anne, had served Queen Claude and Marguerite of Angoulême. Baron Herbert of Cherbury (1583-1648) also wrote that Anne was "said by the French writers to have lived in that court", referring to the French court.[17]

Even if you discount the evidence from the ambassadors and Francis I as referring to Mary Boleyn, which cannot be correct because of the dates, Renée of France, sister of Queen Claude, and Lancelot de Carles, secretary to the French ambassador, were in positions to know whether or not Anne served Queen Claude. There was no reason for them to lie.

I really cannot see there being any reason to doubt that Anne was sent to Margaret of Austria's court and that she went on to serve Queen Claude of France. There is certainly more solid evidence for her having attended them than for her not doing so.

Notes and Sources

1   Zupanec, The Daring Truth About Anne Boleyn: Cutting Through the Myth, chap. 2 – Mademoiselle Boleyn: Did Anne Boleyn really spend her childhood and adolescence abroad.
2   Correspondance de L'empereur Maximilien Ier et de Marguerite d'Autriche, Sa Fille, Gouvernante de Pays-Bas, de 1507 à 1519, 2:461, note 2.
3   Ives, The Life and Death of Anne Boleyn, 19.
4   Paget, "The Youth of Anne Boleyn."
5   Baron de Reiffenberg, Chronique Métrique de Chastellain et de Molinet: Avec Des Notices Sur Ces Auteurs et Des Remarques Sur Le Texte Corrigé, 154.
6   Sergeant, The Life of Anne Boleyn, sec. Appendix D.
7   Ives, The Life and Death of Anne Boleyn, 20.
8   Correspondance de L'empereur Maximilien Ier et de Marguerite d'Autriche, Sa Fille, Gouvernante de Pays-Bas, de 1507 à 1519, 2:273.
9   The Manuscripts of J. Eliot Hodgkin, Fifteenth Report: Appendix, Part II:30.
10   "Letters and Papers, Foreign and Domestic, Henry VIII, Volume 1: 1509-1514," n. 3357.
11   "Letters and Papers, Foreign and Domestic, Henry VIII, Volume 3: 1519-1523," n. 1994.

12 "Calendar of State Papers, Spain: Further Supplement to Volumes 1 and 2," 30.

13 "Calendar of State Papers Foreign, Elizabeth, Volume 3: 1560-1561," n. 870.

14 Ascoli, La Grande-Bretagne Devant L'opinion Française Depuis La Guerre de Cent Ans Jusqu'à La Fin Du XVIe Siècle, 233–34, De la Royne d'Angleterre, Lancelot de Carles, lines 37–42 and 49–51.

15 Camden, Annales Rerum Anglicarum et Hibernicarum Regnante Elizabetha.

16 Russell, "The Age of Anne Boleyn."

17 Herbert, The Life and Raigne of King Henry the Eighth., 55, 110.

6. Anne Boleyn and James Butler

In this chapter, I am going to look at the negotiations which aimed to marry Anne Boleyn off to James Butler, son of Sir Piers Butler, and to settle the dispute over the title of Earl of Ormond. But before we look at the negotiations, we need to consider who the Butlers actually were, how they linked with the Boleyn family, and why the Ormond title was under dispute.

The Butler link came from Anne Boleyn's paternal grandmother, Lady Margaret Butler, who married Sir William Boleyn. William Boleyn was the son of the wealthy mercer (and Lord Mayor of London), Geoffrey Boleyn from Blickling, Norfolk, and of his wife Anne Hoo. Margaret was born at Kilkenny Castle in Ireland, somewhere between 1454 and 1465. She was the daughter of Thomas Butler, 7th Earl of Ormond, (known as "The Wool Earl"), and of his first wife, Anne Hankford. Thomas Butler served on Henry VII's privy council and was Catherine of Aragon's first Lord Chamberlain, serving her from 1509-1512.[1] Her paternal grandparents were James Butler, 4th Earl of Ormond, and Joan Beauchamp. James Butler was known as "The White Earl" and was the patron of "The Book of the White Earl", an Irish religious and literary miscellany.

The simplified family tree in figure 8 shows how Anne Boleyn and James Butler were related, both being descended from James Butler, 3rd Earl of Ormond.

The Butler family were descended from Theobald Walter, 1st Baron Butler (d. 1205), who was of Norman origin. The family surname changed from Walter to Butler during the reign of Henry II and came from Theobald's title, Chief Butler of Ireland. You can read more about Theobald in the chapter "Anne Boleyn's Royal Blood".

The Boleyn/Butler Marriage Negotiations

On 3rd August 1515, Thomas Butler, 7th Earl of Ormond and maternal grandfather of Thomas Boleyn, died in his late eighties. He was one of the wealthiest noblemen in England and, according to Thomas Carte,[2] he inherited more than £40,000 sterling plus plate. He also held two peerages – Earl of Ormond and Baron of Ormond, Irish and English peerages. Thomas Butler had no direct male heirs but he left two daughters: Anne (married to Sir James St.Leger) and Margaret (wife of Sir William Boleyn), Thomas Boleyn's mother.

Both Thomas Butler and his brother, Sir John Butler, 6th Earl of Ormond, before him, had been absent from their Irish estates for a long period due to the Wars of the Roses. Their Ormond estates were managed by their cousin, Sir James Butler (d. 1487), a member of the Polestown branch of the Butler family, who came to regard the estates as his own. When Thomas Butler died in 1515, therefore, James's son, Sir Piers, considered himself to be the rightful heir because Thomas Butler only had daughters. However, the Ormond title was entailed to heirs general, not just male heirs, so Thomas Butler's daughters, Anne St. Leger and Margaret Boleyn, were the rightful heirs. Margaret's son, Thomas Boleyn, father of Anne Boleyn, put forward his claim to the Earldom with the support of his King, Henry VIII.

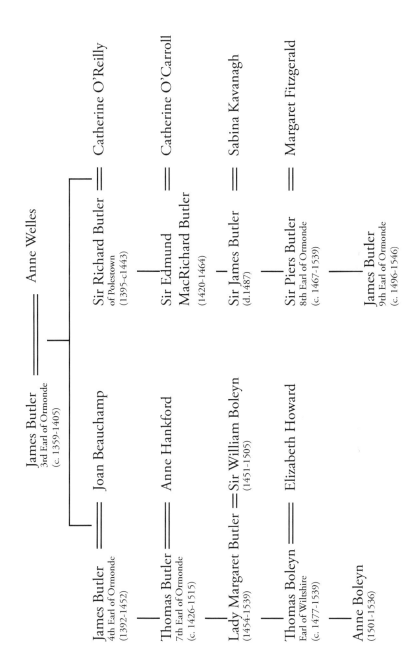

Figure 8 - The genealogical link between James Butler,
9th Earl of Ormonde and Anne Boleyn

Thomas had obviously been close to his grandfather because Thomas Butler left him an important bequest – a white horn of ivory garnished at both ends with gold, covered with gold-barred white silk and with a gold terret ring so that it could be connected to a chain.[3] Family legend had it that this horn had been in the family since the time of Theobald Walter, in the reign of Henry II, and that the famous martyr, Thomas à Becket had drunk from it.[4] In his will, Thomas Butler gave instructions for it to be passed on to Sir Thomas Boleyn "to keep it for the use of his male issue." The fact that Butler left it to Thomas Boleyn, rather than the son of his eldest daughter, Anne, shows that the two men must have been close.[5]

Regardless of the fact that the Boleyns and St. Legers were the rightful heirs to the title and lands, Sir Piers Butler, who was on the ground in Ireland, seized the estates and started styling himself Earl. He had the backing of the Irish Lords and people, but Thomas Boleyn had the backing of Henry VIII. It was a problem. A solution needed to be found to keep both the Boleyns and St. Legers happy, but also to keep the peace in Ireland; Piers could help the English government control the troublesome Irish factions.

On 12th December, 1515, the Crown issued a directive granting Anne St. Leger and Margaret Boleyn "livery of lands as coheirs of their father."[6] The sisters divided the 72 manors equally, with Margaret taking the ones in Essex and the counties near London. The Boleyns and St. Legers had already begun proceedings to obtain the Irish lands before the Earl's death. In July 1515, Sir Thomas Boleyn had asked Henry VIII to write to Lord Kildare, Lord Deputy in Ireland, to examine the claims of Anne St Leger and Margaret Boleyn versus those of Sir Piers Butler. Kildare replied that he'd asked Piers to appear before him and the King's council on 14th October 1515, but that Piers did not show up on that day, his wife pleading war as an excuse for his non-attendance. A date of 19th November was set for a hearing in Dublin.[7] The Earl of Kildare wrote to Henry VIII to report on the hearing:

*"On that day the ladies' counsel showed a livery, under the Great
Seal of England, of all the lands, &c. belonging to the late Earl and
an inspeximus under the Great Seal of Ireland, reciting the creation
of the Earl, with a gift of 10l. yearly to be paid to him and his heirs by
the mayor and bailiffs of Waterford, and certain tails by fines levied
to the said Earl and his heirs general, of his manors, &c. in Dublin
and Meath. To all the residue of the Earl's lands the ladies asserted
their title as heirs general, and Sir Piers and his counsel would show
no evidence or counsel, but prayed to be remitted to the common law."*[8]

The ladies' evidence was impressive.

On 12th December 1515, William Rokeby, Archbishop of
Dublin and Lord Chancellor of Ireland, wrote to Thomas Wolsey
to inform him that he had "been much occupied with the Lord
Deputy in Sir Thos. Bullene's cause."[9] He went on to say that
Piers wanted the case to be tried under common law but that this
would not suit Thomas Boleyn. It was a delicate situation. Rokeby
explained that "The Deputy would have ordered him to appear
before the King in England on a certain day, on pain of allegiance,
but was dissuaded by the Abp. and others, who urged the danger
of rebellion, for he has now made peace and confederation with
Desmond and the three greatest Irish Lords of his party. Moreover,
as he calls himself an Earl, he would be loth to lose the name"
and then asked Wolsey for instructions on how to proceed. No
settlement was reached and the earldom was still under dispute in
spring 1520 when Thomas Howard, Earl of Surrey and Thomas
Boleyn's brother-in-law, was sent to Ireland as Lord Lieutenant. He
quickly became on good terms with Sir Piers and this relationship,
combined with his desire to get home to England as quickly as
possible, caused him to try and come up with a solution that would
solve the dispute and keep everyone happy.

It is not clear how the idea came about, but in September
1520 Henry VIII wrote to Surrey thanking him for his reports
and letters from August and September, and instructing Surrey
"to ascertain whether the earl of Ormond is minded to marry his

son to the daughter of Sir Thomas Boleyn," adding, "The King will advance the matter with Sir Thomas."[10] Surrey and the Council of Ireland wrote to Wolsey on 6th October 1520, saying that they thought "it would be advantageous if a marriage were solemnised between the earl of Ormond's son, now in England, and Sir Thomas Boleyn's daughter." [11] The daughter in question was obviously Anne Boleyn, because Mary Boleyn was already married, and the son in question was James Butler, who had been born around 1496 and so was about twenty-four at this time. He'd spent his early life on the Ormond estates (in the counties of Kilkenny and Tipperary) and had made his debut at the English court in 1513 when he had joined Henry VIII's forces for the invasion of France. He took part in the siege of Thérouanne in August 1513 but suffered a serious leg injury. As a consequence, he limped for the rest of his life and became known as "Bocach" or "Bacach" ("the lame"). A marriage match between Anne and James would mean that the earldom of Ormond would pass to James and Anne on Piers' death and therefore be in the Boleyn and Butler family. However, this would also mean that Thomas Boleyn would not inherit the title, and although his feelings are unrecorded I cannot imagine him being best pleased with this compromise.

James had returned to Ireland after the siege of Thérouanne but was sent back to England when the marriage negotiations began, joining the household of Thomas Wolsey and accompanying Wolsey to Calais on embassy in August 1521. His time in Wolsey's household would further his education but also allow England to keep him as a hostage to ensure his father's good behaviour, as shown by Wolsey's letter to the King in November 1521:

"Thinks the request made to the King in Sir Piers Butler's letter very reasonable. He would do the King great service in that land, considering the towardness of his son, who is right active and discreet. Yet it would be well to see how the said Sir Piers shall acquit himself in the authority lately committed to him; no doubt, his son being in England, he will do all the better in order to get him home the sooner.

Figure 9 - Kilkenny Castle

*On my return I will talk with you how to bring about the marriage
between his son and Sir Thos. Boleyn's daughter, which will be a good
pretext for delaying to send his son over."*[12]

It must have been around this time that Anne was recalled
from France. Although Francis I, King of France, was worried that
the recall of his wife's lady-in-waiting, along with that of various
English students in Paris, "seemed to indicate an English intention
to make war on France",[13] Cardinal Wolsey assured the French King
that Anne Boleyn was being recalled to marry. Here is a report of
this from the Spanish Calendar of State Papers:

*"The ambassadors complained that Boleyn's daughter, who was
in the service of the French queen, had been called home, and said
this was not a sign of continued friendship. The cardinal said that
he himself was responsible for her recall, because he intended, by her
marriage, to pacify certain quarrels and litigation between Boleyn
and other English nobles."*[14]

This report was dated around 17th January 1522. Eric Ives
points out that, seeing as the ambassador who made the original
complaint on behalf of Francis I left France before 6th January
1522, we can be sure that Anne left France in late 1521.[15]

This is the last record we have of the marriage negotiations. We
don't know exactly when the negotiations fizzled out, or why, but
it seems likely that Thomas Boleyn was not happy with the plan.
Anne's feelings are unknown, but I suspect she would have had little
choice in the matter anyway. We do know that James Butler was
still in England in October 1522 when he was recruited into the
King's household, becoming an esquire-at-arms, and that he served
the King for six years, returning to Ireland in 1528. Henry VIII
obviously liked the man because he referred to him as "our faithful
servant, James le Butler"[16] and granted him land in Meath.

William Dean,[17] in his thesis on Thomas Boleyn, ponders
whether the relationship in about 1523 between Anne Boleyn and
Henry Percy, the son and heir of the Earl of Northumberland, was

broken off to keep up the pretext of the Boleyn/Butler marriage, thereby preventing trouble in Ireland. Percy was quickly married off to Mary Talbot, "the cause for such haste being the desire to break up Anne and Percy before the Butlers learned that the marriage idea was just a ruse to insure their good behaviour."[18] Dean believes that Anne was used "as a decoy for the objective of keeping peace in Ireland as long as Piers believed the marriage offer to be genuine." However, Piers Butler must have discovered the truth by May 1523 because the Earl of Kildare wrote to Henry VIII telling him that that Piers had "made new bonds with the Irishry, especially with O'Keroll, by whose aid he means to defend his title to the earldom of Ormond."[19]

It took until 1528 for the dispute to finally be solved. A deal was brokered which involved Piers Butler receiving fourteen of the Ormond manors on a thirty-year lease, and also being elevated to the peerage, in return for relinquishing the earldom of Ormond to Thomas Boleyn. Here is the record of this deal from Letters and Papers:

"*Indenture tripartite between Henry VIII. on the one part; dame Ann Seyntleger, widow, and dame Marg. Boleyn, widow, daughters and heirs of Sir Thos. Butler, earl of Ormond, and Thos. Viscount Rochford, son and heir apparent of dame Margaret, and Sir Geo. Seyntleger, son and heir apparent of dame Anne, on the second part; and Sir Pierce Butler, cousin and heir male of the said Earl, and Jas. Butler, his son and heir apparent, on the third part; witnessing an agreement between the parties through the mediation of Wolsey;—that the title of the earl of Ormond, with the annuity of 10l. out of the fee farm of Waterford, shall be henceforth at the King's disposal; that Sir Pierce shall be allowed peaceable possession of the manors of Cloncurry and Turvy in Ireland, and the said dame Ann and dame Margaret of the castles and manors of Carrykmakgryffen, Roskre, Kilkenny, and a number of others; that dame Ann and dame Margaret grant to farm, to the said Sir Pierce and James his son, the castle of Kilkenny, and other lands on the west side of the river Barowe,*

*in the counties of Kilkenny, Tipperary, and Ormond, for the term of
30 years, at a rent of 40l.; that if Sir Pierce Butler, and James, or any
of their heirs, do within that time recover possession from the wild
Irish of other lands west of the Barowe which should belong to dame
Ann and dame Margaret, the said Viscount and Sir George, they shall
enjoy them to the end of that term without paying any more rent; that
dame Anne, dame Margaret, the said Viscount and Sir George, and
their heirs for ever, shall enjoy the castle of Carrykmakgryffen, and
other lands east of the Barowe, without let or hindrance, except the
manors of Cloncurry and Turvy, but that they will grant Sir Pierce
and James reasonable leases, a year after the feast of the Annunciation
of Our Lady next, &c. Dated 18 Feb. 19 Hen. VIII.”*[20]

Piers became 1st Earl of Ossory on 22nd February 1528[21][22]
and Thomas Boleyn became the 9th Earl of Ormond (as well as
Wiltshire) on 8th December 1529.[23] Both men were finally happy.

After the fall of the Boleyns in 1536, Acts of Parliament were
passed to cancel the agreement made between Piers, the Boleyns
and St Legers and to allow Piers to benefit from the Ormond
inheritance.[24] In October 1537, Piers pleaded his case for the title
of Earl of Ormond, giving proof that the earldom was “tailed to
heirs male”[25] and following that it was recorded that “The earl
of Wiltshire is content that he [Butler] should be called earl of
Ormond in Ireland, like as the two lord Dacres are called, one of
the North, the other of the South.”[26] Thus, Butler began styling
himself Earl of Ormond again, as well as Earl of Ossory.

Anne Boleyn obviously ended up marrying King Henry VIII;
but what happened to James?

- James Butler returned to Ireland in 1528, and in 1530
  he married Joan Fitzgerald, daughter and heir of James
  Fitzgerald, late Earl of Desmond, and then set about being
  a “warlord”. Here are some highlights of his life and career:

- May 1528 - After he, his father and brothers confronted the
  Fitzgeralds at Leinster, he was held prisoner briefly by Brian

O'Connor Faly, an ally of Gerald Fitzgerald, Earl Kildare.

- 1532-1533 - James raided the estates of Fitzgerald supporters in County Wexford. It was recorded that "John Sherlock, merchant of Waterford, did cause and procure Perse, Earle of Ossory, and Lord James Butler, to come with their great oste violently, with force and arms unto the parish of Mulrankan in the county of Wexford on the 2nd day of February the 24th year of the raigne of our soveraine lord; and then and there did feloniously take away from Walter Browne of Mulrankan, and John Devereux, and certain goods from James Keating, to the valew of £100 and more; and then the said Lord James Butler with part of the said oste did menace the commonalty of Federt (Fethard on Sea) to have coyne and livery of them; and in eschewing of the same were compelled to pay unto the said James 20 marks."[27] He didn't get into trouble for his actions and instead was rewarded by being made Lord Treasurer of Ireland in July 1532.[28]

- September 1532 - The Fitzgeralds retaliated by attacking the Butlers in Upper Ossory. James survived, but his brother, Thomas, was killed. In the Calendar of Ormond Deeds, there is the following record:

"Examination of witnesses made on September 24 in the 25th year of Henry VIII at the request of Piers, Earl of Ossory, by Nicholas Wise, mayor of Waterford, and the privy council of the same, Nicholas, bishop of Waterford and Lismore, and Miles, bishop of Ossory, concerning the assault made on the Lord James Butler and his brethren, and the murder of his son, Thomas Butler..."[29]

James testified concerning the involvement of the servants of the Earl of Kildare in his brother's murder, and how the Earl "rejoiced in the murder". Kildare was summoned to England by the King.

- 1534-1535 - James fought the rebels of the Kildare Revolt and was rewarded by being appointed Lord Admiral of Ireland and Warden of the Ports in May 1535.

- Autumn 1535 - He was made Viscount Thurles.

- 1538 - He wrote to Henry VIII of "the longe fraudulent tradicions and detestable abusyons of the papisticall secte" and supporting his reform. He was also friends with Bishop Hugh Latimer.

- August 1539 - James became Earl of Ormond (9th Earl of Ormond) after the death of his father.

- 1539 - He successfully challenged Lord Deputy Leonard Grey's position, writing to Cromwell to compare Grey to Kildare, and plotting against Grey. Grey was dismissed in 1540 and executed in 1541.

- 1544 - He gathered 300 men from Kilkenny and Tipperary to serve in the King's forces in France.

- November 1545 - He was joint commander, with the Earl of Lennox, of the Irish army which was prepared to invade Western Scotland on behalf of Henry VIII. His biographer, David Edward, writes that "Comprising a force of 2000 kerne, it was reckoned to be the largest Irish levy to serve the English monarchy outside Ireland for 200 years. Although the invasion was aborted near Dumbarton in response to political developments in Scotland, Ormond had attained a position of great importance as one of the King's most trusted and most experienced military commanders."[30]

- 1546 - A feud between Ormond and Sir Anthony St Leger, Lord Deputy, led to them denouncing each other. Henry VIII had to intervene and summoned the two men to Whitehall to attend an official enquiry.

- October 1546 - St Leger was exonerated, but Ormond and seventeen of his followers died of poisoning after a banquet at Limehouse in London. Some believe that Ormond was poisoned by St Leger, but David Edwards writes that "a close examination of the evidence surrounding the fatal banquet does not support this suspicion, revealing that St Leger had neither the motive nor the opportunity to plot such an outcome."[31] Edwards further points out that the dying Ormond named St Leger as the supervisor of his will, and so must not have suspected foul play. Chronicler Richard Stanihurst, who helped with Holinshed's Irish Chronicles (Holinshed Volume 6), recorded "For whether it were that one caitife [coward or wretch] or other did poison the meat, or that some other false measures were used."[32] Edwards takes this to mean accidental food poisoning, but I don't read it as such.

Ormond died on 28th October and his body was buried at the Church of St Thomas d'Acres in Cheapside, London. However, his heart was interred at St Canice's in Kilkenny, according to his instructions. He left a wife and seven sons. Stanihurst described Ormond:

"This earle was a goodlie and personable noble man, full of honour, which was not onelie lodged inwardlie in his mind, but also he bare it outwardlie in countance: as franke & as liberall as his calling required, a deepe and a farre reaching head. In a good quarell rather stout than stubborne, bearing himselfe with no lesse courage when he resisted, than with honorable discretion where he yielded. A favourer of peace, no furtherer of warre, as one that procured unlawfull quietnesse before upright troubles, being notwithstanding of as great wisedome in the one, as of valour in the other. An earnest and a zealous vpholder of his countrie, in all attempts rather respecting the publike weale than his priuat gaine. Whereby he bound his countrie so greatlie vnto him, that Ireland might with good cause wish, that either he had neuer beene borne, or else that he had neuer deceased; so it were lawfull to craue him to be immortall, that by course of nature was framed mortall."[33]

His widow, Joan, went on to marry courtier Sir Francis Bryan, a cousin of Anne Boleyn. After his death, Joan married her cousin, Gerald Fitzgerald, 15th Earl of Desmond. Joan was known as a peacemaker in Ireland and Elizabeth I relied on her to keep the peace between the warring Butlers and Fitzgeralds. Joan died on 2nd January 1565. With the peacemaker gone, war broke out, notably the Battle of Affane between the two families. Joan's son, Thomas, was the victor.

How different Anne's life would have been if she had married James Butler instead of Henry VIII. It is impossible to "what if?", but it's reasonable to assume that she would have had a life similar to James's wife, Joan.

- Her home would have been Kilkenny Castle. It may not be as grand as Hampton Court Palace, but it is a beautiful castle with extensive grounds, covering around fifty acres.

- Joan had seven sons, including Thomas Butler who succeeded his father as 10th Earl of Ormond. Trivia: Thomas met Elizabeth I when they were both children and Elizabeth referred to him as her "black husband". There is even a story that she bore him an illegitimate son, although there is, of course, no evidence of this.

- Joan was widowed in 1546 when James died of poisoning and, as I have already said, she went on to marry Sir Francis Bryan, and then, after his death, the Earl of Desmond.

Like Joan, Anne would have been an influential political figure and would have been important to the English monarch for keeping the peace between the Irish factions. However, if Anne had not married Henry VIII, Elizabeth I would never have existed. If Anne had married James Butler, then she certainly would not have been the iconic historical figure she is known as today, but she would still have been important. Papers and books have been written about Joan; I can imagine Anne, with her wit and intelligence, being just as influential as Joan, if not more so.

Final Thoughts

As I said earlier, it's impossible to "what if?" If she'd married James then she would never have been executed, but she also wouldn't have been Queen. My good friend Clare Cherry once said of Anne Boleyn and her brother, George, "I think those amazing people would rather have had those ten years in the sunlight than a lifetime in the shadows", and she may well be right. Anne has gone down in history as Queen Anne Boleyn, a saint to some, a witch to others, the subject of a multitude of history books, novels, movies and websites. I doubt that all that would have happened if she'd married James and moved to Ireland. And who knows what would have happened with Henry VIII and Catherine of Aragon, and the English Reformation?

Notes and Sources

1   "Letters and Papers, Foreign and Domestic, Henry VIII, Volume 1: 1509-1514," n. 82.
2   Carte, The Life of James, Duke of Ormond, Introduction, lxxxiii.
3   Dean, "Sir Thomas Boleyn: The Courtier Diplomat (1477-1539)," 54.
4   Carte, An History of the Life of James Duke of Ormonde, 1:xliii – xliv.
5   Archaeologia: Or Miscellaneous Tracts Relating to Antiquity, III:20–21.
6   "Letters and Papers, Foreign and Domestic, Henry VIII, Volume 2: 1515-1518," n. 1277.
7   Ibid., n. 1230, 1269.
8   Ibid., n. 1230.
9   Ibid., n. 1269.
10   "Letters and Papers, Foreign and Domestic, Henry VIII, Volume 3: 1519-1523," n. 1004.
11   Ibid., n. 1011.
12   Ibid., n. 1762.
13   "Calendar of State Papers, Spain: Further Supplement to Volumes 1 and 2," 30.
14   Ibid.
15   Ives, The Life and Death of Anne Boleyn, 372, note 71.
16   "Oxford Dictionary of National Biography," chap. James Butler, 9th Earl of Ormond and 2nd Earl of Ossory (b. in or after 1496, d. 1546), David Edwards.

17   Dean, "Sir Thomas Boleyn: The Courtier Diplomat (1477-1539)," 95.
18   Ibid.
19   "Letters and Papers, Foreign and Domestic, Henry VIII, Volume 3: 1519-1523," n. 3048.
20   "Letters and Papers, Foreign and Domestic, Henry VIII, Volume 4: 1524-1530," n. 3937.
21   Ibid., n. 3950.
22   "Calendar of Carew Manuscripts, 1515-1574," 37–39.
23   "Letters and Papers, Foreign and Domestic, Henry VIII, Volume 4: 1524-1530," n. 6083.
24   "Letters and Papers, Foreign and Domestic, Henry VIII, Volume 10 - January-June 1536," n. 1030.
25   "Letters and Papers, Foreign and Domestic, Henry VIII, Volume 12 Part 2: June-December 1537," n. 963.
26   Ibid., n. 964.
27   Hore and Graves, The Social State of the Southern and Eastern Counties of Ireland in the 16th Century, 45–46.
28   "Letters and Papers, Foreign and Domestic, Henry VIII, Volume 5: 1531-1532," n. 1207.15.
29   Curtis, "Calendar of Ormond Deeds, Volume IV: 1509-1547," n. 191.
30   "Oxford Dictionary of National Biography," chap. James Butler, 9th Earl of Ormond and 2nd Earl of Ossory (b. in or after 1496, d. 1546), David Edwards.
31   Ibid.
32   Holinshed, Holinshed's Chronicles of England, Scotland, and Ireland, 6:318.
33   Ibid.

7. Anne Boleyn's Love life

In May 1536, while Anne Boleyn was imprisoned in the Tower awaiting her death, her husband, King Henry VIII, was heard to comment that he thought that "upwards of 100 gentlemen have had criminal connexion with her",[1] i.e. that Anne had slept with over one hundred men. I believe that we can put this comment down to bluster, to Henry defending his actions and the treatment of Anne. Even Chapuys was sceptical, commenting that "You never saw a prince or husband show or wear his horns more patiently and lightly than this one does. I leave you to guess the cause of it."[2] Obviously Henry was not showing any signs of distress at his wife making a mockery of their marriage, not like he did when he broke down in tears in front of his privy council over Catherine Howard's alleged betrayal. However, even if we put Henry's words down to bluster, Anne Boleyn has been called many names, in the sixteenth century and today, which relate to her sexuality and her love life:

- The scandal of Christendom
- Goggle-eyed whore
- The concubine
- The putain (whore)
- Harlot

- The English Mare
- The Royal Mule

These are names used by her enemies, men such as Nicholas Sander, who also wrote of her having an extra finger, a wen and a projecting tooth; and of course by Eustace Chapuys, who just couldn't bring himself to call the woman he viewed as a usurper by her actual name. These men had an agenda, a need to discredit Anne. In addition, Sander may well have been confusing Anne and her sister, Mary, who Francis I allegedly nicknamed his "English Mare". But had Anne done anything to earn herself these nicknames? Had she, as one book's blurb claims, before she met Henry VIII, "wandered down love's winding path....[and] learned its twists and turns during her youth spent at the courts of the Low Countries and France"?[3] Let's examine the love life of this fascinating Queen...

Sinning with the Family Chaplain and Butler?

According to the afore mentioned Nicholas Sander, Anne was actually banished to France by her father at the age of fifteen because she had "sinned first with her father's butler, and then with his chaplain".[4] I think we can take this claim with a very hefty pinch of salt. We know that Anne was sent to Margaret of Austria's court at the age of twelve to finish her education and then, a year later, to France to serve Mary Tudor, Queen of France. She was already in France at the age of fifteen and Sander is the only one to make this claim.

Corrupted by the French Court

Alison Weir questions Anne Boleyn's virtue in her recent biography of Mary Boleyn, writing that she had "risked becoming the subject of scandal at the French court".[5] Weir uses two pieces of evidence to back this up:

1. Francis I, King of France, confiding in Rodolfo Pio, Bishop of Faenza: "Francis also spoke three days ago of the new queen of England, how little virtuously she has always lived and now lives, and how she and her brother and adherents suspect the duke of Norfolk of wishing to make his son King, and marry him to the King's legitimate daughter, though they are near relations."[6]

2. Eustace Chapuys, imperial ambassador, reporting that Henry VIII had confided in him that Anne had been "corrupted" during her time in France.

What Chapuys actually reported was that after Anne's fall Henry did not want to marry Madeleine of Valois, Francis I's daughter, because "he had had too much experience of French bringing up and manners".[7] Not quite the same as saying that Anne Boleyn had been corrupted.

There is no evidence to back up Francis I's claim that Anne had lived "little virtuously" and we don't even know that Francis really said it. Surely someone would have warned Henry VIII. before their marriage, if Anne Boleyn had been corrupted in France; scandal would certainly have been attached to her name. Chapuys, one of Anne's main enemies, does not repeat any gossip about her time in France or her alleged sexual experience. Since Anne served the virtuous Queen Claude in France, I suspect that Anne kept her virtue. Anne would have known that her future marriage prospects rested on her keeping her virginity and her reputation.

First Love – Henry Percy

Anne Boleyn returned to England in late 1521 after being recalled to marry James Butler, one of her Irish relations, and to serve Catherine of Aragon, Henry VIII's first wife. According to Cardinal Wolsey's gentleman-usher, George Cavendish, it was in 1523, while Anne was serving Catherine, that she met Henry Percy. Percy was the son and heir of the Earl of Northumberland

and a member of Wolsey's household. Anne and Percy fell in love and were apparently intending to marry when Wolsey and the King put a stop to their relationship.

Cavendish claims that the King ordered Wolsey to stop the marriage because of his "secret affection"[8] for Anne, but there is no other evidence that the King was attracted to Anne at this time. It is thought that Henry was involved with her sister, Mary, in 1523, and that the marriage was more likely to have been stopped due to Wolsey's plans for Anne to marry Butler. Anne and Percy were separated and Percy was quickly married off to Mary Talbot. It was not a happy marriage.

Thomas Wyatt - The Lover Confesseth Him in Love

In Hilary Mantel's recent novel, *Bring Up the Bodies*, Henry VIII suspects his wife of having had a sexual relationship with Thomas Wyatt the Elder, poet and courtier, but is there any truth to this claim?

Thomas Wyatt grew up at Allington Castle, around twenty miles from Hever Castle, the Boleyn family home, and he and Anne were a similar age. However, Anne was abroad for her teenage years so they probably did not meet until Anne began serving Catherine of Aragon in the 1520s. Wyatt was a married man, albeit unhappily married. His love for Anne is recorded by his grandson, George Wyatt, in his memoir of Anne Boleyn, *The Life of Queen Anne Boleigne*.[9] George records that when Wyatt first saw Anne at court, he was "surprised by the sight thereof." He also records a story about Wyatt and King Henry VIII arguing over Anne. In this story, Wyatt manages to snatch a jewel from Anne and keeps it as a trophy. Later, when he is playing playing bowls with the King and arguing over a shot, the King points to the wood, showing a finger on which is he is wearing Anne's ring, and declares "Wyatt, I tell thee it is mine". Wyatt, seeing the ring, replies "If it may like your majesty to give me leave to measure it, I hope it will be mine", and

Figure 10 - Vintage engraving of Sir Thomas Wyatt

then takes Anne's jewel, which was hanging around his neck, and begins to measure the cast with its ribbon. An angry Henry VIII stomped off in search of Anne for an explanation.

Of course, we don't know the truth of this story, but it could well have been handed down the family. However, it does not mean that Anne and Wyatt necessarily had a relationship. Wyatt's poem, *Whoso List to Hunt* tells of a man hunting a hind, with little chance of success, and then being forced to withdraw from the hunt because of another hunter. Wyatt may have been referring to his unrequited love for Anne and his forced withdrawal of his suit because of Henry VIII's interest in her:

> "There is written, her fair neck round about:
> *Noli me tangere*, for Caesar's I am"

Anne belonged to another, more important man than Wyatt.

The Spanish Chronicle[10] tells an interesting story. In it, Wyatt visits Anne at Hever Castle and begins kissing her and touching her breast. All of a sudden, the couple are disturbed by a stamping noise from upstairs, the stamping of a jealous and impatient lover whose liaison with Anne had been interrupted by Wyatt's arrival. This story just cannot be taken seriously. It is pure tabloid journalism and simply an attempt to blacken Anne's name. No other source backs it up.

Henry VIII – For Caesar's I Am

Nobody knows exactly when Anne caught Henry VIII's eye, but Henry rode out to the Shrovetide joust of 1526 motto with the motto "*Declare je nos*" (Declare I dare not) embroidered on his costume below a picture of a man's heart engulfed in flames. He was declaring his love and passion for a new flame; it is likely that she was Anne Boleyn.

What we do know, because we still have them, is that Henry

Figure 11 - Vintage Engraving of King Henry VIII

bombarded Anne with love letters between spring 1527 and autumn 1528. We also know that the couple agreed to marry in the summer of 1527. Following Anne's acceptance of his proposal, Henry VIII decided, in August 1527, to ask the Pope for a dispensation to marry Anne. He had no idea at that time that he'd have to wait so long to marry Anne, but he didn't give up. The couple were married in a secret ceremony on 25th January 1533.

Their relationship sounds pretty sordid. He was a married man, she was his wife's lady-in-waiting, and they actually married before his annulment had come through, but Henry was intent on replacing Catherine and having a fertile wife who would give him an heir to the throne. Anne was his chance.

Her Frail and Carnal Appetites

In 1536, Anne Boleyn was accused of committing adultery and incest, and of conspiring with her lovers to kill the King. The Middlesex and Kent indictments accused Anne of "following daily her frail and carnal appetites" and procuring Sir Henry Norris, Sir Francis Weston, Sir William Brereton, Mark Smeaton and her own brother, George Boleyn, to "violate" her by "sweet words, kisses, touches and otherwise".[11] In a letter to the King's ambassadors in France, Thomas Cromwell referred to Anne's "abominable" deeds and her "incontinent living".[12] He painted her as the Queen of debauchery, a woman whose sexual appetite knew no ends.

We know now that the dates of Anne's alleged crimes just do not make sense. Three quarters of them have been disproved by historians, the majority of whom believe that Anne and the five men were framed. There is no evidence that Anne was unfaithful to the King; it appears that this was simply a plot to get rid of her once and for all.

Conclusion

When I read through these stories of Anne's alleged lovers it makes me think of the tabloid magazines you see advertised on TV, the ones giving the latest salacious gossip about celebrities – who's sleeping with whom, who's having an affair, who's having whose baby. We take these stories with a pinch of salt because we generally find out later that they have no basis. Well, the propaganda machinery was in full swing in Tudor times too, and Chapuys was a great one for repeating gossip and then correcting himself later. And don't get me started on *The Spanish Chronicle*, according to which Thomas Cromwell allegedly interrogated Catherine Howard at a time when he was actually dead!

Anne Boleyn was and is a fascinating lady, but her love life was far from salacious. OK, she got involved with a married man; but that's the most salacious it gets. Married man: yes, 100+ lovers: not likely. She wasn't an angel, but she was far from a whore.

Notes and Sources

1   "Calendar of State Papers, Spain, Volume 5 Part 2: 1536-1538," 121.
2   Ibid.
3   Wilkinson, The Early Loves of Anne Boleyn.
4   Sander, Rise and Growth of the Anglican Schism.
5   Weir, Mary Boleyn: The Great and Infamous Whore, 76.
6   "Letters and Papers, Foreign and Domestic, Henry VIII, Volume 8," n. 985.
7   "Calendar of State Papers, Spain, Volume 5 Part 2: 1536-1538," chap. Additions and corrections to No.61, 6th June 1536 .
8   Cavendish, The Life of Cardinal Wolsey, 1:58.
9   Cavendish, The Life of Cardinal Wolsey, Volume 2.
10   Hume, Chronicle of King Henry VIII. of England, 99.
11   "Letters and Papers, Foreign and Domestic, Henry VIII, Volume 10 - January-June 1536," n. 876.
12   Ibid., n. 873.

8. Anne Boleyn, Nanny McPhee and Nicholas Sander

This chapter was inspired by a comment left on The Anne Boleyn Files which read, "Henry fell in love with Anne because she was a stunning, smart woman, not because she looked like Nanny McPhee." Now Nanny McPhee, played by actress Emma Thompson, had a bulbous nose, warts, and a protruding tooth. It is hard to see Henry VIII abandoning Catherine of Aragon and breaking with Rome simply in order to marry a Nanny McPhee look alike, so what on earth is the link?

Well, Nicholas Sander's 1585 book *De Origine ac Progressu schismatis Anglicani*, more commonly known as "Rise and Growth of the Anglican Schism", has the following passage about Anne:

"Anne Boleyn was rather tall of stature, with black hair, and an oval face of a sallow complexion as if troubled with jaundice. She had a projecting tooth under the upper lip, and on her right hand six fingers. There was a large wen under her chin, and therefore to hide its ugliness she wore a high dress covering her throat. In this she was followed by the ladies of the court, who also wore high dresses, having

Figure 12 - Vintage engraving of Anne Boleyn

before been in the habit of leaving their necks and the upper portion of their persons uncovered. She was handsome to look at, with a pretty mouth, amusing in her ways, playing well on the lute, and was a good dancer."[1]

Sander really could have been describing Nanny McPhee, couldn't he? But Sander was writing in the 16th century so shouldn't we put some store in his words?

No, not really. Sander was born in 1530 and so was only six when Anne Boleyn was executed. He never met her, he never saw her. He was a Catholic recusant who wrote *De Origine* while in forced exile during the reign of Elizabeth I, a woman he hated. While *De Origine* has been hailed by some as "an excellent, popular account of the period from a Catholic point of view",[2] others describe Sander as "Dr Slander, the most violent of anti-Elizabethan propagandists... an enemy agent and no bones about it, an emissary from the Pope to a rebel army".[3] While acting as the procurator for the English exiles in Spain in the 1570s, Sander urged Philip to attack Protestant England, believing that "The state of christendom dependeth upon the stout assailing of England."[4]

As J.H. Pollen points out in his biography of Sander, "Heylin calls him Dr. Slander, Strype 'a most profligate fellow, a very slave to the Roman see, a sworn enemy to his own country,' Burnet's opinion is that 'Sanders had so given himself up to vent reproaches and lies, that he often does it for nothing, without any end but to carry on a trade that had been so long driven by him that he knew not how to lay it down.'"[5] Pollen goes on to describe how Francis Mason described Sander's work as "libel" wherein "the number of lies may seem to vie with the multitude of lines." It is worth noting that Peter Heylin, John Strype and Gilbert Burnet were all 17th century historians and Mason was a 16th and 17th century English churchman. They were not modern day historians examining Sander's work out of context, and they knew their history; this was recent history for them. 19th century historian James Anthony Froude described Sander's work as "the most venomous and successful of libels", describing how Sander "collected into focus every charge which malignity had imagined against Henry VIII and his ministers" and how Sander made use of every "scandalous story" going around at the time.[6]

In my opinion, Sander was going by the old saying "A grain of truth is needed to make a mountain of lies believable" by making use of contemporary descriptions of Anne Boleyn and then embellishing them so as to blacken her name and that of her daughter Elizabeth I. The Venetian ambassador described Anne as "not one of the handsomest women in the world; she is of middling stature, swarthy complexion, long neck, wide mouth, bosom not much raised... and her eyes which are black and beautiful...",[7] and reformer Simon Grynée wrote that "she is young, good-looking, of a rather dark complexion, and likely enough to have children."[8] It is likely also that Sander relied on the hostile account of Anne's coronation which was once in a catalogue of papers at Brussels:

> "Her dress was covered with tongues pierced with nails, to show the treatment which those who spoke against her might expect. Her car was so low that the ears of the last mule appeared to those who stood behind to belong to her. The letters H. A. were painted in several places, for Henry and Anne, but were laughed at by many. The crown became her very ill, and a wart disfigured her very much. She wore a violet velvet mantle, with a high ruff (goulgiel) of gold thread and pearls, which concealed a swelling she has, resembling goître."[9]

This is the only contemporary account of Anne having a wart. However, as Eric Ives[10] points out, if Anne's coronation garb was like the surcoat and mantle that Elizabeth I wore at her coronation, it would have covered Anne's neck anyway. It was not an attempt to hide her neck; and how could the observer have seen the wart in any case? Contrary to what some historians and authors have said, it is the mystery account of Brussels, not Chapuys, which mentions a swelling on Anne's neck at her coronation. The account is lost, so we do not know who wrote it. Chapuys' account of the coronation processions and pageants is not a glowing one – he compares the pageant to a funeral and describes it as "a cold, poor, and most unpleasing sight"[11] – but he certainly does not give Anne a wen.

So, the wen, goitre or wart is not mentioned by any valid contemporary report and, contrary to Sander's account, Anne was not known for wearing high-necked dresses or for bringing in this fashion; high necked dresses came later. Although one historian[12] has quoted George Wyatt, grandson of poet Thomas Wyatt and author of *The Life of Anne Boleigne*, as saying that Anne had a pronounced Adam's apple, I have been unable to find any mention of this in Wyatt's work.

Lancelot de Carles, secretary to the French ambassador, wrote that Anne was "belle et de taille elegante",[13] beautiful with an elegant figure, and he had no reason to lie. Would de Carles really have described a woman with a projecting tooth, an extra finger, yellow skin and a wen as "belle"? I don't think so.

As for Anne being "a thin, old, and vicious hack", another description of Anne which is often given as a reason for her losing Henry's interest, this is a translation of Chapuys' 1536 words "Que sentoit fort a linterpretation de plusieurs la ioyssance destre quiete de maigre, vielle et meschante bague avec espoir de rechargement quest chose fort peculiarie [ment] aggreable au dict roy."[14] Actually, "maigre, vielle et meschante bague" translates to "skinny, old and nasty ring" so Chapuys may be saying that Henry VIII wanted to replace a thin, old, nasty wedding ring with a more agreeable one, i.e. Jane Seymour, but it doesn't necessarily mean that Anne was thin and old. Chapuys is commenting more on Henry VIII's whim than on Anne's appearance.

An Extra Finger?

A six-fingered (on one hand) Anne Boleyn has appeared in Robin Maxwell's *The Secret Diary of Anne Boleyn*, Karen Harper's *The Queen's Governess*, Norah Lofts' fictional *The Concubine* and non-fiction *Anne Boleyn*, and in the Ludlow Castle Lodge portrait of Anne, a modern painting based on the National Portrait Gallery portrait. Anne Boleyn Files visitor, Sonetka, commented recently on one of my web page articles, "The major source for many earlier novelists was Agnes Strickland's *Lives of the Queens of England*, which had a sympathetic account of Anne but which also stated that she had a sixth finger which is why Lofts et al gave her one and made it a way to set her apart from the crowd, both literally and symbolically."[15] She is probably right. However, it's not just in fiction or in old books that we hear about this deformity. One Tudor history website, which is usually very accurate, explains that Anne Boleyn disguised her deformities by "creating new fashions at the Tudor court".[16] Apparently, she wore a black velvet ribbon around her neck to cover up an "unsightly mole", and used long sleeves to hide her extra finger. Alison Weir writes of Anne having a second nail on one of her fingers and how she "took pains to hide it with long hanging oversleeves, another of her fashionable inventions."[17] I've also heard a Yeoman Warder at the Tower of London tell tourists that an extra finger was found when the Victorians exhumed Anne Boleyn's remains in the Chapel of St Peter ad Vincula, and a recent London Dungeon Henry VIII themed "infographic" declared that "Henry's wife, Anne Boleyn, had 6 fingers on each hand", along with a few other dubious facts about the King. This, of course, sparked off outrage on Tudor Facebook pages, particularly as nobody has ever gone as far to say that Anne had an extra finger on both her hands! Obviously the Yeoman Warders and London Dungeon are using the myth as a salacious fact to interest tourists and to entertain, but it means that the myth is propagated.

When we were discussing the six-finger legend over at The Anne Boleyn Files, costume expert Molly Housego tackled the long sleeve theory:

"[It's] rubbish about the extra material in the sleeves being invented by Anne to hide her hands. The large cuffed turn-back sleeves were already known, and continued to grow in size due to fashion

from the 1510s onwards. Check out the National Portrait Gallery (London) 1520s painting of Catherine of Aragon to see her wearing large turn-back cuffs as well."

Catherine would, of course, have been very unlikely to have taken fashion advice from Anne Boleyn.

The Holbein portrait of Lady Mary Guildford, which dates to around 1527, shows Mary with turned back sleeves before Anne was prominent at court. Long sleeves, therefore, just cannot be attributed solely to Anne Boleyn and her desire to hide her fingers. They were simply the fashion of that time.

This legend, like that of the deformed foetus, is rooted in the work of Catholic recusant Nicholas Sander. However, Sander is not the only Elizabethan writer to mention Anne's deformity. George Wyatt, grandson of Thomas Wyatt the Elder, wrote:

"There was found, indeed, upon the side of her nail upon one of her fingers, some little show of a nail, which yet was so small, by the report of those that have seen her, as the workmaster seemed to leave it an occasion of greater grace to her hand, which, with the tip of one of her other fingers, might be and was usually by her hidden without any least blemish to it. Likewise there were said to be upon some parts of her body certain small moles incident to the clearest complexions."[18]

Now Wyatt had nothing to gain by blackening Anne's name and his book is actually a treatise in defence of her, so perhaps there was some kind of blemish on Anne's hand. Wyatt was born in 1553 and never knew Anne Boleyn or his own grandfather, who was a close friend of Anne's, but perhaps this information had been handed down in the family. It is impossible to know, but "some little show of a nail" is far from an extra finger.

I agree with historian Retha Warnicke when she points out that Sander's description of Anne Boleyn "cannot be logically reconciled" with that of the Venetian ambassador who saw Anne in Calais in 1532. He wrote:

"Madam Boleyn is not one of the handsomest women in the world; she is of middling stature, swarthy complexion, long neck, wide mouth, a bosom not much raised, and in fact has nothing but the English king's great appetite and her eyes, which are black and beautiful."[19]

It's not the most flattering description, but does not mention a wen, goitre or mole on her neck, nor an extra finger.

Not one ambassador hints at an extra finger in their reports, yet these are men who would have seen Anne at court and who also had dealings with her diplomat father and brother. An extra finger would surely have caused some contemporary gossip. It is hard to believe that Henry VIII, a man to whom looks were important and who was paranoid about illness and disease, would have accepted such a deformity in a woman who was going to be his wife, Queen, and mother to the heir to the throne. I'm sure that he would have worried about this deformity being passed on to their child.

As far as Anne's remains being proof that she had a extra finger, Dr Mouat, who examined all the remains exhumed from the chancel of the Chapel of St Peter ad Vincula in 1876, recorded that the remains belonged to "a female of between twenty-five and thirty years of age, of a delicate frame of body, and who had been of slender and perfect proportions; the forehead and lower jaw were small and especially well formed. The vertebrae were particularly small, especially one joint (the atlas), which was that next to the skull, and they bore witness to the Queen's 'lyttel neck.'" He also commented that "the hands and feet bones indicate delicate and well-shaped hands and feet, with tapering fingers and a narrow foot."[20] He had found nothing unusual on the hand bones and certainly no extra finger bones. Of course, there is speculation that these remains were not in fact those of Anne Boleyn; but no extra finger bones were found in any of the remains.

The extra finger makes a good story for guides to tell tourists and novelists to explore, but it's just that: a story. Yet another myth that surrounds this fascinating historical woman.

It is frustrating that we do not know exactly what Anne Boleyn looked like, but I think it is safe to say that she had dark hair and eyes, olive skin and moles, and that she was of medium build with small breasts. It is impossible to say what the blemish/deformity was on her hand, but there was obviously something on it.

Notes and Sources

1   Sander, Rise and Growth of the Anglican Schism, 25.
2   "Nicholas Sander."
3   Rose, Cases of Conscience: Alternatives Open to Recusants and Puritans Under Elizabeth I and James I, 47.
4   Ibid.
5   Pollen, "Dr. Niholas Sander," 36.
6   Froude, History of England from the Fall of Wolsey to the Defeat of the Spanish Armada, 11: Reign of Elizabeth Part V:203–4.
7   "Calendar of State Papers and Manuscripts, Venice, Vol. 4 (1527-1533)," n. 824.
8   Sergeant, The Life of Anne Boleyn, 129.
9   "Letters and Papers, Foreign and Domestic, Henry VIII, Volume 6 - 1533," n. 585.
10   Ives, The Life and Death of Anne Boleyn, 30.
11   "Calendar of State Papers, Spain, Volume 4: Part 2," n. 1077, 1081.
12   Weir, The Six Wives of Henry VIII, 151.
13   Ascoli, La Grande-Bretagne Devant L'opinion Française Depuis La Guerre de Cent Ans Jusqu'à La Fin Du XVIe Siècle, 234, line 61.
14   "Calendar of State Papers, Spain, Volume 5 Part 2: 1536-1538," 127.
15   Ridgway, "Anne Boleyn Myths Coming Soon."
16   "Anne Boleyn, Six Wives Info."
17   Weir, The Six Wives of Henry VIII, 151.
18   Cavendish, The Life of Cardinal Wolsey, Volume 2, 2:188.
19   "Calendar of State Papers and Manuscripts, Venice, Volume 4: 1527-33," n. 824.
20   Bell, Notices of the Historic Persons Buried in the Chapel of St Peter Ad Vincula in the Tower of London, 19–21,26.

9. 29 May 1533 – Anne Boleyn's Coronation River Pageant

The coronation of Anne Boleyn in 1533 was a huge, four-day affair and was more like the coronation of a monarch, rather than that of a queen consort. It was a PR exercise; a statement by Henry VIII that Anne Boleyn was his rightful wife and queen, whatever people thought of her or of the annulment of his marriage to Catherine of Aragon. The Milanese ambassador estimated that Anne's coronation cost the City of London was £46,000, or 200,000 ducats, and that Henry VIII spent half that sum again.[1] We don't know how accurate that figure is, but there's no denying that the coronation was a sumptuous and a lavish occasion.

The coronation celebrations began on 29th May 1533, the day after Archbishop Cranmer had proclaimed valid Anne's marriage to Henry VIII. They culminated in the coronation ceremony on Whitsun (1st June). *Hall's Chronicle*[2] and *The Noble Tryumphaunt Coronacyon of Quene Anne*, the latter printed by Wynkyn de Worde, give us all the details of what happened on 29th May.[3] The pageantry began at 1pm, when the London livery companies' fifty barges set off from Billingsgate. These sixty- to seventy-foot long barges,[4] escorted by small boats, were decorated with streamers, bunting, cloth of gold, and banners displaying the arms of the companies. Minstrels entertained the fleet with music and in front of the Mayor's barge was a "foyst", or wherry, bearing a great dragon which was was "continually moving and casting wildfire".[5] This dragon was surrounded by "terrible monsters" and "wild men" also casting fire and making "hideous noises". It sounds like quite a spectacle.

Then came the Mayor's barge and the bachelors' barge, the latter being full of musicians playing trumpets and other instruments. The bachelors' barge was hung with cloth of gold and silk, and bore two huge banners displaying the arms of the King and Queen, along with streamers and bells. It also bore the arms of the company of "Haberdashers" and "Merchant Adventurers." On its starboard gunwale were thirty-six "scochyons", or metal shields, showing the King and Queen's arms impaled (the King's colours on the right and the Queen's colours on the left). These shields were fastened to hangings of cloth of gold and silver. Another feature of this river procession was a wherry carrying a representation of Anne's falcon badge. This crowned, white falcon stood on a gold tree stump surrounded by white and red roses, and "virgins singing and playing sweetly".

The procession arrived at Greenwich Palace at 3pm to pick up the pregnant Queen and escort her to the Tower of London. Anne appeared, dressed in cloth of gold, and boarded her barge. Her ladies boarded a second barge, then the King's guard boarded the King's barge – the King was not part of the procession. These three barges were joined by the barges of bishops and of courtiers. Noblemen in attendance that day included the Duke of Suffolk, the Marquess of Dorset, the Earls of Arundel, Derby, Rutland, Worcester, Huntingdon, Sussex and Oxford, as well as Anne's father, Thomas Boleyn, Earl of Wiltshire. By this time there were "some 120 large craft and 200 small ones"[6] on the Thames.

Letters and Papers[7] describes how gun salutes heralded the

Queen as she made her way along the Thames and that "when she came over against Wapping mills the Tower 'lousyd their ordinaunce' most triumphantly, shooting four guns at once." Anne landed at Tower Wharf and was greeted by dignitaries lined up across the King's bridge to the Tower's private royal entrance, the Court Gate of the Byward Tower. Among the dignitaries were Sir Edward Walsingham, Lieutenant of the Tower, and Sir William Kingston, Constable of the Tower. When Anne entered the Tower, she was received by her husband, the King, "who laid his hands on both her sides, kissing her with great reverence and a joyful countenance", before leading her to her chamber. The King and Queen then supped together.

Notes and Sources

1   Ives, The Life and Death of Anne Boleyn, 181.
2   Hall, Hall's Chronicle, 798–800.
3   The Maner of the Tryumphe of Caleys and Bulleyn and The Noble Tryumphaunt Coronacyon of Quene Anne, Wyfe Unto the Most Noble Kynge Henry VIII.
4   Ives, The Life and Death of Anne Boleyn, 173.
5   Hall, Hall's Chronicle, 799.
6   Ives, The Life and Death of Anne Boleyn, 173.
7   "Letters and Papers, Foreign and Domestic, Henry VIII, Volume 6 - 1533," n. 563.

10.   30 May 1533 –
The Knights of the Bath

*Figure 13 - Engraving showing the Ceremony of
The Knights of The Bath*

Part of coronation celebrations in medieval and Tudor times was the Order of the Bath ceremony, where favoured courtiers were created Knights of the Bath. In 1533, during Anne Boleyn's coronation celebrations, this event took place in the Tower of London on the night of 30th/31st May. Eighteen Knights of the Bath were created:[1]

- Henry Grey, Marquess of Dorset
- Edward Stanley, Earl of Derby
- Henry Clifford, Lord Clifford
- Henry Ratcliffe, Lord Fitzwalter
- Francis Hastings, Lord Hastings
- William Stanley, Lord Monteagle
- Thomas Vaux, Lord Vaux
- Henry Parker, son of Henry, Lord Morley
- William Windsor, son of Lord Windsor
- John Mordaunt, son of Lord Mordaunt
- Francis Weston
- Thomas Arundell
- John Hudletson
- Thomas Poynings
- Henry Savile
- George Fitzwilliam
- John Tyndall
- John (or Henry?) Germayne (Edward Hall says Thomas Germayne[2])

A record in Letters and Papers adds further names: "Mr. Corbet, Mr. Wyndham, John Barkely... Ric. Verney of Penley... Rob. Whitneye of Gloucestershire".[3]

In his book on the Tower, George Younghusband describes this traditional coronation ceremony in relation to the coronation

Figure 14 - Engraving showing the Ceremony of The Knights of The Bath

of Henry IV.[4] He writes that forty-six baths were arranged in one of the halls of the White Tower. Each bath had a canopy over it and was filled with warm water and draped with clean sheets. The forty-six knights bathed and then a procession, led by the King, entered the hall. The King the approached each Knight, still in his bath, and dipped his finger into the bath water and made the sign of the cross on the Knight's bare back. While he did this, the King said:

"You shall honor God above all things; you shall be steadfast in the faith of Christ; you shall love the King your Sovereign Lord, and him and his right defend to your power; you shall defend maidens, widows, and orphans in their rights, and shall suffer no extortion, as far as you may prevent it; and of as great honor be this Order unto you, as ever it was to any of your progenitors or others."

When he had done this to all forty-six knights, King Henry IV processed out of the hall. The knights then dried themselves off and were put to bed in "beds with rich hangings", which had been placed behind their baths. After they had rested for a while, they were summoned to rise by the curfew bell of the Bell Tower. Their esquires helped them dress as monks in long brown woollen cassocks, with cowls, then they processed into St John's Chapel as music played. Their new helmets, armour, swords and spurs had been arranged around the high altar, "and before these each Knight knelt in devotion, and watched his armour all night".

That is what happened at Henry IV's coronation in 1399 and it gives us a good idea of what might have taken place on the night of 30th May 1533. Of course, because he was monarch King Henry VIII, not Anne, would have dubbed the Knights.

Notes and Sources

1   Shaw, The Knights of England: A Complete Record from the Earliest Time to the Present Day of the Knights of All the Orders of Chivalry in England, Scotland, and Ireland, 1:149–50.

2   Hall, Hall's Chronicle, 800.

3   "Letters and Papers, Foreign and Domestic, Henry VIII, Volume 6 - 1533," n. 562.

4   Younghusband, The Tower from Within, 107–108.

11. 31st May 1533 – Anne Boleyn's Coronation Procession

At 5pm on 31st May 1533, Anne Boleyn left the Tower of London to begin her procession through the streets of London to Westminster Hall. Chronicler Edward Hall[1] describes how the streets were gravelled. and railed off so that people would not get hurt. Cornhill and Gracehurch Street were decorated with scarlet and crimson cloth, arras, tapestries and carpets, while Cheapside was decorated with "cloth of tissue, gold, velvet and many rich hangings".

The mayor was clothed in crimson velvet and escorted by footmen dressed in white and red damask, and the Queen's part of the procession was led by the servants of Jean de Dinteville, the French ambassador. These servants were dressed in blue velvet coats with sleeves of blue and yellow velvet. Their horses were "trapped with close trappers of blue sarcenet powdered with white crosses".[2] After them came "gentlemen, squires and knights", followed by the judges, and the Knights of the Bath, dressed in ermine trimmed violet gowns and hoods. Next were abbots, barons, bishops, earls, marquesses, the Lord Chancellor, the Archbishop of York, the

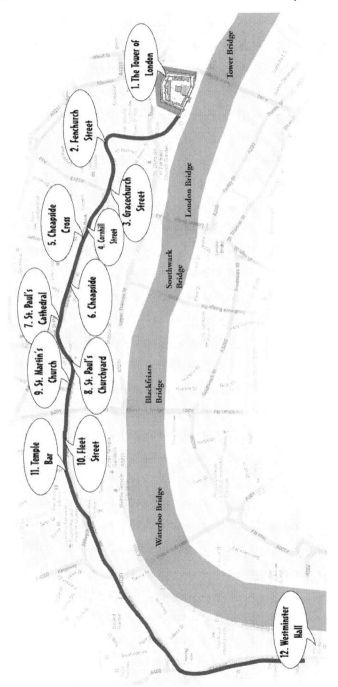

Figure 15 - The Route of the Coronation Procession

Venetian ambassador, the Archbishop of Canterbury, the French ambassador, the Mayor of London, William Howard (acting as Deputy Earl Marshal for his brother, Thomas Howard, Duke of Norfolk) and Charles Brandon, Duke of Suffolk, acting as Constable of England.

Behind her chancellor, "sergeants and officers of arms", came Queen Anne Boleyn in a litter decorated with white cloth of gold and led by two palfreys clad in white damask. Hall describes Anne as wearing a surcoat of white cloth of gold, a mantle, of the same cloth but trimmed with ermine, and a coif with a circlet of "rich stones". Her hair was loose and flowing. Above her was a canopy of cloth of gold, decorated with gilt statues and silver bells, and carried by the barons of the Cinque Ports. Following the Queen were her chamberlain, Lord Borough, and her master of the horses, William Coffin, then her ladies clothed in crimson velvet and cloth of gold and tissue. Then came chariots carrying the Dowager Duchess of Norfolk and the Marchioness of Dorset (or possibly Elizabeth Boleyn, Anne's mother), as well as other ladies of the court.

Rather than simply progressing Westminster, the procession stopped at points on the route to enjoy various pageants and displays. One pageant, on the corner of Gracechurch Street, depicted Apollo and the nine muses on Mount Parnassus. This "ryght costly" pageant had been designed by Hans Holbein the Younger. Another pageant, at Leadenhall, was of Anne's falcon badge. It had a castle with a green, and a "root", or stump, out of which white and red roses spilled. A white falcon descended from Heaven and landed on the stump, then an angel wearing armour descended and crowned the falcon. Yet another pageant consisted of St Anne, surrounded by her children, the three Marys, and their children. In this pageant, Queen Anne Boleyn was read poetry, the verses of which emphasised England's hope for her and for the child she was carrying. Other pageants included a recreation of the Judgement of Paris in which angels held out crowns to Anne whilst a lady prophesied that "Quene Anne whan you shalte beare a newe sone of y e kynges bloode there shalbe a golden worlde unto thy people."³ Other displays included a fountain running with wine, children reading poems of praise for Anne and the King, the Virtues promising to never abandon the Queen, and children singing.

Finally, Anne reached Westminster Hall, which was described by Hall as newly glazed and decorated with "cloth of arras". There, Anne enjoyed refreshments such as "spice plates" and hippocras and wine, which she shared with her ladies. She then gave thanks to the lords, ladies and Mayor, and retired for the night. Both Hall and *The Noble Tryumphaunt Coronacyon of Quene Anne, Wyfe Unto the Most Noble Kynge Henry VIII* record that Anne was then taken secretly to spend the night with the King at his "Manor of Westminster".

Notes and Sources

1   Hall, Hall's Chronicle, 800–802.

2   Ibid., 800.

3   The Maner of the Tryumphe of Caleys and Bulleyn and The Noble Tryumphaunt Coronacyon of Quene Anne, Wyfe Unto the Most Noble Kynge Henry VIII.

12. 1st June 1533 – Anne Boleyn's Coronation

The 1st June 1533, Whitsun, was the day of Anne Boleyn's coronation ceremony at Westminster Abbey. The chronicler Edward Hall[1] records that the Mayor, clad in scarlet and wearing his chain of office, took a barge to Westminster at 7am. He was accompanied by the aldermen, by the sheriffs, and by the Council of the City of London. At Westminster they waited for the Queen. She arrived between 8 o'clock and 9 o'clock, and stood under the cloth of state as the royal court and peers gathered, dressed in their parliament robes. A railed blue "ray cloth" was spread all the way from the high dais of the King's bench to the high altar of the abbey, and the officers of arms helped organise those gathered into a procession.

Figure 16 - Westminster Abbey

Figure 17 - Westminster Hall

Hall records the procession order as:

- Gentleman
- Squires
- Knights
- Alderman of the City
- Judges
- Knights of the Bath
- Barons and viscounts
- Earls, marquesses and dukes
- Lord Chancellor
- Staff of the Chapel Royal and monks
- Abbots and bishops
- Sergeants and officers of arms
- The Mayor of London
- Marquess of Dorset, bearing the sceptre of gold
- Earl of Arundel, bearing the rod of ivory topped with a dove
- Earl of Oxford, High Chamberlain of England, carrying the crown of St Edward
- Charles Brandon, Duke of Suffolk and High Steward of England for the day
- William Howard, carrying the rod of the Marshal of England
- The Garter Knights

Following this procession came the woman of the day, the pregnant Queen Anne Boleyn. Anne was wearing a surcoat and robe of purple velvet, trimmed with ermine, and the coif and circlet she had worn for the procession the previous day. Her train was carried by the Dowager Duchess of Norfolk, and she walked barefoot under a canopy of cloth of gold carried by the barons of the Cinque Ports. Anne made her way to the "great chair", the chair of St Edward, where she rested for a while before descending to the high altar. There, Anne prostrated herself while Thomas Cranmer, Archbishop of Canterbury, prayed over her. When she got up, he anointed her. She was then able to rest once again in St Edward's chair while orations were said. Cranmer crowned Anne with the crown of St Edward, which was usually reserved for crowning the reigning monarch. He placed the sceptre in her right hand and the rod in her left. The Te Deum was sung and Cranmer helped Anne exchange the heavy crown for a custom-made lighter version.

Mass was celebrated, and Anne took the sacrament before visiting St Edward's shrine and giving the traditional offering. She then rested for a few moments while everybody formed into a line to process back to Westminster Hall for the coronation banquet. Anne walked back, her right hand "sustained" by her father, the Earl of Wiltshire, and her left hand by Lord Talbot, who was acting as a deputy for his father, the Earl of Shrewsbury. Trumpets played as they processed to the hall. It was time for the celebratory banquet.

At the banquet, Anne sat on the King's marble chair, which has been set under a cloth of state. She sat next to Thomas Cranmer, Archbishop of Canterbury, and was attended by the Dowager Countess of Oxford and by the Countess of Worcester, whose job was to "hold a fine cloth before the Queen's face when she list to spit or do otherwise at her pleasure."[2] This was not so that she could vomit between courses, as one website has suggested,[3] it was simply so that she could take care of personal hygiene (wiping her face, spitting etc.) in private. Anne was also attended by two gentlewomen positioned at her feet. The Earl of Oxford was high chamberlain, the Earl of Essex was the carver, the Earl of Sussex the sewer, the Earl of Derby the cupbearer, the Earl of Arundel the chief butler and Thomas Wyatt, on behalf of his father, the chief ewer. Between Anne and the Archbishop stood the Earl of Oxford with his white staff of office.

Figure 18 - Vintage Engraving of Thomas Cranmer

When everyone was seated, the Duke of Suffolk and William Howard entered the hall on horseback to announce the first course, which was being carried by the Knights of the Bath. Suffolk is described by Hall as wearing a jacket and doublet "set with orient perle" and a gown of embroidered crimson velvet. He was sitting on a horse draped with crimson velvet which reached the ground and was embroidered with real gold letters. "Trumpets and hautbois sounded at each course, and heralds cried "largesse."" Henry VIII did not join the banquet but watched proceedings, accompanied by the ambassadors of France and Venice, from a special "little closet" which Hall described as situated "out of the cloyster of S. Stephens".

The banquet was followed by wafers and hippocras, then the Queen washed and enjoyed "a voyde of spice and comfettes", after over eighty dishes! After that, the Mayor passed her a gold cup, from which she drank, before giving it back to him. Anne then retired to her chambers where she had to go through the formalities of thanking everyone before she could rest. At 6pm it was finally over. It had been a long and exhausting day for her.

The coronation celebrations were not actually at an end. The four days of processions and pageantry were followed by jousts and further banqueting. King Henry VIII and Queen Anne Boleyn were triumphant.

Notes and Sources

1   Hall, Hall's Chronicle, 802.
2   Ibid., 804.
3   "Odd Food and Drink Facts,". Author Susan Higginbotham has noted that Elizabeth of York was also attended at her coronation by two women who at "certain times held a kerchief before her grace."

13.   Anne the Mother

It is impossible to talk about Anne, her pregnancies and motherhood without looking at what life was like for a Tudor woman who was pregnant or recovering from childbirth. The beliefs and rituals surrounding motherhood were part of Anne's life and the world she lived in. Procreation was a Tudor woman's duty, and a queen was expected to provide her king with a son and heir, as well as with "spares".

Upper class women like Anne married younger than their lower-class counterparts, and also had more children, often having a child every year. For example, Anne's niece, Catherine Carey, had fourteen children. However, it is estimated that 19% of "landed families" in the 17th century died childless either because they had trouble conceiving or because they lost their children to disease.[1] Infant mortality was high - 13% in 1550-99 for children under 1 and 6% for 1-4 yr olds[2] - so it was important for women to have lots of children to ensure that the family name and line were carried on. Families who were keen on having a particular first name carried on would even give two of their children the exact same name, just in case one of them died. This explains why there were two Thomas Culpepers – one who served Thomas Cromwell, and the other who served in Henry VIII's privy chamber and who was known for being Queen Catherine Howard's lover.

Childbirth was also dangerous, although a mortality rate of 1% for each birth made it no more than a woman's chance of dying from disease.[3] Women feared it though, because they all knew someone who had died in childbirth or shortly afterwards due to puerperal fever or some other type of infection.

The Conception of Elizabeth

Anne was around thirty-one[4] when she became pregnant with her first child, Elizabeth. It was perfectly common for women to have children between their mid 20s and late 30s, so in that respect Anne was perfectly normal, although perhaps slightly old for a first child.

Elizabeth was born on 7th September 1533. If she was born around Anne's due date for her, then she was conceived between 12th and 20th December 1532, before Anne and Henry VIII's secret wedding ceremony on 25th January 1533. It appears that Anne and Henry began cohabiting on their return from Calais in November 1532, a trip on which Anne had acted as Henry's consort, and it is possible that they had some kind of betrothal ceremony or wedding ceremony around then. The Tudor chronicler, Edward Hall, wrote:

"The king, after his return [from Calais] married privily the Lady Anne Bulleyn on Saint Erkenwald's Day, which marriage was kept so secret that very few knew it, till she was great with child, at Easter after."[5]

St Erkenwald's Day was 14th November, the day after the couple's return from Calais. We do not know where Hall got his information about the wedding, but a formal commitment at that time fits in with the couple beginning sexual relations. Alternatively, Henry and Anne may have held off consummating their relationship until after their wedding in January 1533 and

Elizabeth may have been born slightly prematurely. Anne took to her chamber fewer than two weeks before Elizabeth's birth, rather than the usual four to six weeks so it is a possibility. But even if Elizabeth was actually due between 23rd September and 7th October, she still would have been conceived before the January wedding (a conception date of between 28th December and 19th January, depending on Anne's menstrual cycles and ovulation date. Anne is unlikely, in this scenario, to have realised she was pregnant as early as she actually did.

By February 1533, Anne's pregnancy was common knowledge at court. According to Chapuys, in open court in mid February Anne told her uncle, the Duke of Norfolk, that if she wasn't pregnant soon she would go on a pilgrimage after Easter.[6] Then, on 22nd February, Anne came out of her apartment into the hall and, spotting Thomas Wyatt, told him that a few days previously, she had had a violent desire to eat apples. She informed Wyatt that, when she had told the King, he'd said that it was a sign that she was pregnant, but she had denied it. She then burst out laughing.[7] Anne obviously knew that this would be gossiped about and was perfectly happy for her pregnancy to be hot news around court.

Historian Eric Ives writes that after Anne's coronation on 1st June 1533, reports of her health continued to be good. However, Ives tells us, the latter stages of Anne's pregnancy were difficult. He writes that the King "had been at his wits' end, even hoping for a miscarriage if it would save Anne's life."[8] Ives' source for this is the poetry of Lancelot de Carles. Here is what de Carles says:

"Quant commença de sentir remuer
Les petitz piedz, et qu'elle se veit prise,
O! qu'elle estoit bien saigement apprise
De se bien plaindre, et faire la dolente,
En voix piteuse et parolle tremblante,
Pour demonstrer la doulleur qu'elle avoit!
O! quel ennuy le Roy en recevoit,
De veoir sa mye en si piteuse sorte!
Je croy qu'il eust voullu sa fille morte,
Mais qu'elle en fust delivree sans tournament,
Tant la faisoit traicter songnieusement,
S'y travaillant de toute son envye,
Qui n'eust tant faict pour conserver sa vye.
Or pensez doncq, puis que le roy lui-mesmes
Estoit en deuil et soucy tant extresme,
Si ung chacun s'efforçoit de trouver
Mille moiens pour plaisir recouvrer!"⁹

It is in 16th century French, but it roughly translates as:

"When she began to feel stirrings
and she felt the kicking of the little feet
how quickly did she learn to complain of the pain in a
pitiful and trembling voice
to show how great was the pain!
And how worried was the King at the sight of his dearest
in such a predicament
why I believe he may have wanted his daughter dead
but she was delivered without a hitch.
So much did he care that he would have done anything to
save her life.
He was like a man in mourning overwhelmed with cares
needing a 1000 diversions to get over it."

It is hard to know whether the "stirrings" mentioned in the poem were Anne simply feeling the baby move, and being in discomfort, or whether the words referred to her contractions beginning. Whatever it means, Henry was obviously very worried about Anne's health and safety, and he didn't go on his usual royal progress that summer.

Pregnancy

We know nothing more about Anne's pregnancy, her feelings about it, or how she looked after herself; but we do know some facts about pregnancy in Tudor times. There was little pre-natal care, and women didn't have much choice about the food they ate or what they drank.[10] Water wasn't safe to drink, so Anne would have continued with wine or ale, but these were not as strong as today's wine and beer. There is some evidence that women were advised to eat protein and to avoid highly spiced foods, to wear low-heeled shoes, to loosen lacings on their garments and to avoid strenuous lifting.[11] There were also debates on whether sexual intercourse and blood-letting were safe during pregnancy.

The ingestion of herbal remedies was very common. Sage was known as the "holy herb" and was thought to strengthen the womb. Seventeenth century midwife Jane Sharp advised women to drink a "good draught" of sage ale every morning during pregnancy and to either drink "Garden Tansie Ale" or to apply tansy and muscatel to the navel to prevent miscarriage. Sharp advised a woman nearing her due date to boil mallows or hollyhocks in spring water with honey and salt, and to use this as an enema. The woman could also bathe in warm water infused with hollyhock leaves, betony, mallows, mugwort, marjoram, mint, camomile, linseed and parsley, and then be "anointed" on her back and belly with an ointment made from sweet almond oil, lilies, violets, duck and hen fat, hollyhock roots, fenugreek seeds and butter.[12]

Pregnancy was surrounded by superstition, and there a strong belief in the power of the maternal imagination. It was believed that what a woman saw or experienced during pregnancy affected the child. For example, a strawberry birthmark was thought to be caused by eating strawberries or by drinking red wine, and a hare lip by seeing a hare.[13] Deformities and miscarriages were linked to sudden frights, bad experiences during pregnancy or contact with animals. Women were advised, therefore, to avoid shocks, funerals, ugly sights and pictures. They put their faith in amulets, charms and objects like eagle stones. An eagle stone, which symbolised the pregnant woman, was a hollow stone with a smaller stone inside. It was worn around the woman's neck so that it touched her skin and it was thought to prevent miscarriage by acting a bit like a magnet and anchoring the unborn child to the woman's body, preventing miscarriage.

Royal astrologers would predict whether the queen was expecting a boy or a girl based on astral arrangements at the time of conception, and there were also superstitions to predict the sex of the unborn baby. Signs that the woman was expecting a boy included:

- The woman being "better coloured"
- Her right breast being more swollen than her left
- The right side of her tummy being more rounded
- The baby moving more on the right side
- The woman being more cheerful
- Her right breast being harder and the nipple being redder
- The woman using her right foot first when she rose from sitting to standing
- The woman choosing to lean on her right hand when she rested
- Drops of breast milk floating on top of the water in a basin, rather than sinking.[14]

Taking Her Chamber

One of the rituals associated with childbirth was called "taking her chamber". A Tudor woman usually "took to her chamber", or went into confinement, four to six weeks before her due date. Anne took to her chamber on 26th August 1533, fewer than two weeks before Elizabeth was born. As I said earlier, Elizabeth may have been premature, Anne may have miscalculated her dates, or she may have purposely entered confinement late to suggest that Elizabeth had been conceived legitimately. Ives suggests that the rapid appointment of Thomas Cranmer as Archbishop of Canterbury, the promotion of Thomas Audley, the burst of parliamentary drafting and the hurried secret ceremony on 25th January 1533 were because Anne suddenly realised that she was pregnant. However, conception was hard to recognise in the early stages of pregnancy, so this burst of activity may simply have been because the couple were sleeping together and so were risking pregnancy.

Anne's "taking her chamber" ceremony took place at Greenwich Palace. A heavily pregnant Queen Anne Boleyn attended a special mass at the palace's Chapel Royal and then processed with her ladies to the Queen's great chamber. There, the group enjoyed wine and spices before Anne's lord chamberlain prayed that God would give the Queen a safe delivery. After the prayer, Anne and her ladies retired to her chamber, which, from that moment on, would be a male-free zone. The fifteenth century "Royalle Book"[15] and the ordinances added to it by Lady Margaret Beaufort stipulated that the birthing chamber should:

- Be carpeted
- Have its walls, ceilings and windows covered with blue arras; these beautiful tapestries were to have calming and romantic images
- Have one window slightly uncovered to let in light and air when needed

- Be furnished with a bed for the Queen and a pallet at the foot of it. The Queen would give birth on the pallet and it was set at a height appropriate for the midwife. This was set up close to the fire and away from cold draughts.

- Have soft furnishings of crimson satin embroidered with gold crowns and the Queen's arms

- Have an altar

- Have a tapestry covered cupboard to house the birthing equipment and swaddling bands

- Have a font in case of a sickly baby needing to be baptised straight after the birth

- Have a display of gold and silver plate items from the Jewel House[16] - It was important for the Queen and her baby to be surrounded by symbols of her wealth and status.

This was the norm. Birth rooms were fastened up against fresh air, which was thought to be harmful; candles were lit in the darkened room and special objects to speed delivery were brought in – objects such as amulets, relics of saints and herbs. It was thought that this womb-like chamber would protect the baby from evil spirits as it came into the world. The woman was advised to remove all types of knots, fastenings, laces, buckles and rings so that she wouldn't be restricted in any way and so that they wouldn't get in the way. This was also a symbolic gesture, with their removal being seen as promoting an easier birth.

Although "taking her chamber" is often referred to as "confinement", the woman was not actually alone. Men were banned from the chamber, but close female friends and relatives joined the woman there, and a Queen would have a certain number of her ladies. It was a social occasion; when the labour began, the ladies would spring into action helping the midwife and making the caudle, which was a spiced wine or ale that was given to the woman during labour to give her strength.

The Tudor Midwife

The midwife was the one in charge in the birthing chamber. She was there to comfort the woman, to ease her pains with remedies and to deliver the baby. She would come armed "with a convenient stool or chair, with a knife, sponge, binders, and with oil of lilies warmed, with which she may profitably anoint both the womb of the labouring woman and her own hands."[17] Unfortunately, though, midwives and doctors didn't know the importance of washing their hands and so left the woman and baby at risk of infection. Once the baby was born, the midwife would swaddle the child with bands of cloth and hand it to its father with the traditional words "Father, see there is your child, God give you much joy with it, or take it speedily to his bliss."[18]

The midwife's job was not finished after the birth. She was also an important part of the baptism ceremony and would carry the child to the font. She also attended the mother's churching ceremony.

The Birth of Elizabeth

We don't know the details of Princess Elizabeth's birth, only that she was born at 3 o'clock on the afternoon of 7th September and that she was named after her paternal grandmother, Elizabeth of York, and possibly also after her maternal grandmother, Elizabeth Howard. The little girl had her father's red hair and long nose, and her mother's dark eyes.

The birth appears to have been straightforward; the baby was healthy, and so was Anne. However, the baby was a girl, and not the predicted son and heir. So sure were Henry and Anne that the baby would be a prince that a celebratory tournament had been organised and a letter announcing the birth of a prince had been written. The joust was cancelled and the word "prince" had an "s" added in the birth announcement letter, but it is easy to read too much into the cancellation of the festivities. As Eric Ives points out, the celebratory jousts were cancelled in 1516 too, when Catherine of Aragon gave birth to Mary, and it was traditional for the celebrations of the birth of a princess to be low-key. Although the joust was cancelled, Ives writes that "a herald immediately proclaimed this first of Henry's 'legitimate' children, while the choristers of the Chapel Royal sang the Te Deum".[19] In addition, preparations were already underway for a lavish christening.

Tudor Childbirth

While we don't know the details of Elizabeth's birth, we do know what traditionally happened at Tudor births. When her time was near, the woman was encouraged to confess her sins and to celebrate the mass. The 1549 Book of Common Prayer included masses on behalf of woman in labour, showing that religion was a big part of the birth process. As well as using herbal remedies and ointments to ease labour, the midwife would use certain phrases and charms. David Cressy[20] writes of how one phrase used during labour was "O infans sive vivus, sive mortuus, exi foras, quia Christus te vocat ad lucem", or "Oh, a child whether living, or dead, come forth, because Christ calls you to the light". Holy relics from monasteries were also loaned to pregnant women to help them through labour. Pregnancy and labour were a strange mixture of religion and superstition.

After delivery, the midwife would use further remedies to deliver the afterbirth, deal with any tearing or problems, promote milk production and make the woman comfortable. Hellebore powder could be given to the mother as snuff to make her sneeze and thereby loosen the afterbirth; alternatively, herbal draughts could be given. The afterbirth was buried later. The cutting of the umbilical cord, or "navel string" as it was known, was thought to be important because it kept "the blood and spirits in, after the child was born."[21] Midwife Jane Sharp advised that it be cut straight after birth and that it be left longer for a boy, so that his penis would be bigger, and shorter for a girl so that she would be modest and bear children more easily. A powder of aloes and frankincense was applied to the navel as an astringent and then the baby was bathed, after which s/he was swaddled to protect the limbs and to keep them straight. The Catholic tradition was to cross the child after swaddling, to sprinkle it with salt and to place a coin in the cradle or baby's hand, for protection.

If there were complications, then things could go very wrong. There were no forceps in Tudor England, only metal hooks which could kill the child and tear the woman. Moreover, there were no caesareans to help mother and baby if the baby got stuck. Puerperal fever was common, and infections could be caused by dirty cloths and unwashed hands. There were, obviously, no antibiotics, so an infection could lead to the death of the mother or baby. Jane Seymour and Catherine Parr both died of infections following childbirth.

After the birth, it was recommended that a woman should be kept from sleeping for the first few hours, so her friends would entertain her and keep her merry. This post-natal gossiping was a real bonding experience for women. The new mother was then confined to her bed for three days in a darkened room, because it was believed that labour weakened the eyes. Instructions for "child bed women" included praising God for the safe delivery of a child, bathing her womb and "privies" in "a decoction of chervil", tailoring her diet according to whether she was tender or strong stomached, and the drinking of certain draughts to close and fortify her womb, help her with any fevers, ease afterpains and deal with any other problems.

A woman was generally "confined" for a month, but the exact length of time depended upon her recovery and also upon her domestic circumstances. Two to three weeks after the birth, there would be the "upsitting". This involved the family potentially holding a feast to celebrate the woman's recovery and neighbours bringing gifts. The woman could now bathe and change, but was confined to her chamber, although no longer to her bed. Sometimes there would also be a second gossips' supper.

Christening

The next ritual after the birth of the child and the upsitting was the baptism or christening. Baptism was the foundation of Christian life and it opened the doors to eternal life. The Elizabethan prayer book instructed pastors and curates to tell people to make sure that baptism took place no later than the Sunday or first holy day after the birth, but obviously weaker babies were baptised by the midwife at birth. Tudor people believed that man was born in sin, because of original sin, but that he could be born anew of the water and the Holy Spirit.

In baptism, the priest named the child, dipped it in water or poured water on it, then marked a cross on its forehead as the baby was received into "the congregation of Christ's flock". During Elizabeth I's reign, 2% of babies died on their first day of life, 5% within the first week, 8-9% within a month and 12-13% within a year, so baptism was an important rite of passage.[22] It saved the child from God's wrath. If a priest was not available, any Christian male or female was permitted to conduct a baptism; the 1549 prayer book had instructions for a private baptism. In 1537, Bishop Rowland Lee instructed his clergy to "teach and instruct your parishioners, at the least twelve times in the year, the spiritual manner and form of christenings in English; and that the midwife may use it in time of necessity; commanding the woman when the time of birth draweth near, to have at all seasons a vessel of clean water for the same purpose."[23]

At the baptism (or christening) service, the baby was wrapped in the "chrisom cloth", a white cloth which symbolised the child's innocence. The midwife would present the baby at the font. A baby boy would generally have two godfathers and one godmother, and a baby girl would have two godmothers and one godfather. The godparents would name the baby, although this was purely symbolic as the name would have already been chosen by the parents in advance of the service. The godparents would also give the baby gifts; in the upper classes, this tended to be silverware. Edward VI's christening gifts included a gold cup from his half-sister Mary, three bowls and two pots of silver and gilt from the Archbishop of Canterbury, the same from the Duke of Norfolk, and two flagons and two pots of silver and gilt from the Duke of Suffolk. A christening was usually followed by a christening supper, where the men enjoyed drinking copious amounts of alcohol and the women enjoyed gossiping. Gifts were put on display at the christening supper.

David Cressy writes that "The Orders and Regulations for an Earl's House" (1525) specified how the church should be decorated for a noble child's christening. It also specified the processional order for the guests and what gifts were appropriate. At the 1589 christening of the Earl of Huntingdon's baby, the church was decorated with arras and cloth of gold and silk, the font was draped with cloth of gold and silk, and the baby was wrapped in silk, lawn and wool. This was obviously a wealthy child's christening, but it gives us an idea of just how important this rite of passage was.

Mothers did not attend their baby's christening because they had not yet been churched, so guests would visit the mother and baby after the service. They would also make sure that food and drink was taken up to the mother so that she too could enjoy a part of the celebrations.

Princess Elizabeth's christening

On 10th September 1533, when Elizabeth was three days old, she was christened at the Church of Observant Friars in Greenwich. She was processed along a carpet of green rushes from the Great Hall at Greenwich to the church. A contemporary record give us details of the christening:

"*The mayor, Sir Stephen Pecock, with his brethren and 40 of the* chief citizens, were ordered to be at the christening on the Wednesday following; on which day the mayor and council, in scarlet, with their collars, rowed to Greenwich, and the citizens went in another barge.

All the walls between the King's place and the Friars were hanged with arras, and the way strewed with rushes. The Friars' church was also hanged with arras. The font, of silver, stood in the midst of the church three steps high, covered with a fine cloth, and surrounded by gentlewomen with aprons and towels about their necks, that no filth should come into it. Over it hung a crimson satin canopy fringed with gold, and round it was a rail covered with red say.

Between the choir and the body of the church was a close place with a pan of fire, to make the child ready in. When the child was brought to the hall every man set forward. The citizens of London, two and two ; then gentlemen, squires, and chaplains, the aldermen, the mayor alone, the King's council, his chapel, in copes ; barons, bishops, earls ; the earl of Essex bearing the covered gilt basons ; the marquis of Exeter with a taper of virgin wax. The marquis of Dorset bare the salt. The lady Mary of Norfolk bare the chrisom, of pearl and stone. The officers of arms. The old duchess of Norfolk bare the child in a mantle of purple velvet, with a long train held by the earl of Wiltshire, the countess of Kent, and the earl of Derby. The dukes of Suffolk and Norfolk were on each side of the Duchess. A canopy was borne over the child by lord Rochford, lord Hussy, lord William Howard, and lord Thomas Howard the elder. Then ladies and gentlewomen.

The bishop of London and other bishops and abbots met the child at the church door, and christened it. The archbishop of Canterbury was godfather, and the old duchess of Norfolk and the old marchioness of Dorset godmothers. This done, Garter, with a loud voice, bid God send her long life. The archbishop of Canterbury then confirmed her, the marchioness of Exeter being godmother. Then the trumpets blew, and the gifts were given ; after which wafers, comfits, and hypocras were brought in. In going out the gifts were borne before the child, to the Queen's chamber, by Sir John Dudley, lord Thos. Howard, the *younger, lord Fitzwater, and the earl of Worcester. One side was full of the Guard and King's servants holding 500 staff torches, and many other torches were borne beside the child by gentlemen. The mayor and aldermen were thanked in the King's name by the dukes of Norfolk and Suffolk, and after drinking in the cellar went to their barge."*[24]

In his chronicle, Windsor Herald Charles Wriothesley writes that "and the morrowe after their was fiers[bonfires] made in London, and at everie fire a vessell of wyne[wine] for people to drinke for the said solempnitie."[25] However, the imperial ambassador, Eustace Chapuys, contradicts this in his report to Charles V on the 15th September, saying "the christening has been like her mother's coronation, very cold and disagreeable, both to the Court and to the city, and there has been no thought of having the bonfires and rejoicings usual in such cases."[26] We know that Anne Boleyn's coronation was lavish, so I'm not sure that we can believe Chapuys.

Anne and Breastfeeding

There were some rather strange ideas about breastfeeding in Tudor England, one of them being that the milk was actually menstrual blood turned white. Some also believed that colostrum, the highly nutritious milk produced in the first few days after birth, was harmful, so the baby was sometimes given to a wet nurse for a few days.

Breastfeeding was recommended in Richard Jonas' 1540 book *The Byrth of Mankynde*, a translation of an earlier manual, recommended breastfeeding, but noblewomen ignored this advice and hired wet nurses because it was important for the new mothers to conceive again quickly. Wet nurses were chosen carefully because it was believed that the mother could pass on her characteristics via breast milk. In the early days, when feeding was frequent, babies would often live with the wet nurse to make things easier.

As a queen, Anne would have been expected to hand over

Elizabeth to a wet nurse. The wet nurse would have been well vetted to make sure that she had the right temperament and plenty of milk for the royal princess. In her book on Elizabeth, historian Tracy Borman writes of how Anne wanted to breast-feed Elizabeth. However, David Starkey states that the story that Anne wanted to breastfeed, and was prevented from doing so by Henry VIII, is just a "tale... derived from Leti's fictionalised account and is without foundation."[27] Gregorio Leti was an historian, but he was known for mixing facts with fiction; other than Leti, there is no source for Anne wanting to feed Elizabeth herself. Perhaps she did want to breastfeed, but it was not the done thing and she would have had to have followed royal protocol.

The advice of the time was that babies should be breastfed for two years, but in reality it tended to be one year. The Tudor equivalents of baby rice and rusks as weaning foods were gruel, bread and sugar, or bread dipped in water or milk to make it soft. Finger food for older babies included chicken legs, if the family could afford the meat. In poorer families, the baby would eat the same food as the rest of the family: gruel.

Instructions were given to Lady Bryan, Princess Elizabeth's nurse, to wean the little princess at twenty-five months of age. The instructions were from the King, "with the assent of the queen's grace", and records show that with this order was included a letter from Anne Boleyn. We do not know what the letter said, but perhaps Anne was giving Lady Bryan instructions regarding weaning.[28]

Churching

Although churching is often seen as a purification ceremony, cleansing the woman after the unclean business of childbirth, it was more a celebration of her survival, a thanksgiving service, and a rite of passage marking her return to normal life after her confinement. It also marked the woman's survival and her return to everyday life. It was celebrated with more drinking, feasting and gossiping, and the actual ritual involved the woman dressing in fresh, clean clothes, leaving her chamber and attending her local church. The priest would meet her at the church door, where he would sprinkle her with holy water. The woman would then enter the church, accompanied by two married female friends and wearing a white veil and carrying a candle. The priest would then recite psalms – such as Psalm 121, a psalm of thanksgiving for God's protection – and talk about how the woman had been delivered from the dangers associated with childbirth. He would finish with the Lord's Prayer and a prayer of thanks. As an offering, the woman would then give the church either the chrisom cloth which had been used for her baby's christening, or a cash equivalent.

We don't have any details of Anne's churching ceremony but it would have taken place a few weeks after Elizabeth's birth. It was usual for the service to take place about a month after the birth, but records from a church in Lancashire show that women were churched anywhere from eight to forty-eight days after the baptism of the child.[29]

Anne and Elizabeth

Whatever the truth about Anne's wish to suckle her own child, and go against the usual royal protocol and tradition, Anne was quite clearly pleased with and proud of her little girl. Courtiers were often embarrassed by Anne's displays of affection for her baby and by her preference for placing Elizabeth next to her on a cushion, rather than shutting her away in a nursery.[30] Elizabeth's removal from court to her own household at Hatfield on the 10th December 1533 must have been a huge wrench for Anne. Even though it was just a few miles away, Anne would not have been expected to visit her daughter very much and, instead, would have been expected to get on with her queenly duties and to leave Elizabeth's upbringing to Lady Bryan and her staff. Anne had to concentrate on conceiving again and providing Henry VIII with a prince.

We don't know exactly how much time Anne was able to spend with Elizabeth, but we know the following:

- That Anne visited Elizabeth at Hatfield in Spring 1534[31] [32]

- That Elizabeth was moved to Eltham, just 5 miles from Greenwich, at the end of March 1534 and that her parents visited her there a few weeks later[33]

- That she was at court with her parents for five weeks in the first quarter of 1535[34] [35]

- That she was at court at Christmas 1535, and that she was still there at the end of January 1536 when news reached the court of Catherine of Aragon's death. Henry paraded his daughter around in celebration.[36]

- That she was at court at the end of April 1536, shortly before Anne's fall. Alexander Alesius described Anne holding Elizabeth In her arms while she appealed to her husband.[37] David Starkey discounts this report, saying that Elizabeth was most probably at Hunsdon at the time.

- That Anne kept in touch with Elizabeth's nurse, Lady Bryan.

At the end of the day, Henry and his council had the last word regarding Elizabeth's upbringing, but the stylish Anne Boleyn involved herself in buying items for her daughter's chamber and for her clothing. *The Account of materials furnished for the use of Anne Boleyn and Princess Elizabeth 1535-36*[38] by Anne's mercer, William Loke, included the following items for Elizabeth:

- White sarsenet to line an orange velvet gown
- Black velvet for a partlet
- Black satin for a partlet
- Russet velvet
- Black buckram
- Crimson, purple, white, yellow sarsenet

- Yellow velvet to edge a yellow kirtle
- White damask for a kirtle
- White velvet for edging the kirtle
- Russet damask for a bed cover
- Black satin for a muffler and taffeta for its lining
- Embroidered purple satin sleeves
- Green velvet for edging a green satin kirtlet
- Black velvet for mufflers

We learn more about the Queen's expenses in *The Queen's reckoning, beginning in December 1535. Hen. VIII.*[39] (the debts owed by Anne at her death. This account includes the following items for Elizabeth:

- "Boat-hire from Greenwich to London and back to take measure of caps for my lady Princess, and again to fetch the Princess's purple satin cap to mend it."
- "A purple satin cap, laid with a rich caul of gold, the work being roundelles of damask gold, made for my lady Princess."
- "A pair of pyrwykes for my lady Princess, delivered to my lady mistress." Eric Ives explains that pyrwykes were a device to straighten the fingers.[40]
- "2¼ yds. crimson satin, at 15s., an ell of "tuke" and crimson fringe for the Princess's cradle head."
- "2 fine pieces of "nydle rybande" [ribbon] to roll her Grace's hair withal."
- " A white satin cap laid with a rich caul of gold for the Princess, 4l., and another of crimson satin."
- "A fringe of Venice gold and silver for the little bed."
- "A cap of taffeta covered with a caul of damask gold for the Princess."

Anne obviously made sure that Elizabeth looked the part of a royal princess and Henry's heir.

Anne and Elizabeth's Future

On 26th April 1536, just days before her arrest, Queen Anne Boleyn met with her chaplain of two years, her "countryman", thirty-two year-old Matthew Parker. Parker recorded later that Anne had asked him to watch over her daughter, the two year-old Princess Elizabeth, if anything happened to her. In other words, Anne was entrusting him with her daughter's spiritual care.[41] Eric Ives writes that this was a request that Parker never forgot and something which stayed with him for ever.[42] Parker obviously came to be important to Elizabeth, because in 1559 she made him her Archbishop of Canterbury. This was a post which, Parker admitted to Lord Burghley, he would not have accepted if he "had not been so much bound to the mother".[43]

By getting Parker involved with Elizabeth's upbringing and her future, Anne was putting her daughter into the hands of a man with important connections, connections with a set of men with humanist and Protestant ideals who would influence and help her daughter. This cohort included John Cheke, Roger Ascham, William Cecil, Anthony Cooke, William Grindal and John Dee. Three of these men – Grindal, Cheke and Ashcam – tutored Elizabeth, and Dee may even have spent time with the young Elizabeth. He certainly taught Edward VI and Robert Dudley. It is no coincidence that Elizabeth relied on these men when she became queen. Her mother had made sure that she was surrounded by men who could help her in the future.

Elizabeth's Household of Boleyn Relatives

The young Elizabeth was also surrounded by Boleyn relatives:

- Anne Boleyn's uncle, Sir John Shelton, was comptroller of the joint household of Elizabeth and Mary, and was helped by his wife, Lady Anne (née Boleyn).

- Lady Margaret Bryan, Elizabeth's nurse, was related to Anne Boleyn by marriage.

- Katherine Champernon (or Champernowne) was appointed to Elizabeth's household in July 1536 and became her governess in 1537. She became related to the Boleyns when she married Sir John Ashley (Astley) in 1545. Ashley's mother, Anne Wood, was the sister of Lady Elizabeth Boleyn whose husband, James Boleyn, was Anne Boleyn's paternal uncle.

- Thomas Parry, Elizabeth's "cofferer", or treasurer, was was also connected to the Boleyns. His wife, Anne Reade, was the widow of Sir Adrian Fortescue, whose mother, Alice Boleyn, was an aunt of Queen Anne Boleyn.

J.L. McIntosh writes:

"The presence of these Boleyn relations and the evidence of Queen Anne's interest in the material splendor of her daughter's environment indicates that Anne, before her death, was an important, if indirect, early influence on the development of her daughter's household's culture. Henry VIII funded the household and had the final say in all important aspects of his daughter's upbringing, such as when she was weaned, but it was Anne who was guiding the routine behavior and agenda of the household...The queen also may have begun to draw up plans for Elizabeth to receive a Protestant humanist education."[44]

Although Anne was unable to bring up her daughter herself, because she died before Elizabeth turned three, she made sure from the start that her daughter was well taken care of and had the appropriate household for a royal princess. Anne's instructions to Matthew Parker, one of the Cambridge cohort I have already mentioned, is evidence that Anne was not just ensuring that Elizabeth's spiritual needs would be met. She was also making sure that Elizabeth would have the connections she needed to become a formidable woman and queen. I believe that Anne's influence was kept alive by those who surrounded the young Elizabeth.

Notes and Sources

1   Sim, The Tudor Housewife, 19, citing Patricia Crawford in "The Construction and Experience of Maternity in Seventeenth Century England."

2   Youings, Sixteenth Century England, 372.

3   Cressy, Birth, Marriage, and Death: Ritual, Religion, and the Life-Cycle in Tudor and Stuart England.

4   Ridgway, The Anne Boleyn Collection Volume 2, chap. Anne Boleyn's Birth Date.

5   Hall, Hall's Chronicle, 794.

6   Friedmann, Anne Boleyn: A Chapter of English History, 1527-1536, 1:189, note 2.

7   Friedmann, Anne Boleyn, A Chapter of English History, 1527-1536, 190, note 1.

8   Ives, The Life and Death of Anne Boleyn, 183.

9   Ascoli, La Grande-Bretagne Devant L'opinion Française Depuis La Guerre de Cent Ans Jusqu'à La Fin Du XVIe Siècle, l. 148–164.

10   Sim, The Tudor Housewife, 17.

11   Weisner, Women and Gender in Early Modern Europe, 79.

12   Sharp, The Midwives Book: Or the Whole Art of Midwifry Discovered, 132–133.

13   Weisner, Women and Gender in Early Modern Europe, 43.

14   Sharp, The Midwives Book: Or the Whole Art of Midwifry Discovered, 80–82.

15   Edwards, Mary I: England's Catholic Queen, 5.

16   Starkey, Elizabeth: Apprenticeship, 2.

17   Cressy, Birth, Marriage, and Death: Ritual, Religion, and the Life-Cycle in Tudor and Stuart England.

18   Ibid.

19   Ives, The Life and Death of Anne Boleyn, 184.

20   Cressy, Birth, Marriage, and Death: Ritual, Religion, and the Life-Cycle in Tudor and Stuart England.

21   Sharp, The Midwives Book: Or the Whole Art of Midwifry Discovered, 157.

22   Cressy, Birth, Marriage, and Death: Ritual, Religion, and the Life-Cycle in Tudor and Stuart England.

23   Ibid.

24   "Letters and Papers, Foreign and Domestic, Henry VIII, Volume 6 - 1533," n. 1111.

25 Wriothesley, A Chronicle of England During the Reigns of the Tudors, from A.D. 1485 to 1559, 23.

26 "Letters and Papers, Foreign and Domestic, Henry VIII, Volume 6 - 1533," n. 1125.

27 Starkey, Six Wives: The Queens of Henry VIII, 511.

28 "Letters and Papers, Foreign and Domestic, Henry VIII, Volume 9 : August-December 1535," n. 568.

29 Sim, The Tudor Housewife, 26.

30 Borman, Elizabeth's Women: The Hidden Story of the Virgin Queen, 21.

31 "Letters and Papers, Foreign and Domestic, Henry VIII, Volume 7," n. 296.

32 "Letters and Papers, Foreign and Domestic, Henry VIII, Volume 10 - January-June 1536," n. 913.

33 "Letters and Papers, Foreign and Domestic, Henry VIII, Volume 7," n. 509.

34 "Letters and Papers, Foreign and Domestic, Henry VIII, Volume 6 - 1533," n. 1486.

35 "Letters and Papers, Foreign and Domestic, Henry VIII, Volume 8," n. 440.

36 "Letters and Papers, Foreign and Domestic, Henry VIII, Volume 10 - January-June 1536," n. 141.

37 "Calendar of State Papers Foreign, Elizabeth, Volume 1 - 1558-1559," n. 1303.

38 Loke, "Account of Materials Furnished for the Use of Anne Boleyn and Princess Elizabeth 1535-36."

39 "Letters and Papers, Foreign and Domestic, Henry VIII, Volume 10 - January-June 1536," n. 913.

40 Ives, The Life and Death of Anne Boleyn, 255.

41 ed. Bruce and ed. Perowne, Correspondence of Matthew Parker, 59.

42 Ives, The Life and Death of Anne Boleyn, 267.

43 ed. Bruce and ed. Perowne, Correspondence of Matthew Parker, 391.

44 McIntosh, "From Heads of Household to Heads of State: The Preaccession Households of Mary and Elizabeth Tudor 1516-1558."

14.   Pregnancies and Miscarriages 1533-1536

In the previous chapter, I looked at Anne's Boleyn's first pregnancy, which resulted in the birth of a healthy baby girl, Elizabeth. I'll now look at Anne's complete obstetric history.

In her book *Blood Will Tell: A Medical Explanation of the Tyranny of Henry VIII*, Kyra Kramer writes that both Catherine of Aragon and Anne Boleyn "endured myriad stillbirths, miscarriages and neonatal deaths."[1] It is often said that Anne's series of miscarriages and her inability to provide Henry VIII with a living son factored greatly in her fall. Kramer is not the only one to believe that Anne had a series of pregnancy disasters. G.R. Elton wrote that after the birth of Elizabeth "the dreary tale of miscarriages was resumed";[2] Marie Bruce said " during the first six months of 1534 she appears to have had one miscarriage after another";[3] and Hester W. Chapman believed that Anne suffered three miscarriages in 1534 alone plus the miscarriage of January 1536.[4] Whilst I believe that a son would have protected Anne and would have prevented the plots of April and May 1536 ever happening, I simply do not believe that Anne had "myriad stillbirths, miscarriages and neonatal deaths."

Let us consider the evidence for Anne's pregnancies...

September 1533

We know that Anne was heavily pregnant at her coronation on 1st June 1533 and that she gave birth to a healthy baby girl on 7th September 1533, the future Elizabeth I. There is no evidence of a pregnancy before this time, so that's pregnancy number one.

January 1534

On 28th January 1534, the imperial ambassador, Eustace Chapuys, commented that "Anne Boleyn is now pregnant and in condition to have more children."[5] For Chapuys to have known that Anne was pregnant, Anne and the King must have been sure of her pregnancy. This means she must have conceived soon after her churching; Anne obviously did not suffer with fertility issues.

The next mention of this pregnancy is in a letter dated 27th April 1534 from George Taylor, Anne Boleyn's receiver-general, to Lady Lisle, in which he says that "The Queen hath a goodly belly, praying our Lord to send us a prince".[6] There is further evidence of this pregnancy; in July 1534, Anne's brother George, Lord Rochford, was sent on a diplomatic mission to France to ask for the postponement of a meeting between Henry VIII and Francis I because of Anne's condition. Anne was described as "being so far gone with child she could not cross the sea with the King".[7] Chapuys backs this up in a letter dated the 27th July, where he refers to the King delaying his meeting with the French King because "the lady de Boulans (Anne Boleyn) wishes to be present, which is impossible on account of her condition".[8] If, for example, Anne was twelve weeks pregnant when Chapuys reported it on 28th January, her baby would have been due around 12th August. This would have made her very heavily pregnant in July 1534, hence her being described as "being so far gone". The frustrating thing is that we don't know what happened to this pregnancy. There is no mention of Anne taking to her chamber, having a late miscarriage, premature birth or stillbirth. There is just Chapuys' report on 27th September 1534:

> *"Since the King began to doubt whether his lady was enceinte or not, he has renewed and increased the love he formerly had for a beautiful damsel of the court".*[9]

Chapuys doesn't say that Anne had a miscarriage or stillbirth; he merely writes of Henry no longer believing Anne to be pregnant. Now, it is not clear whether this is Chapuys' reading of the situation or whether it is him passing on a fact. It may well be that Anne gave birth to a stillborn baby and that the news was hushed up. However, this seems unlikely since ambassadors and Tudor chroniclers recorded Catherine of Aragon's stillbirths and miscarriages when this situation arose. I find it hard to believe that Anne could have faked a pregnancy, when she would have been dressed and bathed by her ladies, and would have had her sheets examined for menstrual blood. Perhaps she experienced a false (phantom) pregnancy (pseudocyesis). The symptoms of a false pregnancy, which can last months, are the same as pregnancy: the cessation of menstrual periods, a swollen abdomen, enlarged and tender breasts, nipple changes and even the production of milk. They also include feeling of the baby moving, morning sickness and weight gain. There would have been no way for Anne to differentiate between a real pregnancy and a false one; Catherine of Aragon and Mary I both suffered false pregnancies which fooled their doctors.

It is not known exactly what causes a false pregnancy, but one factor is thought to be an intense desire to get pregnant. Although Eric Ives believes that Anne "had no reason to be under stress at this date, having produced a healthy female child eight months earlier",[10] I have to respectfully disagree. Anne was under immense pressure. It was her duty to provide Henry with a son and heir, that was that. Henry had got over the disappointment of Elizabeth's gender because of the hope of a prince to come; now Anne had to provide that prince. That was pressure! Ives argues that Anne must have miscarried, rather than having a stillbirth, because there is no evidence of her taking her chamber. However, in medical terms the loss of a baby after 24 weeks is termed a stillbirth, and Anne must have been over 24 weeks pregnant in the July. It is odd that there was no mention of such a tragedy.

None of this explains Chapuys' comment in the September about Henry now doubting that Anne was pregnant. Perhaps Chapuys was not kept 'in the loop', or perhaps Anne's miscarriage or stillbirth was hushed up. It is impossible to know. Henry may well have wanted to keep it quiet rather than having to admit that Anne's pregnancy had ended in tragedy like so many of Catherine's.

1535

The only evidence for a pregnancy in 1535 is a sentence from a letter written by Sir William Kingston to Lord Lisle on 24th June 1535. Kingston wrote:

"No news here worth writing. The King and Queen are well, and her Grace has a fair belly as I have seen".[11]

Sir John Dewhurst,[12] believes that there is actually an error in the dating of this letter because Kingston asks to be remembered to "Master Porter", Sir Christopher Garneys, who actually died in 1534. It is likely, therefore, that the letter was written in either June 1533 or June 1534, and that Anne was not pregnant in 1535.

29th January 1536 – Anne's Final Pregnancy

The majority of historians and authors believe that Anne Boleyn's final pregnancy ended with a miscarriage on 29th January 1536, the day of Catherine of Aragon's burial and a few days after Henry VIII suffered a serious jousting accident. There are five main pieces of contemporary evidence for the miscarriage: a letter written by Eustace Chapuys, the imperial ambassador; the individual chronicles of Charles Wriothesley, Edward Hall and Raphael Holinshed; and the poem by Lancelot de Carles, secretary to the French ambassador:

1. "On the day of the interment [Catherine of Aragon's funeral] the Concubine had an abortion which seemed to be a male child which she had not borne 3½ months, at which the King has shown great distress. The said concubine wished to lay the blame on the duke of Norfolk, whom she hates, saying he frightened her by bringing the news of the fall the King had six days before. But it is well known that is not the cause, for it was told her in a way that she should not be alarmed or attach much importance to it. Some think it was owing to her own incapacity to bear children, others to a fear that the King would treat her like the late Queen, especially considering the treatment shown to a lady of the Court, named Mistress Semel, to whom, as many say, he has lately made great presents."[13] Eustace Chapuys to Charles V, 10th February 1536.

2. "And in February folowyng was quene Anne brought a bedde of a childe before her tyme, whiche was born dead."[14] Edward Hall

3. "This yeare also, three daies before Candlemas, Queene Anne was brought a bedd and delivered of a man child, as it was said, afore her tyme, for she said that she had reckoned herself at that tyme but fiftene weekes gonne with chield..."[15] Charles Wriothesley

4. "The nine and twentith of Januarie queen Anne was delivered of a child before hir time, which was borne dead."[16] Raphael Holinshed

Figure 19 - Queen Anne Boleyn, from "The Tower From Within"

In his "Poème sur la Mort d'Anne Boleyn", Lancelot de Carles, writes:

> "Adoncq le Roy, s'en allant a la chasse,
> Cheut de cheval rudement en la place,
> Dont bien cuydoit que pur ceste adventure
> Il dust payer le tribut de nature :
> Quant la Royne eut la nouvelle entendue,
> Peu s'en faillut qu'el ne chuet estendue
> Morte d'ennuy, tant que fort offensa
> Son ventre plain et son fruict advança,
> Et enfanta ung beau filz avant terme,
> Qui nasquit mort dont versa mainte lerme."[17]

Here, de Carles is saying that the news of Henry VIII's jousting accident caused Anne to collapse, landing on her stomach, and that this caused her to give birth "avant terme", prematurely, to "ung beau filz", a beautiful son, who was born dead.

All five sources state that Anne miscarried her baby, and three of them state that it was a boy. Wriothesley goes on to put forward the idea that the miscarriage was caused by Anne suffering shock at the news of Henry VIII's jousting accident, as does Chapuys. The dates differ, with Chapuys and Holinshed stating that the miscarriage happened on 29th January, Wriothesley saying the 30th January, Hall saying February and de Carles stating that it happened after Henry VIII's jousting accident. However, I think we can safely assume that it happened at the end of January.

In Philippa Gregory's novel, *The Other Boleyn Girl*, Anne Boleyn miscarries "a baby horridly malformed, with a spine flayed open and a huge head, twice as large as the spindly little body".[18] Now, obviously this is just a novel, but Gregory used the work of historian Retha Warnicke as a source and Warnicke believes that Anne did miscarry a deformed foetus. In both *The Rise and Fall of Anne Boleyn* and her essay *Sexual Heresy at the Court of Henry VIII*, Warnicke puts forward the idea that Anne's miscarriage was a factor in her downfall because it was "no ordinary miscarriage"[19] and that it was "an unforgivable act".[20] According to Warnicke, the foetus was deformed; this was seen as an evil omen and a sign that Anne had committed illicit sexual acts or been involved in witchcraft. Warnicke believes this because:

- Anne was charged with committing incest with her brother, George, who Warnicke believes to have been Mark Smeaton's lover.

- Anne was charged with adultery with Smeaton, Norris, Brereton and Weston, who Warnicke believes to have been "suspected of having violated the Buggery Statute" and who "were known for their licentious behaviour."[21]

- There seems to have been a delay between the miscarriage and the news being announced, showing that there was something odd about it. Chapuys did not report it until 10th February 1536.

- From late January 1536 Henry VIII councillors took steps to protect the King's honour "by leaking erroneous information about his consort before the public announcement of her miscarriage."[22] Warnicke believes that they did this so that the 'sin' would be seen as Anne's, and not that of the King.

In my own reading on pregnancy and childbirth in Tudor times,[23][24] however, I have learned that deformities, or things like birthmarks, were actually thought to have been caused by things the mother had seen during pregnancy, rather than by the parents necessarily having committed a sexual sin. These were superstitious times.

The only source, anyway, for Anne miscarrying a deformed foetus is Nicholas Sander, a Catholic recusant writing in the reign of Anne's daughter, Elizabeth I. His book *De origine ac progressu schismatis Anglicani* was published in 1585; in 1877 it was translated from Latin into English by David Lewis as "Rise and Growth of the Anglican Schism". In the English translation,

Sander's record of Anne's miscarriage reads:

"The time had now come when Anne was to be again a mother, but she brought forth only a shapeless mass of flesh."[25]

Sander went on to write about how Anne blamed Henry VIII for the miscarriage, crying "See, how well I must be since the day I caught that abandoned woman Jane sitting on your knees". However, Sander did not attempt to explain the "shapeless mass" or to give any more details. I'm sure that if he had thought it was important and suggestive of sin or witchcraft, then he would have mentioned it. Sander is the only source that describes Anne's baby in this way, and he was writing much later (he wasn't born until ca.1530). As Eric Ives pointed out, "no deformed foetus was mentioned at the time or later in Henry's reign, despite Anne's disgrace"; nor was it mentioned in Mary I's reign "when there was every motive and opportunity to blacken Anne".[26] Ives concluded that "it is as little worthy of credence as his assertion that Henry VIII was Anne's father"; I agree wholeheartedly. Sander, as a Catholic exile, had every reason to blacken the name of Elizabeth I and her mother, and he had no first hand knowledge of events that had happened in 1536.

There is also no evidence that the five men executed in May 1536 were involved in "illicit" sexual acts, or that Anne was involved in witchcraft.

In her recent book on Anne Boleyn, Sylwia Zupanec[27] discusses Anne's 1536 miscarriage and puts forward the idea that it may not have been a miscarriage at all, but a phantom/false pregnancy. The evidence she puts forward for this is:

- That Sander did not actually mention a "shapeless mass of flesh" but, according to Zupanec, "in Latin described the outcome of Anne's pregnancy as *'mola'*". She goes on to say that "Sander's account is not précising the information about what had happened on 29 January 1536 so he could have meant that Anne Boleyn had suffered from phantom pregnancy, miscarried an undeveloped foetus or expelled some kind of tumour."[28] Zupanec believes that Sander's work was "incorrectly translated" and that as a result of this historians have misinterpreted it. To back up her translation of *"mola"* as a false conception, she cites two Latin works: *M. Verrii Flacci Quae Extant: Et Sexti Pompeii Festi De Verborum Significatione*[29] and Johannes Micraelius' *Lexicon Philosophicum Terminorum Philosophis Usitatorum*.[30] These are both Latin glossaries of terms.

- That rumours spread around Europe saying that Anne had pretended to miscarry and that she hadn't been pregnant at all. Zupanec quotes the Bishop of Faenza writing to Prothonotary Ambrogio on 10th March 1536. The bishop stated that Francis I had said "that 'that woman' pretended to have miscarried of a son, not being really with child, and, to keep up the deceit, would allow no one to attend on her but her sister, whom the French king knew here in France 'per una grandissima ribalda et infame sopre tutte.'"[31] Zupanec also quotes Dr Ortiz writing to the Empress on 22nd March 1536: "La Ana feared that the King would leave her, and it was thought that the reason of her pretending the miscarriage of a son was that the King might not leave her, seeing that she conceived sons."[32]

Zupanec believes that Sander's words and these reports, when combined, suggest that Anne may have been "simply suffering from illness unknown to her contemporaries",[33] i.e. a phantom or false pregnancy. However, if you read Sander's original Latin, as I have done, Sander does not use the word *"mola"*. Here is what Sander says about Anne's miscarriage in his book:

"Venerat tempus quo Anna iterum pareret, peperit autem informem quandum carnis molem, ac praeterea nihil."[34]

So, he says *"molem"* and not *"mola"*; the two words have completely different meanings.

My Latin is not very good at all, so I asked Phillipa Madams, a Latin teacher and expert, to translate the sentence by Nicholas Sander as well as the Latin references given by Zupanec. Phillipa translated Sander's words as "there came the time when Anne was preparing again to give birth, however, she gave birth to something that was an unformed shapeless mass of flesh, and nothing else", which was in keeping with Lewis's 19th century translation.

With regard to the references cited by Zupanec to back up the idea that "*mola*" meant a "false conception", Phillipa stated that the first one (by famous Roman grammarians Marcus Verrius Flaccus and Sextus Pompeius Festus) gave a definition of the word "*mola*" as "a millstone", used for milling grain; there was nothing about conception or pregnancy in the definition. The second one, Johannes Micraelius' glossary of Latin terms, was a definition of "*mola carnis*" (not "*carnis molem*", as written by Sander), and thus stated that this pregnancy had been a "useless conception". Indeed, as one of Phillipa's students, Ellen, found, there is a condition called a molar pregnancy which is caused by problems with fertilization; perhaps this, rather than a phantom pregancy, is what Zupanec is referring to when she says "false conception"? However, this is a very rare condition, more commonly found today in teenage pregnancies or in women over 45. In a molar pregnancy, the cells of the placenta behave abnormally and "grow as fluid-filled sacs (cysts) with the appearance of white grapes".[35] In a complete molar pregnancy, a mass of abnormal cells grows but no foetus develops, and in the case of a partial molar pregnancy some normal placental tissue forms along with an abnormal foetus, which dies in early pregnancy. In most current-day cases, there are no signs that the pregnancy is anything but normal until the woman has a scan, but in some cases the woman can experience bleeding or can lose the developing foetus. The treatment is for the woman to have the "mole" removed by surgery (a dilatation and curettage, or D&C), because if it is left then there can be complications, such as the growth becoming cancerous. The woman does not miscarry the "mole" or "tumour", yet Sander is quite specific in saying that Anne "brought forth only a shapeless mass of flesh", i.e. that she miscarried or gave birth to something. A foetus in the early stages of pregnancy may, in any case, have appeared to untrained eyes as a "shapeless mass of flesh".

A phantom pregnancy, or false pregnancy (pseudocyesis), is when a woman experiences many of the symptoms of a real pregnancy and believes herself to be pregnant, but there is no foetus, or placenta. This just doesn't fit with what we know about Anne in January 1536 – Chapuys, Hall, Wriothesley, Holinshed, de Carles and Sander all write of Anne miscarrying rather than of her being "pregnant" for months and then there being no baby born at the end of it. We can rule out a false pregnancy in this case.

As I said earlier, "*mola*" and "*molem*" are two completely different words; neither Phillipa nor I can understand why the references cited by Zupanec were definitions of a word not used by Sander in his book. Sander clearly wrote "*informem quandum carnis molem*" and "*molem*" simply means "mass". Phillipa explained to me, "*Carnis* is clearly and unambiguously referring to flesh and *informem* can have a range of meanings from shapeless to monstrous. Even without the misunderstanding of mola/molem Anne clearly gave birth to something."[36] The Latin translation by David Lewis is, therefore, correct and has not been misinterpreted by historians. There is no way, in my opinion, that Sander's words can be read as suggesting that Anne was suffering from a phantom pregnancy; nor does this account fit the symptoms or outcome of a molar pregnancy. That's even if we take Sander's words seriously. We don't know what he was basing his story on. Furthermore, nobody takes seriously his description of Anne – the six fingers, projecting tooth etc.; we should apply the same hefty pinch of salt to his description of the miscarriage.

As far as the rumours of Anne pretending to be pregnant are concerned, they are likely to have been just that: rumours. We have Chapuys, Wriothesley, Hall and de Carles, and later Holinshed and Sander, all writing of a miscarriage. Eric Ives pointed out in his biography of Anne Boleyn that Wriothesley was Windsor Herald, a man whose "post gave him a ready entrée to the court" and that "his cousin Thomas was clerk of the signet and close to Cromwell",[37] so Wriothesley would have been well informed. De Carles, whose account backs up those of Wriothesley, Hall, Chapuys and Holinshed, was the secretary of the French ambassador, so is likely to have received information from Thomas Cromwell. I don't believe that there is any reason to doubt these reports.

Having looked at the various theories and having examined the contemporary sources, I believe that Anne suffered an ordinary, but tragic, miscarriage in January 1536. That is what the evidence points to. It was obviously a huge blow to the royal couple, and may have been a factor in her downfall, but there was nothing strange about this miscarriage.

How Many Pregnancies?

There is no evidence of Anne having any other pregnancies. So, she either had one successful pregnancy and two miscarriages, or one successful pregnancy, a false pregnancy and a miscarriage. That's hardly "myriad stillbirths, miscarriages and neonatal deaths", is it?

Miscarriages

Before I look at miscarriages in Tudor times, I'd like to consider miscarriage statistics today, in an age where we have good nutrition and advanced medical care. According to the UK charity Tommy's:

- Up to 1 in 4 women who get pregnant will experience a miscarriage
- Women under the age of 30 have a 10% risk of miscarriage
- Women between the ages of 35 and 40 have a 20% chance of miscarriage[38]

The US March of Dimes website gives another statistic, saying "As many as 40 percent of all pregnancies may end in miscarriage, because many losses occur before a woman realizes she is pregnant".[39] So even today miscarriages are very common; we all know women who have experienced a miscarriage, or even a number of miscarriages.

In Tudor times too, miscarriage was a common occurrence. David Cressy, author of *Birth, Marriage, and Death: Ritual, Religion, and the Life Cycle in Tudor and Stuart England*, quotes from Isaac Archer's diary of his wife's pregnancies and labours in the late 17th century, i.e. the Stuart era. In fifteen years of marriage, Anne Archer was pregnant at least ten times and had only one surviving child, a daughter. She came close to death at several points, experienced miscarriages and lost the baby either in birth or shortly afterwards. This was not uncommon; therefore, Anne experiencing one or two miscarriages was certainly not unusual or anything to jump to conclusions about.[40]

Even today, with our medical advances, the Tommy's Charity points out that miscarriages are often unexplained. The March of Dimes website lists the following possible causes:

- Chromosomal abnormality in the foetus
- A blighted ovum, when the pregnancy sac is empty because either the embryo never formed or it stopped developing early in the pregnancy.
- Maternal health conditions: for example, hormonal problems, infections, diabetes, thyroid disease, systemic lupus erythematosus and other autoimmune disorders.
- Lifestyle factors: for example, alcohol, smoking and the use of drugs.

But again, they point out that miscarriages are still not completely understood and many cannot be explained.

But was Henry *actually* responsible for his wives' miscarriages?

Well, that's what Kyra Kramer believes. In *Blood Will Tell*, not only does Kramer argue that Henry VIII had McLeod Syndrome, and that this explains his tyrannical and irrational behaviour, she also argues that Henry had Kell Positive Blood Type and that this explains his wives' "reproductive woes". As I said earlier, Kramer believes that both Catherine of Aragon and Anne Boleyn experienced a series of miscarriages and stillbirths, and that "It seems unlikely that the two women's experiences could mirror each other so closely simply due to chance".[41] Kramer argues, "It seems more plausible that something about Henry VIII himself was actually the reason there were so few children in the royal nurseries. After all, he was the common factor in every single pregnancy." She goes on to explain that the miscarriages and stillbirths experienced by Catherine and Anne "are similar to documented cases of Kell-affected pregnancies, which only occur when the father of the fetus has a Kell positive blood type but the mother has the more common Kell negative blood type." When a Kell negative woman gets pregnant by a Kell positive man and the foetus is Kell positive, her body reacts and attacks the developing foetus. This doesn't usually happen in a first pregnancy with a Kell positive baby, but there will be problems with any subsequent Kell positive pregnancies. The pregnancy ends in a late miscarriage, stillbirth or the death of the baby shortly after birth. Kramer comments that, "This is exactly what happened to any woman who had more than one pregnancy with Henry VIII."

But what about Mary I, the result of Catherine of Aragon's fifth pregnancy? Well, Kramer argues that Mary was a Kell negative baby and so was not attacked by her mother's antibodies. She also believes that Henry, Duke of Cornwell, the baby boy born to Catherine and Henry who survived fifty-two days was a Kell negative baby. Kramer concludes:

"Putting together the reproductive records of Henry's first two Queens, they had at least nine, and possibly even thirteen, pregnancies between them. It is blatantly obvious that they, and Henry, were

fertile. Yet very few pregnancies ended successfully and only two of the babies who were born alive survived infancy. Given the relative rarity of this type of obstetrical history... it seems likely that the King was the source of their troubles. If he was Kell positive, it would explain all the reproductive misfortune he and his wives endured."

I'm just not convinced though. Yes, Catherine was unlucky. She had four stillbirths, one son who died in infancy and just one healthy baby, Mary, who survived into adulthood. However, Catherine sounds similar to Anne Archer, the Stuart lady I mentioned earlier, who was pregnant at least ten times and had only one surviving daughter. Then we have Anne Boleyn, who had three pregnancies at the most and suffered one miscarriage that we're sure of. That's not unusual even today. So I don't agree that Catherine and Anne were unusual.

Kramer's argument for Kell also rests on her argument for Henry having McLeod Syndrome, a syndrome which can only be manifested in people who have a Kell positive blood type.

Here are some facts about McLeod Syndrome:

- Symptoms of McLeod syndrome begin to appear near the patient's fortieth birthday
- The symptoms grow progressively worse over time
- The symptoms include muscle and nerve deterioration, facial tics, malformed blood cells, and damage of the internal organs like the liver and the heart
- There is also often an erosion of mental stability, wherein the patient becomes more and more irrational and erratic.
- Patients usually display symptoms like memory deterioration, depression, paranoia and even schizophrenia-like behaviours.

Kramer believes that "there is a plethora of evidence to show how Henry's personality and mental processes had changed", particularly after his 40th birthday. Examples she cites include:

- The banishment of Catherine of Aragon and Henry's cruel treatment of her and of Mary
- The executions of the Carthusian monks
- The executions of Bishop John Fisher and Sir Thomas More
- The fall of Anne Boleyn and her execution, along with the executions of men he'd been friends with, e.g. Norris
- His mood swings and the way that he could just turn against those he'd loved
- His behaviour when Jane Seymour was dying; he was more concerned with hunting
- His response to Anne of Cleves when she didn't recognise him at their first meeting in Rochester. Kramer writes, "The mental impairment caused by McLeod syndrome likely exacerbated Henry's response to Anna's gaffe" and "he developed a deep-seated revulsion towards Anna."
- The fall of Thomas Cromwell and his subsequent execution.
- His decision to execute the frail and elderly Margaret Pole
- The falls and executions of Catherine Howard, Lady Rochford, Francis Dereham and Thomas Culpeper.
- Bad foreign policy decisions

Kramer comments that Henry VIII changed from knight to nightmare, and that this was the result of McCleod Syndrome. I don't agree. Thomas More, who served Henry VIII as his Lord Chancellor, was very close to the King, more like a father figure to him. Nonetheless, he once famously said of Henry, "I have no cause to be proud thereof, for if my head would win him a castle in France, it should not fail to go", knowing that Henry was capable of tyranny when it suited his ambition. And I have to agree with the great historian, J. J. Scarisbrick who remarked, in response to the argument that Henry's behaviour became more tyrannical after 1536, "Henry was not notably more cruel afterwards than he had been before".[42]

Before he turned forty, Henry had made scapegoats of his father's chief advisors, Richard Empson and Edmund Dudley, and he had executed Edmund de la Pole and the Duke of Buckingham. Yes, there were many executions after he turned forty, but Henry was having to deal with the aftermath of the break with Rome, with those who challenged his authority by not accepting his supremacy or who were a threat to him. I'm not excusing his tyranny, and I do believe he was a tyrant, but I just can't see that there was a radical change in his behaviour after his fortieth birthday. He always had those tendencies and they simply got worse when he felt threatened.

So, I don't believe that Henry had McLeod Syndrome and I don't believe that he was Kell Positive. I therefore don't believe that he was to blame for his wives' reproductive woes, and I don't actually think that you can say that Anne Boleyn did, in fact, experience reproductive woes.

Alison Weir puts forward the theory that Anne Boleyn may have been Rhesus negative and that this explains why she experienced stillbirths. Rhesus disease does not occur in a first pregnancy, but in subsequent pregnancies when a mother has been sensitised to Rhesus positive blood cells by carrying a Rhesus positive baby. After sensitisation, when the woman is carrying a Rhesus positive baby, her immune system will produce antibodies which attack and destroy her baby's blood cells.[43] Weir concludes that this theory explains why "Anne's first pregnancy had resulted in a healthy child, but her three subsequent pregnancies had ended in stillbirth".[44] But, I don't believe that Anne had that many pregnancies; what's more, the one that ended in January 1536 was a miscarriage, not a stillbirth. Rhesus disease, when untreated, results in stillbirth or deafness, blindness, cerebral palsy or learning difficulties; but it doesn't result in miscarriage. Today, Rhesus negative women are given a special injection, an anti-D injection, between 28 and 30 weeks of pregnancy, to stop their body making antibodies which would harm their baby. Anne lost her baby in 1536 at around 15 ½ weeks, so it was too early for it to be affected by her Rhesus negative blood type, if indeed she had it. I don't believe that Rhesus disease explains Anne's obstretic history at all.

In my opinion, Anne, and Catherine of Aragon too, were just unlucky. They were living at a time when miscarriages were common, infant mortality was high, and there was no prenatal care. They were not unusual. Anne, in particular, cannot be said to have suffered a series of miscarriages because there is only firm evidence for one such miscarriage. It is human nature to want to explain something, but I think it's time to stop trying to find medical reasons for what happened to these women and to stop trying to lay blame.

Was Anne Boleyn Pregnant at her Execution?

I'm often asked this question, which you also see being asked on forums and blogs. The idea that Anne was pregnant when she went to her death on 19th May 1536 was put forward by Alison Weir in her book *Henry VIII: The King and His Court*, first published in 2008.[45] Weir argued that Henry VIII's comment to Chapuys in April 1536, when he said "Am I not a man like other men? Am I not? Am I not? You do not know all my secrets", was a reference to Anne's pregnancy. Furthermore, Weir argues, this was backed up by Henry's words to his ambassadors in Rome and France regarding "the likelihood and appearance that God will send us heirs male," thus implying that Anne was actually already pregnant. The problem is that Chapuys actually recorded this conversation in a letter to Emperor Charles V on 15th April *1533*, not 1536. He wrote:

> *"He asked me three times if he was not a man like other men (si nestoit point home comme les autres), adding that I had no reason to affirm the contrary, seeing I was not privy to all his secrets ; leaving me clearly to understand that his beloved lady was enceinte."*[46]

Well, of course, Anne *was* pregnant in April 1533, with Elizabeth, so Chapuys' comment makes sense. Weir obviously made a mistake with the date; Chapuys cannot be recording a conversation which took place in 1536 in a letter in 1533. In any case, Weir has changed her mind on this matter and refutes it in her more recent book, *The Lady in the Tower*. Unfortunately, the idea is still out there being discussed.

Notes and Sources

1   Kramer, Blood Will Tell: A Medical Explanation of the Tyranny of Henry VIII.
2   Elton, England Under the Tudors, 152.
3   Bruce, Anne Boleyn, 251.
4   Chapman, Anne Boleyn, 161.
5   "Letters and Papers, Foreign and Domestic, Henry VIII, Volume 7," n. 114.
6   Ibid., n. 556.
7   Ibid., n. 958.
8   Ibid., n. 1013.
9   Ibid., n. 1193.
10 Ives, The Life and Death of Anne Boleyn, 394, note 12.
11 "Letters and Papers, Foreign and Domestic, Henry VIII, Volume 8," n. 919.
12 Dewhurst, "The Alleged Miscarriages of Catherine of Aragon and Anne Boleyn."
13 "Letters and Papers, Foreign and Domestic, Henry VIII, Volume 10 - January-June 1536," n. 282.
14 Hall, Hall's Chronicle, 818.
15 Wriothesley, A Chronicle of England During the Reigns of the Tudors, from A.D. 1485 to 1559, 33.
16 Holinshed, Holinshed's Chronicles of England, Scotland, and Ireland, 6:796.
17 Ascoli, La Grande-Bretagne Devant L'opinion Française Depuis La Guerre de Cent Ans Jusqu'à La Fin Du XVIe Siècle, chap. Poème sur la Mort d'Anne Boleyn, lines 317–326.
18 Gregory, The Other Boleyn Girl, 589.
19 Warnicke, The Rise and Fall of Anne Boleyn: Family Politics at the Court of Henry VIII, 191.
20 Warnicke, "Sexual Heresy at the Court of Henry VIII," 260.
21 Warnicke, The Rise and Fall of Anne Boleyn: Family Politics at the Court of Henry VIII, 214.
22 Warnicke, "Sexual Heresy at the Court of Henry VIII," 258.

23   Cressy, Birth, Marriage, and Death: Ritual, Religion, and the Life-Cycle in Tudor and Stuart England.

24   Weisner, Women and Gender in Early Modern Europe.

25   Sander, Rise and Growth of the Anglican Schism, 132.

26   Ives, The Life and Death of Anne Boleyn, 297.

27   Zupanec, The Daring Truth About Anne Boleyn: Cutting Through the Myth, chap. 9.

28   Ibid.

29   Flaccus and Festus, M. Verrii Flacci Quae Extant: Et Sexti Pompeii Festi De Verborum Significatione, XX:424.

30   Micraelius, Lexicon Philosophicum Terminorum Philosophis Usitatorum, 825.

31   "Letters and Papers, Foreign and Domestic, Henry VIII, Volume 10 - January-June 1536," n. 450.

32   Ibid., n. 528.

33   Zupanec, The Daring Truth About Anne Boleyn: Cutting Through the Myth, chap. 9.

34   Sander, De Origine Ac Progressu Schismatis Anglicani, 166.

35   "Molar Pregnancy."

36   Madams, "Carnis Molem."

37   Ives, The Life and Death of Anne Boleyn, 296.

38   "Miscarriage Statitsics."

39   "Pregnancy Loss."

40   Cressy, Birth, Marriage, and Death: Ritual, Religion, and the Life-Cycle in Tudor and Stuart England.

41   Kramer, Blood Will Tell: A Medical Explanation of the Tyranny of Henry VIII.

42   Scarisbrick, Henry VIII, 655.

43   "Rhesus Disease."

44   Weir, The Lady in the Tower: The Fall of Anne Boleyn, 35.

45   Weir, Henry VIII: The King and His Court, chap. 47: Thunder Rolls Around the Throne.

46   "Letters and Papers, Foreign and Domestic, Henry VIII, Volume 6 - 1533," n. 351.

15. Anne Boleyn and the Charge of Witchcraft

Every year in the lead-up to the anniversary of Anne Boleyn's execution on 19th May, I notice a multitude of tweets and Facebook comments referring to Anne Boleyn being charged with witchcraft. This is in addition to her charges of treason, adultery and incest. I bite my tongue and sit on my hands, resisting the urge to point out the glaring error in these posts. In 2012, there was even an article by author Hilary Mantel in *The Guardian* newspaper entitled "Anne Boleyn: witch, bitch, temptress, feminist".

Now, Mantel was not actually suggesting that Anne was a witch or that she had been charged with witchcraft. In fact, Mantel writes, "Anne was not charged with witchcraft, as some people believe. She was charged with treasonable conspiracy to procure the king's death, a charge supported by details of adultery."[1] In this, Mantel is correct; Anne was not charged with witchcraft. But Anne Boleyn's name is too often linked with witchcraft and many people, even Tudor history buffs, assume that she was indeed charged with it. It's no wonder that people make that assumption; depictions of Anne as a witch are ubiquitous. Her portrait is on the wall at Hogwarts (not that this allusion should be taken seriously, though, of course). In addition, the 2009 Hampton Court Palace Flower

Show had a Witch's Garden to represent Anne Boleyn. Finally, Philippa Gregory's famous novel *The Other Boleyn Girl*[2] depicted Anne Boleyn dabbling in witchcraft, taking a potion to bring on the miscarriage of a baby (which turns out to be monstrously deformed) and having a "witch taker" help to bring her down. You only have to Google "Anne Boleyn witchcraft" to find sites claiming that Anne was charged with and executed for witchcraft, or mentions of her having an extra finger and moles all over her body, which could have been seen as "witch's teats" and the marks of a witch. Even an article on the BBC history website refers to her being accused of being "a disciple of witchcraft".[3]

Some non-fiction authors and historians give credence to the witchcraft theory. In her biography of Anne Boleyn, Norah Lofts[4] writes of Anne bearing a mole known as the "Devil's Pawmark," and of making a "typical witch's threat" when she was in the Tower, claiming that there would be no rain in England for seven years. Lofts explains that seven was the magic number and that witches were thought to control the weather. What's more, Anne had a dog named Urian, a name for Satan. In addition to this, she managed to cast a spell on Henry which eventually ran out in 1536, hence his violent reaction, "the passing from adoration to hatred". Lofts goes even further when she writes about the story of Anne haunting Salle Church in Norfolk, where, according to legend, Anne's body was really buried. Loft writes of meeting the sexton of the church; he told Lofts that he kept vigil one 19th May to see if Anne's ghost appeared. He didn't see a ghost, but he did see a huge hare "which seemed to come from nowhere". It jumped around the church before vanishing into thin air. According to Lofts, "a hare was one of the shapes that a witch was supposed to be able to take at will"; she pondered if it was indeed Anne Boleyn.

That all sounds rather far-fetched, but reputable historian Retha Warnicke[5] also mentions witchcraft in her book on Anne. Warnicke writes that sodomy and incest were associated with witchcraft. Warnicke believes that the men executed for adultery

Figure 20 - St. Peter & St. Paul, Salle, Norfolk

with Anne were "libertines" who practised "buggery". In addition, of course, Anne and George were charged with incest. Warnicke also thinks that the rather lurid mentions in the indictments of Anne procuring the men and inciting them to have sexual relations with her was "consistent with the need to prove that she was a witch". She continues, saying that "the licentious charges against the queen, even if the rumours of her attempted poisonings and of her causing her husband's impotence were never introduced into any of the trials, indicate that Henry believed that she was a witch."[6] Now, Henry VIII may well have said that he had been "forced into this second marriage by sortilèges and charms",[7] but I don't for one second believe that Henry was convinced that Anne was a witch. If he had believed it, then surely Cromwell would have used this claim to get Henry's marriage to Anne annulled. If Anne was a witch, then it could have been said that Henry had been bewitched and tricked into the marriage, that the marriage was, therefore, invalid. Anne Boleyn was charged with adultery, with plotting the King's death and with committing incest with her brother, George Boleyn, Lord Rochford. There was no mention or suggestion of witchcraft or sorcery in the Middlesex or Kent indictments. What's more, at her trial, Anne was found guilty of committing treason against the King – again, no mention of witchcraft. Although witchcraft was not a felony or a crime punishable by death until the act of 1542, a suggestion of witchcraft could still have helped the Crown's case and served as propaganda. I believe that the details of the indictments were simply there for shock value, rather than to prove that Anne was a witch.

So, where does the whole witchcraft charge come from if it was not mentioned in 1536? Well, I think we can put some of the blame on the Catholic recusant Nicholas Sander who in 1585 described Anne Boleyn as having "a projecting tooth", six fingers on her right hand and "a large wen under her chin" – very witch-like! He also wrote that Anne miscarried "a shapeless mass of flesh" in January 1536. This "shapeless mass" was turned by historical fiction writer Philippa Gregory into "a monster", "a baby horridly malformed, with a spine flayed open and a huge head, twice as large as the spindly little body", and was used to back up the idea that Anne had committed incest and dabbled in witchcraft. However, Sander's words have to be judged as Catholic propaganda, as an attempt to denigrate Elizabeth I by blackening the name of her mother. Sander was only about six years of age when Anne died, so he could hardly have known her, and he was a priest, not a courtier, so would not have been privy to court gossip about Anne. None of Anne's contemporaries mention an extra finger, projecting tooth or wen; even Anne's enemy, Eustace Chapuys, describes her miscarriage as the loss of "a male child which she had not borne 3½ months". If the baby had been deformed, Chapuys would surely have mentioned this; he would also have recorded any physical deformities that Anne possessed. He nicknamed her "the concubine" and "the putain", or whore, so he wasn't afraid of saying what he thought.

While I cannot prove that Anne Boleyn was not a witch, I can cast doubt on this belief. Norah Lofts' claims can easily be refuted. Anne's mole was simply a mole. Her dog was named after Urian Brereton (brother of William Brereton, who gave the dog to Anne). Anne's mention of the weather in the Tower was simply the ramblings of a terrified and hysterical woman. Finally, the hare was simply a hare! As for Retha Warnicke's views, I have found no evidence to prove that the men executed in May 1536 were homosexual; and the only evidence for the deformed foetus is Nicholas Sander. Also, Henry's words concerning "sortilèges and charms" were more likely to have been bluster than a serious accusation. He also said that Anne had had over a hundred lovers and that she had tried to poison his son, Fitzroy, and his daughter, Mary. I believe this to be the bluster of an angry and defensive man, rather than something to take seriously.

In conclusion, witchcraft was not something that was linked to Anne Boleyn in the sixteenth century, so I feel that it is about time that people stopped talking about Anne and witchcraft in the same breath. Let's get the facts straight.

◇◇◇

Notes and Sources

1   Mantel, "Anne Boleyn: Witch, Bitch, Temptress, Feminist."
2   Gregory, The Other Boleyn Girl.
3   Bevan, "Anne Boleyn and the Downfall of Her Family."
4   Lofts, Anne Boleyn.
5   Warnicke, The Rise and Fall of Anne Boleyn: Family Politics at the Court of Henry VIII.
6   Ibid., 231.
7   "Calendar of State Papers, Spain, Volume 5 Part 2: 1536-1538," 28.

16. Anne Boleyn, Mary Boleyn and Little Henry Carey

I'm often asked about Anne Boleyn's relationship with her sister Mary and the claim made in the book *The Other Boleyn Girl* that Anne stole Mary's son, Henry Carey, from her.

Now, it's impossible to know exactly how close the sisters were and how their relationship was; we just don't have the evidence. What we do know is that they were relatively close in age, if you take 1501 as Anne's birthdate and 1499/1500 as Mary's. They would have also been educated together at home until Anne was sent to the Low Countries in 1513. Anne and Mary would surely have been playmates and friends, but we know nothing about that early sibling relationship; all we can do is guess.

In 1514, Mary Boleyn was chosen to accompany Mary Tudor, sister of Henry VIII, to France. Anne was also recalled, from the Low Countries, to serve Mary Tudor. It is likely that Anne arrived in France in late 1514, so the sisters would have spent a few months together serving Mary Tudor before the Queen went back to England in April 1515. We know that Anne stayed on in France to serve Francis I's wife, Queen Claude, but we do not know what happened to Mary Boleyn. It does appear, however, that the sisters were separated until Anne's return to England in late 1521.

Mary Boleyn was a married woman when Anne returned to the English court, having married courtier William Carey in February 1520. Carey was a member of the King's privy chamber and an Esquire of the Body, so he and his wife would have lived at court. The two sisters would have met again at court when Anne began her duties as a lady-in-waiting to Queen Catherine of Aragon. Both women participated in the Shrovetide Château Vert Pageant of 1522, Anne playing Perseverance and Mary playing Kindness, so they would have spent time together preparing for the pageant. It is thought that Mary began her affair with Henry VIII, Anne's future husband, around this time. Merely being in the same place at the same time is, of course, not evidence of a close relationship, but Mary accompanied Anne and Henry VIII on their trip to Calais in autumn 1532, was one of Anne's ladies in 1533 and attended her sister at her coronation in 1533. The sisters must surely have been close for Anne to choose Mary to attend her at these key events.

Anne Boleyn and Henry Carey

Mary's husband, William Carey, died of sweating sickness in June 1528, leaving his wife with their two young children, Catherine and Henry. William's death left Mary In considerable financial difficulty so she wrote to the King for help. Henry VIII obliged, securing financial help for her from her father, Thomas Boleyn, and granting the wardship of Mary's son, Henry, to Anne Boleyn. This is where the facts get twisted...

In Philippa Gregory's *The Other Boleyn Girl*, Anne Boleyn suggests to Mary Boleyn that she, Anne, should adopt Mary's son. Mary Is shocked and refuses, but then Anne tells her that it is a fait accompli; she has already stolen Mary's son. The wardship is treated as something sinister and as part of Anne's plan to marry

Figure 21 - Vintage engraving of Sir Henry Carey

the King and provide him with a ready-made son, a son that is actually his anyway (according to the novel). The truth is not so exciting. There was actually nothing unusual or sinister about Anne being granted the wardship of Henry Carey. Mary Boleyn was experiencing financial problems and Anne was in a position to help. Anne provided the boy with a good education, appointing the French poet and reformer, Nicholas Bourbon, as his tutor. Carey was educated along with Thomas Howard and Henry Norris (son of Sir Henry Norris, Henry VIII's Groom of the Stool). It was a great start for the young boy.

Anne was not kidnapping Henry Carey, stealing him or even adopting him; she was providing for him. Wardship was standard practice in Tudor times; other examples of it include Charles Brandon being granted the wardship of the teenage Catherine Willoughby, and Lady Jane Grey becoming Thomas Seymour's ward. In the case of a woman being widowed, it was quite usual for a son who was not 'of age' to become the ward of another adult or family. Wardships could actually be purchased from the Crown and the child's property could be controlled by the holder of the wardship until the child came of age, giving the holder extra income during that time. It seems to have been a bit of a win-win situation in that the widow was relieved of some of her financial burden and may have had her child better educated and brought up in an influential family, and the wardship holder received extra income. Anne was a provider not a kidnapper.

Banishment and Survival

In September 1534, Mary Boleyn turned up at court pregnant and announced to her sister, the Queen, that she had secretly married William Stafford. Anne Boleyn was livid that Mary had dared to marry without her permission and had thus undermined her authority. Anne, as queen, was now head of the Boleyn family, and should have been consulted. Anne's reaction was nothing to do with spite and everything to do with protocol.

Although a report by the Bishop of Faenza[1] places Mary at court in January 1536, attending Anne when she miscarried, it is thought that Mary was actually away from court in 1536. Alison Weir, in her recent biography of Mary, puts forward the idea that Mary and Stafford may even have lived in Calais at this time. Wherever she was, Mary was not implicated in the fall of her sister and brother in May 1536, and may not have known that her affair with the King was used to annul Henry's marriage to Anne Boleyn on the grounds of consanguinity.

Anne Boleyn was executed on 19th May 1536 and her ward, Henry Carey, went from being educated by a reformer to being educated by a staunch Catholic – quite a difference. Mary died a natural death in July 1543 and it was her children, Henry and Catherine, who carried on the Boleyn bloodline. Henry went on to serve his cousin, Elizabeth I, as a privy councillor and Catherine became Elizabeth's Chief Lady of the Bedchamber. Whatever the relationship between Anne and Mary, their children were close. Elizabeth gave Catherine a lavish royal-style funeral on her death in 1569, and Henry Carey received a magnificent tomb which is the tallest in Westminster Abbey. Today's royal family descend from Mary Boleyn.

Notes and Sources

1   "Letters and Papers, Foreign and Domestic, Henry VIII, Volume 10 - January-June 1536," n. 450.

17. Anne Boleyn and Charity

It is impossible to talk about Anne the patron and generous giver without looking at what drove Anne to be the person that she was. Her driving force in this respect was her faith. Anne was an evangelical, one who was heavily influenced by French reformers like Jacques Lefèvre d'Étaples and Clément Marot, rather than by German reformers such as Martin Luther. In his 1512 commentary on Romans 3, Lefèvre distinguished between the justification (or salvation) of the law and that of faith, explaining that justification of the law came from works, and justification of faith came from grace.[1] Where Martin Luther emphasised justification by faith, salvation through accepting Christ as one's saviour, Lefèvre insisted that works, or good deeds, were also important for salvation; works that stemmed from a person's faith. To put it simply, he believed that faith without works was not faith, and that works without faith were not works. They were both important and hinged on each other.

This kind of thinking on faith and works must have influenced Anne Boleyn; it featured in the literature she was reading. Historian Maria Dowling points out that "Poor relief was both a humanist and a Lollard preoccupation, and Anne was, according to all her panegyrists, outstandingly generous to the poor",[2] something that was emphasised in *The Ecclesiaste*. This book was given to her by her brother, George Boleyn. It contained a translation based on Lefèvre's translation of Ecclesiastes, as well as a commentary by Johannes Brenz, the German theologian and reformer.

In the Bible, Ecclesiastes 11 verses 1 and 2 say:

"Be generous: Invest in acts of charity. Charity yields high returns. Don't hoard your goods; spread them around. Be a blessing to others. This could be your last night."

And Anne's copy of *The Ecclesiaste* said:

"The court of kings, princes, chancellors, judging places and audiences be the places where one ought to find equity and justice. But, oh good Lord, where is there more injustice, more exactions, more oppressions of poor widows and orphans, where is there more disorder in all manners and more greater company of unjust men than there, whereas should be but all good order and just people of good and holy example of life."[3]

Anne, being first the King's queen-in-waiting and then queen, was in just such a place, and she was also in a position to obey the Bible and help those who needed it. Charity and the dissemination of the English Bible were the two reformist principles that were close to Anne's heart.

But just how generous was Anne? What evidence is there of her charitable giving and how did she help people? Let's consider some 16th century sources...

John Foxe (1516/17-1587)

John Foxe was an English historian, reformer and martyrologist who is known for his accounts of religious martyrs, which were published as *Actes and Monuments* and abridged as *Foxe's Book of Martyrs*. *Actes and Monuments* contains a section on Anne Boleyn, a woman who Foxe clearly saw as a Protestant martyr. Foxe also wrote of Anne's charitable giving:

> "*Also, how bountiful she was to the poor, passing not only the common example of other queens, but also the revenues almost of her estate; insomuch that the alms which she gave in three quarters of a year, in distribution, is summed to the number of fourteen or fifteen thousand pounds; besides the great piece of money which her grace intended to impart into four sundry quarters of the realm, as for a stock there to be employed to the behoof of poor artificers and occupiers.*"[4]

However, historian Eric Ives believes that Foxe is exaggerating when he quotes the sums of £14-15000. We have to remember that Foxe was writing in Elizabeth I's reign; he may have been flattering the Queen or trying to get her to be just as generous as her mother.

William Latymer

William Latymer was a man who knew Anne Boleyn personally. He had acted as her chaplain and had also undertaken travels abroad to bring back religious books for Anne. In his biography of Anne, his *Cronickille of Anne Bulleyne* written in Elizabeth I's reign, he described Anne as "generous to the poor" and gave the following examples of her generosity, charitable giving and kindness:

- Anne's Maundy giving: "For upon a certain Maundy Thursday, after she had most humbly (humbly, I said, because kneeling on her knees she washed and kissed the feet of simple poor women) embased herself to perform the ceremonyies of that day, she commanded to be put pivily into every poor woman's purse one george noble, the which was 6 shillings 8 pence over and besides the almes that wanted to be given."[5] While it was traditional for the monarch and his consort to wash the feet of as many poor people as years they were old, in addition to giving them purses of coins, both Latymer and John Foxe record how the amount in the royal Maundy purses increased when Anne was Queen. Indeed, the 1536 court expenses show that the "costs of the Queen's maundy" were 31 pounds, 3 shillings and 9 and a half pence.

- Her "myndefull remembrance of the poore" when she was on royal progresses. She would "give in special commandment to her officers to buy a great quantity of canvas to be made into shirts and smocks and sheets to those of the poor."

- Her orders to her ladies to make shirts, smocks and sheets for the poor and her ordering of "flannell" to be made into "pettycotes for poore men, wemen and children." These items were then distributed "to every of whome was distributed by her graces commaundemente a shurte, smok or petticote, and 12 pence [xiid] in money, and to some more, according as here grace understod of their nede and necessitie." Anne also made sure that pregnant women were given two shillings and a pair of sheets.[6]

- Anne's speech to her chaplains where she told them that they should all "take special regard in the choice of such poor people as shall be found most needy, not vagrant and lazy beggars, who in every place besides are relieved abundantly, but poor needy and impotent householders over-charged with children, not having any sustenance, comfort or relief otherwise; and to such I command my alms liberally. In like manner, if you assuredly perceive any poor men of women having cause of suit either to me or my council to be delayed from their answer, whereby they suffer loss of time and goods to their great hindrance, I command you to open the matter to my council and other officers to whom such cases it shall appertain."[7] Anne was asking her chaplains to make sure that they always let her know if they found people in need.

- The example of Mrs Jaskyne, who attended the queen. The former's husband, sergeant of the queen's pantry, was "greviouslye sick" and had called for his wife. One of Anne's chaplains informed Anne and she "not only graunted her licence to depart..., but also most bountyfullye commaunded to be prepared for her sufficiente furniture of horse and other necessarys for her jorney, and tenne pounds in monye towarde the charge of her travaill."[8]

- The story of a Mr Ive at Kingston who lost most of his cattle "almost to his utter undoing". Anne gave his wife a purse of gold with xxli in it (£20) and said to tell her if they needed further help.[9]

- The aid she gave to refugees and reformers in danger. This is mentioned by Latymer, Nicholas Bourbon and Thomas Alwaye. Latymer writes of a Mrs Marye who fled France and was helped by Anne.[10]

- Anne's concern over the use of the money from the dissolution of the monasteries. Anne commanded Hugh Latimer, another of her chaplains, to preach "to dissuade the utter subversion of the said houses and to induce the kinges grace to the mynde to converte them to some better use."[11] Latimer preached in front of the King and based his sermon on Luke 20 verses 9-16, the parable of the vineyard. Here is a modern text of that parable from the New International Bible:

"A man planted a vineyard, rented it to some farmers and went away for a long time. At harvest time he sent a servant to the tenants so they would give him some of the fruit of the vineyard. But the tenants beat him and sent him away empty-handed. He sent another servant, but that one also they beat and treated shamefully and sent away empty-handed. He sent still a third, and they wounded him and threw him out. Then the owner of the vineyard said, 'What shall I do? I will send my son, whom I love; perhaps they will respect him.' But when the tenants saw him, they talked the matter over. 'This is the heir,' they said. 'Let's kill him, and the inheritance will be ours.' So they threw him out of the vineyard and killed him.   What then will the owner of the vineyard do to them? He will come and kill those

tenants and give the vineyard to others."

It is a fitting text when you consider the first fruits and taxes that the monasteries had to pay. William Latymer wrote of this sermon in his *Cronickille of Anne Bulleyne.* He explained that Hugh Latimer emphasised that the owner of the vineyard did not destroy the vineyard when the tenants could not pay him in fruit. Instead, he commanded it "to be farmed and let to others, who should by their industry and husbandry amend the negligence of the other farmers." In other words, the owner let it be used by others who would do the right thing. Latimer, and Anne through him, were saying that instead of dissolving the monasteries, the King could "converte the abbeys and prioryes to places of studye and goode letres and to the contynuall releve of the poore." This was obviously something that Anne felt strongly about. It was backed up by the Passion Sunday sermon of 1536 given by Anne's almoner John Skip. This sermon called on those advising the King to "reject the lure of personal gain". Both sermons were controversial; in order to risk the backlash, Anne must have felt strongly about this issue.

According to Latymer, Anne was of the opinion that "where as God hadd indued her with greate riches, dignitie and estate, even so she wolde not spare thankefuly to dedicate thereof some porcion to his glorye."[12] She had been blessed by God and felt that it was her duty to share that with others who were less fortunate.

Thomas Alwaye

Thomas Alwaye, who is described by historian Maria Dowling as "an otherwise obscure evangelical prosecuted by Wolsey and the bishops for buying English new testaments and other prohibited books",[13] petitioned Anne Boleyn in 1530 or 1531, seeking her help and intervention. In his letter, he wrote:

"But anon I remembered how many deeds of pity your goodness had done within these few years, and that without respect of any

persons, as well to strangers and aliens as to many of this land, as well to poor as to rich."

He also made mention of Anne's "charity" and said that her "Christian mind is everywhere ready to help, succour and comfort them that be afflicted, troubled and vexed". He may well have been flattering Anne to gain her assistance but, as Dowling points out, for him to even turn to her in his hour of need shows that Anne was known for helping reformers. Would he have dared write to her otherwise?

George Wyatt

George Wyatt was the grandson of courtier and poet, Sir Thomas Wyatt the Elder, and author of "The Life of the Virtuous Christian and Renowned Queen Anne Boleigne" which was written towards the end of the 16th century, during the reign of Elizabeth I. His account of Anne's life was based on information given to him by his family and by Anne Gainsford, former lady-in-waiting to Anne Boleyn. Wyatt wrote of Anne:

"And yet far more rich and precious were those works in the sight of God which she caused her maids and those about her daily to work in shirts and smocks for the poor. But not staying here her eye of charity, her hand of bounty passed through the whole land."[14]

He then concurred with Foxe over the sum of money which Anne gave as poor relief:

"Her ordinary amounted to fifteen hundred pounds at the least, yearly to be bestowed on the poor. Her provisions of stock for the poor in sundry needy parishes were very great. Out of her privy purse went not a little to like purposes. To scholars in exhibition very much: so as in three quarters of a year her alms was summed to fourteen or fifteen thousand pounds."

Foxe's book was first published in 1563, so perhaps Wyatt used that as a source; we just don't know. Historian Eric Ives believes that the regular amount of £1500, mentioned by Wyatt, would be more credible. According to Ives a sum of £14-15000 was "twelve times larger than the annual surplus on Anne's expenditure". In this case, the sum does not make sense unless it is a typo, a case of an extra 0 being added.

William Marshall

In 1535, William Marshall, a man who was enlisted by Cromwell to draft legislation for poor relief, dedicated to Anne his work The Form and manner of subvention or helping for poor people, devised and practised in the city of Ypres. Marshall wrote:

"My very mind, intent and meaning is (by putting of this honourable and charitable provision in mind) to occasion your grace (which at all times is ready to further all goodness) to be a mediatrix and mean unto our most dread sovereign lord... for the stablishing and practising of the same (if it shall seem so worthy) or of some other, as good or better, such as by his majesty or his most honourable council shall be devised."

Maria Dowling points out that it is "a telling indication of the distribution of political influence that Marshall, primarily a Cromwell protégé, should consider it more effective to present his work through Anne rather than through his own patron".[15] It shows that Anne had a reputation for being concerned with poor relief, that she had influence over the King and that she did play a part in the government's decision to provide poor relief.

Anne Boleyn and Thomas Cromwell's Poor Law

Contrary to popular opinion, Thomas Cromwell was not a greedy money-grabbing statesman whose main motivation in office was to line Henry VIII's pockets, and his own on the way. Cromwell, like Anne Boleyn, was concerned about poverty. In June 1535, Eustace Chapuys, the imperial ambassador, reported

Figure 22 - Vintage engraving of Thomas Cromwell

to Emperor Charles V that Cromwell had told him that he (Cromwell) "and other privy councillors are now looking out for the means of checking this King's avarice, and making him spend his money for the benefit of the nation".[16] As the Thomas Cromwell Experience website explains, "Cromwell, and his army of staff, spent a year investigating the causes of poverty. Among their conclusions were: cruel employers, ill health/incapacity, crime, and bad living conditions/poor upbringing."[17] With the main causes of poverty identified, Cromwell then began planning how the problem could be tackled. His biographer John Schofield explains that, "an ambitious plan of public works was then laid out. It included new buildings, repairs to harbours, highways, and fortresses, and scouring and cleansing of water courses; all under the direction of officers reporting to a central council."[18]

By Autumn 1535, Cromwell had the draft bill prepared, legislation that would provide help for the unemployed, relief for those in poverty and care for those who were incapacitated. However, the rather conservative House of Commons did not agree to Cromwell's legislation and the resulting "poor law" was much more modest than Cromwell's draft policy. Cromwell's investigations and proposals show that Cromwell was on the same page as Anne with regards to charity. Whether or not they argued on the proceeds from the dissolution of the monasteries, they were both concerned with poor relief.

Did Anne have any input into Cromwell's poor law plans? We don't know, but, as Maria Dowling points out, William Marshall was linked to Cromwell and the Boleyns, and he was definitely involved in Cromwell's plans. Eric Ives goes as far as to describe Marshall as a Boleyn protégé, so Anne may well have been involved.

Patronage

Humanist scholars, who believed that society could be rescued by education and scholarship, dedicated their works to Anne Boleyn. These scholars included Robert Whittington, Robert Wakefield and Louis de Brun.[19] Anne also supported men at Cambridge – John Elmer and William Barker for example – as well as those studying abroad, e.g. Wolsey's illegitimate son, Thomas Winter, and John Beckynsaw, who was given £40 per year. In the dedication of his *Nobility of Women* to Anne's daughter, Elizabeth I, in 1559, William Barker mentioned Anne's "bountiful benevolence".

Men like Edward Fox, Hugh Latimer, Matthew Parker, William Barlow, Nicholas Shaxton, Edward Crome, Thomas Garrett and William Betts were just some of the reformers who gained positions due to Anne's help and patronage. Eric Ives writes of Anne being seen "as someone for reformers to turn to". People in prison for possessing heretical books petitioned her for help; and she was "the prime mover" in rescuing Nicholas Bourbon from trouble in France and then employing him as a schoolmaster for her ward, Henry Carey, along with Henry Norris the Younger and Henry Howard. Nicholas Bourbon thanks and praises Anne for her help in his verses:

> "A poor man, I lie shut in this dark prison:
> There is no one who would be able or would dare
> > to bring help:
> Only you, Oh, Queen:
> You, Oh noble nymph both can and will dare:
> As one whom the King and God Himself loves."[20]

Also, Bourbon's friend, Etienne Dolet, wrote a favourable epitaph on Anne after her execution entitled *Reginae utopiae falso adulterii crimine damnatae et capite mulctatae epitaphium*[21] (Queen of Utopia falsely charged of adultery and condemned and punished, the epitaph).

John Cheke, in a letter to Matthew Parker asking him to intercede with the Queen on behalf of William Bill, "praised Anne's munificence to scholars",[22] so it was obviously no secret that Anne helped those of a reformist persuasion. We also know that Anne supported the universities of Oxford and Cambridge by means of annual subventions, and interceded with her husband, Henry VIII, to secure exemption of both universities from the clerical tax which had been introduced. She also supported the collegiate church of Stoke by Clare, the church to which her chaplain, Matthew Parker, had been appointed dean in 1534. Anne was not only supporting education and scholarship, she was also advancing the cause of reform by supporting men of reformist persuasions and influencing appointments within the Church. When Nicholas Shaxton and Hugh Latimer were made Bishops (of Salisbury and Worcester respectively), neither man could afford to pay their first-fruits to the King. Anne stepped in and lent each of them £200. They were, after all, reformers and men she knew.

Conclusion

Anne Boleyn is often portrayed as a woman who only thought about herself, as someone who was ambitious, greedy and power hungry. However, this is far removed from the truth. Evidence shows that she was a religious woman with a true and living personal faith, and that her faith led her to commit to doing good with what God gave her.

She didn't need to instruct her chaplains to look out for needy people and to tell her about them; she didn't need to increase the amount in the Maundy purses; she didn't need to be so generous with her time, money and influence; but she did so. Yes, it was good for her image, and some might call it public relations or propaganda, but through these deeds she risked her reputation and image to support reformers, so I don't believe that it was all about making Anne look good to the people. Her good deeds and her charity surely came from her faith and her love for her people.

Notes and Sources

1   Lindberg, "Jacques Lefèvre d'Étaples by Guy Bedouelle," 25–26.
2   Dowling, "Anne Boleyn and Reform."
3   Ives, The Life and Death of Anne Boleyn, 283.
4   Fox (Foxe), Fox's Book of Martyrs: Acts and Monuments of the Church in Three Volumes, II:407.
5   Dowling, "William Latymer's Cronickille of Anne Bulleyne," 53.
6   Ibid., 54.
7   Ibid., 49.
8   Ibid., 52–53.
9   Ibid., 54.
10 Ibid., 56.
11 Ibid., 57.
12 Dowling, "William Latymer's Cronickille of Anne Bulleyne."
13 Dowling, "Anne Boleyn and Reform."
14 Cavendish, The Life of Cardinal Wolsey, 443.
15 Dowling, "Anne Boleyn and Reform."
16 "Calendar of State Papers, Spain, Volume 5 Part 1: 1534-1535," n. 170.
17 Stewart, "The Relief of the Poor Bill, 1535."
18 Schofield, The Rise and Fall of Thomas Cromwell: Henry VIII's Most Faithful Servant, 103.
19 Ives, The Life and Death of Anne Boleyn, 285.
20 Ives, "A Frenchman at the Court of Anne Boleyn."
21 Ives, "Anne Boleyn on Trial Again."
22 Dowling, "Anne Boleyn and Reform."

.

18.   Anne Boleyn
and the Tower of London

The Tower of London, or Her Majesty's Royal Palace and Fortress, as it is officially called, is famous for being the site of much bloodshed and for being the prison of many hundreds, if not thousands, of people since it was first built by William the Conqueror in the late 11th century. However, during its 900-year history, it has enjoyed many different roles:

- Fortress
- Prison
- Royal Palace
- Armoury
- Mint
- Place of Execution
- Home of the Royal Menagerie
- Jewel house
- Resting Place

In Tudor times, one of the functions of the Tower of London was a prison. Notable prisoners included:

- Anne Boleyn and the five men condemned to death for committing adultery with her
- Sir Thomas More and Bishop John Fisher
- Thomas Cromwell
- Catherine Howard and Lady Jane Rochford
- Anne Askew
- Thomas Cranmer
- Lady Jane Grey and Guildford Dudley
- Princess Elizabeth Tudor and Robert Dudley during Mary I's reign
- Sir Walter Ralegh

However, the Tower was not just a prison; it was also a Royal Palace, complete with Great Hall and royal lodgings which were used by a monarch traditionally before his/her coronation.

Anne Boleyn and the Tower of London

There is much misinformation out there regarding Anne Boleyn, her execution and her links with the Tower of London. Errors and myths I've come across include:

- Anne Boleyn was executed by an axeman
- She was executed where the glass memorial stands today on Tower Green
- Anne was imprisoned in a room in the Queen's House overlooking Tower Green where she carved "ANNE" into the stonework
- The bodies in the chancel were exhumed and then buried in the crypt or in a mass grave
- An extra finger was found when the Victorians exhumed her

remains

- Anne was escorted through Traitors' Gate

I haven't read these in fiction; I've read them on forums and websites, or heard tour guides like Yeoman Warders and Blue Badge Guides tell them to tourists. When one person confronted a Yeoman Warder and told him that Anne was not executed on the spot being pointed out, she got the rather sarcastic reply, "Oh, you've been reading Alison Weir". Oh dear.

Today, we think of the Tower of London as a prison and fortress. The Yeoman Warders tell you its history, and then concentrate on the grisly goings-on. Of course, this is what tourists want to hear about - executions, daring escapes, murders, the Princes, ghosts, the menagerie and the Polar bear who once swam in the moat. These are all interesting stories, but there is so much more to the Tower. There are plenty of books available on the history of the Tower, but in this chapter I'm going to focus on Anne Boleyn's links with the Tower.

The Tower and Anne's Coronation

It was traditional for monarchs to go to the Tower before their coronations and to process from there to Westminster; hence why Edward V, one of the Princes in the Tower, was housed there after his father's death. Henry VIII wanted his queen consort, Anne Boleyn, to follow this royal tradition, to thus show the people that Anne was his rightful wife and Queen. He spent a fortune refurbishing the royal palace and commissioning lavish timber-framed lodgings for Anne's comfort. Improvements included "a rebuilt great chamber and a rebuilt dining room, while a new bridge across the moat gave access from her private garden into the city."[1] The great gallery had also been restored. It is estimated that Cromwell spent the equivalent of nearly £1.3 million in today's money on the repairs and improvements.[2] It is sad that these apartments became uninhabitable by the end of the 16th century

Figure 23 - A view of the Tower of London

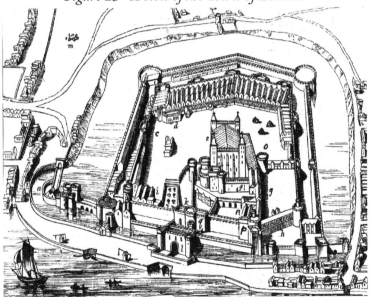

a	Lion's Tower	f	Jewel House	l	St. Thomas' Tower, and
b	Bell Tower	g	Queen's Lodgings		Traitor's Gate
c	Beauchamp Tower	h	Queen's Gallery and Garden	m	Place of Execution on Tower Hill
d	The Chapel	i	Lieutenant's Lodgings	n	Palace buildings inc. Great Hall
e	The Keep, called also Caesar's			o	Wardrobe Tower
	Tower, or White Tower	k	Bloody Tower	p	Lanthorn Tower q Wakefield Tower

Figure 24 - Plan of the Tower in 1597

and were demolished in the 18th century when so much was spent on them and when they had such history.

The royal palace consisted of :-

- The Great Hall, the centre-piece of the palace and a huge hall built by Henry III in the 13th century
- Kitchens
- The Queen's lodgings, which overlooked the palace gardens
- The jewel house
- The Queen's gallery, used for promenades and viewing the gardens
- The palace gardens with their courtyards, railings and posts topped with heraldic beasts

It was a sumptuous royal palace.

In Figure 24, the Great Hall is in the royal palace complex ("n"); the Queen's lodgings are the buildings on the right of it ("g"), running between the White Tower's Wardrobe Tower ("o") and the Lanthorn Tower ("p"). The kitchens were situated beside the Wakefield Tower ("q").

On 29th May 1533, Anne Boleyn's coronation celebrations began with a river pageant from Billingsgate to the Tower of London. The procession paused at Greenwich Palace for Anne to board her barge and then made its way to the Tower, where Anne disembarked at the Court Gate of the Byward Tower. The royal couple spent the next forty-eight hours in the royal palace of the Tower before Anne's procession to Westminster in readiness for her coronation ceremony. The traditional Order of the Bath ceremony took place from the night of 30th May to the morning of the 31st, with eighteen Knights of the Bath being created.

At about 5pm on Saturday 31st May, Anne left the Tower of London to process to Westminster. The lavish rebuilding and refurbishments that Henry VIII had ordered were rather decadent for a mere forty-hour stay; ironically, however, Anne would make uses of the Queen's lodgings once again following her arrest in May 1536.

The Queen's House

Various websites state that Anne Boleyn was imprisoned in a small room within the Queen's House, the Anne Boleyn room. The Queen's House is a part-timbered building which overlooks Tower Green. Victorian visitors interested in the tragic queen were once shown around this bedroom, complete with "Anne" carved into the stonework; but we now know that this building was not built until around 1540. Anne could not have been imprisoned in a building that did not exist in her lifetime.

The Tower and Anne Boleyn's Fall

On 30th April 1536, court musician Mark Smeaton was apprehended and taken to Thomas Cromwell's house in Stepney. There he was interrogated until he confessed to sleeping with the Queen three times. At dawn on 2nd May, Sir Henry Norris, Henry VIII's groom of the stool, was escorted to the Tower of London following his apprehension after the May Day joust the previous day. Smeaton joined Norris at the Tower that morning; George Boleyn, Lord Rochford and the Queen's brother, was taken there in the early afternoon. Smeaton was kept in irons, probably due to his lower status. We do not know whereabouts in the Tower the men were held, but in the stone of the Martin Tower there is a carving of a rose with what looks like a letter "H" and the name "Boullan" etched beside it. In the Beauchamp Tower there is another carving, this time of Anne's falcon badge, but without its crown and sceptre.

On the morning of 2nd May, the Queen was watching a match of real tennis when she received a message telling her to present herself before members of the King's council. She duly presented herself and was informed that she was being accused of committing adultery with three different men: Mark Smeaton, Sir Henry Norris and a third man, at this stage unnamed. She was also told that Smeaton and Norris had confessed. Anne remonstrated with her accusers, but her words had no effect and the royal commission ordered her arrest. Anne was then taken to her apartments until the tide of the Thames turned and then, at two o'clock in the afternoon, she was escorted by barge to the Tower of London.

Upon arrival at the Tower, it is likely that Anne's would have entered through the Court Gate (also called the Tower Gate) of the Byward Tower, the King and Queen's private entrance, rather than through Traitors' Gate. This was the same gate through which she had entered in 1533; she was even met by the same man, Sir Edmund Walsingham, the Lieutenant of the Tower. Anne was then escorted to the Royal Palace where she encountered the Constable of the Tower, Sir William Kingston. Much to Anne's surprise, he informed her that she was to be imprisoned in the Queen's lodgings, rather than a dungeon.

On 4th May, courtiers Sir Francis Weston and Sir William Brereton were arrested and taken to the Tower. They were joined on 5th May by Sir Thomas Wyatt and Sir Richard Page. Wyatt's poem about the executions of the five men includes the words "The bell tower showed me such sight", so he must have been imprisoned there.

The trials of Norris, Smeaton, Weston and Brereton took place in Westminster Hall in front of a special commission of oyer and terminer. The men were taken there and back by barge along the river Thames. Anne and George, however, were tried in front of a jury of their peers in the Great Hall, or King's Hall, of the Tower. A great platform had been erected in the hall so that everybody could see. The Great Hall no longer exists, but we can gain as sense of what it might have looked like by considering the Great Hall at Winchester Castle, which was built at around the same time (in the 13th century) and on the orders of the same man, Henry III.

Figure 25 - The Great Hall in Winchester Castle

Figure 26 - Parade Ground, looking from
St. Peter ad Vincula, Tower of London

Winchester's Great Hall (Figure 25) was built in a "double cube" design, i.e. the height and width measure exactly half its length. It measures 110 ft by 55 ft by 55 ft,[3] so it is easy to imagine how 2,000 spectators managed to fit in the hall for Anne's trial.

Mark Smeaton, Sir Henry Norris, George Boleyn, Sir Francis Weston and Sir William Brereton were executed on Tower Hill on 17th May 1536. Tower Hill is outside the Tower walls and is sometimes missed by tourists and visitors to the Tower because you have to cross a road to get to it. The scaffold site is next to the Tower Hill war memorial and is marked by a simple paved square with plaques commemorating some of the people who were executed there. Eustace Chapuys, the imperial ambassador, recorded Anne Boleyn witnessing the executions of the men, something that she would not have been able to do from her lodgings in the palace complex. Historian Gareth Russell[4] wonders if, therefore, Anne asked Sir William Kingston to move her to one of the towers, such as the Bell Tower.

We know from contemporary accounts that Anne Boleyn's scaffold was not where the present day glass memorial is situated on Tower Green. In the 16th century, Tower Green was much bigger and stretched around the back of the White Tower. Figure 26 is a photo is of the parade ground between the White Tower and the Waterloo Barracks, where the Crown Jewels are, and that's where Anne's scaffold was built.

On the morning of 19th May 1536, Anne exited the Queen's Lodgings, walked past the Great Hall, through Cole Harbour Gate (Cold Harbour Gate), and along the western side of the White Tower to the black-draped scaffold. There, she was executed by the famous Hangman of Calais who used a sword, not an axe. She did not lay her head on a block, she knelt upright; images of Anne with an axeman and block are not at all accurate. After her execution, Anne Boleyn's body and head were wrapped in white cloth and placed in a chest, which had been fetched from the Tower armoury. This chest had once contained bow staves. The chest was buried in the chancel area of the Chapel Royal of St Peter ad Vincula (St Peter in Chains), where it lay in peace until 1876, when much-needed restoration work was carried out on the chapel. During the work, it was found that the pavement of the chancel area, where Anne Boleyn, Catherine Howard and Lady Jane Grey were buried, was sinking. It was decided that proper foundations were needed, so the chancel area was dug up and the remains exhumed.

In the area where Anne Boleyn was recorded to have been buried, the bones of a female were found at a depth of about two feet. The remains were examined by Dr Mouat who confirmed that they belonged to "a female of between twenty-five and thirty years of age, of a delicate frame of body, and who had been of slender and perfect proportions".[5] He went on to say that "the forehead and lower jaw were small and especially well formed. The vertebrae were particularly small, especially one joint (the atlas), which was that next to the skull, and they bore witness to the Queen's 'lyttel neck'." Although the bones were mixed up, they had been heaped together in a small space and there were no further female remains at that spot. Dr Mouat's memorandum said of Anne Boleyn's remains:

"The bones found in the place where Queen Anne Boleyn is said to have been buried are certainly those of a female in the prime of life, all perfectly consolidated and symmetrical, and belong to the same person.

"The bones of the head indicate a well-formed round skull, with an intellectual forehead, straight orbital ridge, large eyes, oval face and rather square full chin. The remains of the vertebrae, and the bones of the lower limbs, indicate a well-formed woman of middle height, with a short and slender neck. The ribs show depth and roundness of chest. The hands and feet bones indicate delicate and well-shaped hands and feet, with tapering fingers and a narrow foot."[6]

He noted that she had been around 5' to 5'3 inches in height. Both hands were entirely normal; no extra finger was found.

Figure 27 - The Glass Memorial, Tower of London

Figure 28 - The Chapel of St. Peter ad Vincula, Tower of London

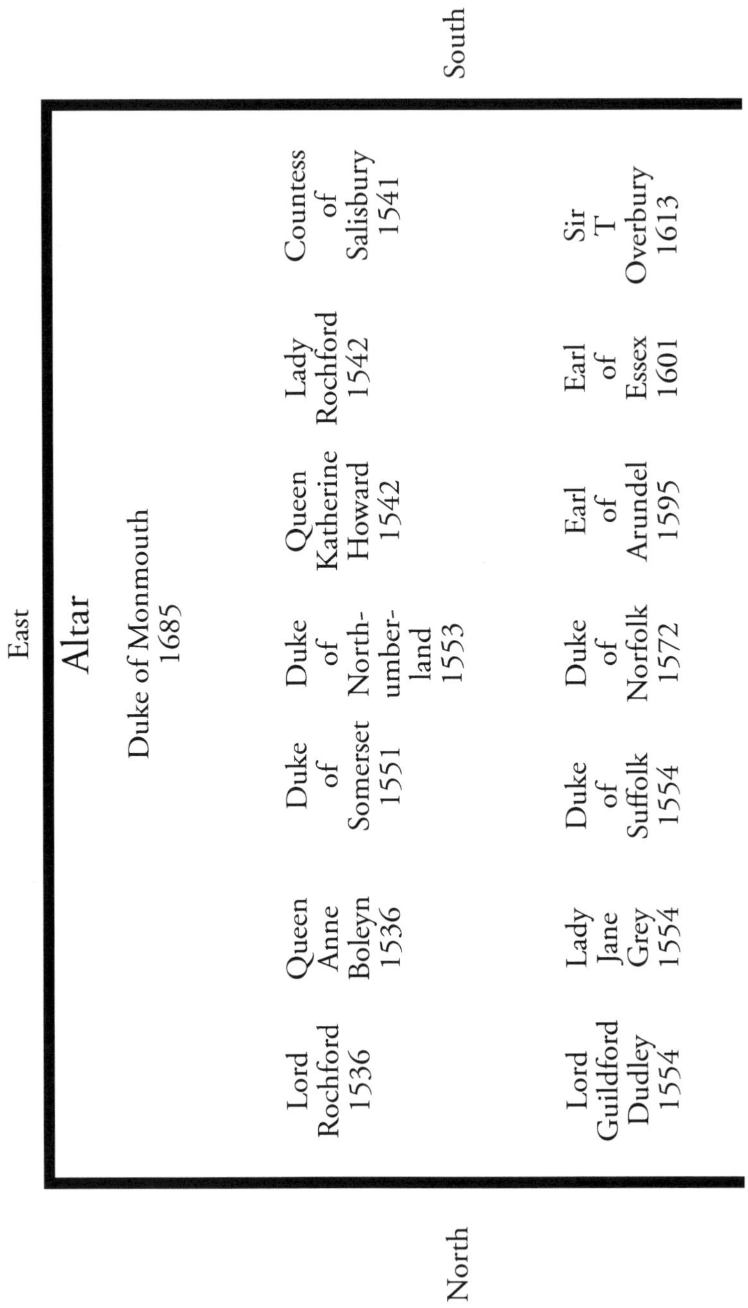

Figure 29 - Probable positions of interments in St. Peter ad Vincula

After the work had been completed in the chapel, the remains found in the chancel area were "soldered up in thick leaden coffers, and then fastened down with copper screws in boxes made of oak plank, one inch in thickness. Each box bore a leaden escutcheon, on which was engraved the name of the person whose supposed remains were thus enclosed, together with the dates of death, and of the year (1877) of the reinterment. They were then placed in the respective positions in the chancel in which the remains had been found, and the ground having been opened, they were all buried about four inches below the surface, the earth was then filled in, and concrete immediately spread over them".[7]

Algernon Bertram Freeman-Mitford, Lord Redesdale, recorded how a plan of the burials was deposited amongst the Tower of London records and a "solemn ceremony" was carried out, presided over by the chaplain, the Reverend E. Jordan Roberts.[8] Beautiful memorial tiles were used to mark the resting places of those buried in the chancel. These can still be seen today, although a rope cordons off the chancel area and some tiles lie underneath the altar table. As you look at the altar, Anne Boleyn's tile is to the left of the table.

Every year, a basket of red roses is delivered to the Tower with instructions to lay them on her memorial tile. The card simply reads "Queen Anne Boleyn 1536." The roses have been delivered every year as far back as anyone can remember. According to one article,[9] Major General Chris Tyler, a former director-general of the Tower, played detective and tried to find out who was sending the rose. He tracked down a family of Boleyn descendants who live in Kent. After polite questioning during a visit to the Tower they admitted that they had been responsible for the flowers, and their relatives before them. The florist shop closest to the Tower confirmed that they had been receiving the order since the 1850s but a few years ago the order was moved to florist in a Kent village close to where the descendants lived. When I spoke to the Chief Yeoman warder about it in 2010, he was under the impression that

Figure 30 - Tiles in the chancel of St. Peter ad Vincula

the flower order was part of a bequest and that it would go on and on until the money ran out.

The Tower Today

The Queen's lodgings once stood in the area between the Wardrobe Tower (D) and the Lanthorn Tower (E) on the plan of the Tower of London as it stands today. The Great Hall stood on the lawn (F) between the Wakefield Tower (J), Lanthorn Tower (E) and the White Tower (A), at right angles to the Queen's Lodgings. Anne's final walk took her past the Great Hall, out of Cole (Cold) Harbour Gate (G) and around the White Tower to the present day parade ground (B) between the White Tower (A) and the entrance to the Crown Jewels (H). You cannot walk in Anne Boleyn's footsteps today because the raven enclosures block the way, but you can walk from Cole Harbour Gate (G) to the parade ground (B).

The glass memorial is on the lawn marked (I) on the plan, but, as I said, it's not where Anne was executed. The real spot is marked (B) on the plan. However, the glass memorial is moving as it has a beautiful verse etched on it in memory of those who died. It reads:

> "Gentle visitor pause a while,
> Where you stand death cut away the light of many
> days.
> Here, jewelled names were broken from the vivid
> thread of life.
> May they rest in peace while we walk the generations
> around their strife and courage,
> Under these restless skies."[10]

A must-see is Anne's resting place in the Chapel of St Peter ad Vincula by Tower Green, marked "C" in Figure 31 on the plan. The Tower always seems to be changing the rules about entry to the Chapel and at the time of writing (summer 2013), you have

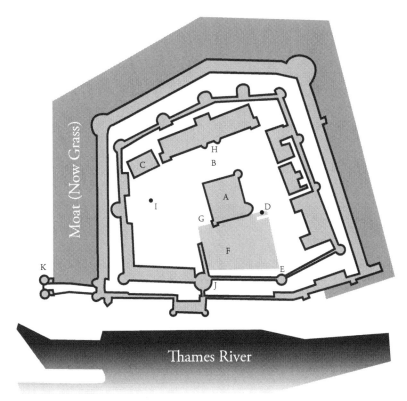

Figure 31 - A modern plan of the Tower of London

to join a Yeoman Warder's tour to go in there, or to wait until after 4.30pm, when it's open to the public. Alternatively, you can worship at the chapel on Sunday mornings. Unfortunately, as I said before, the chancel area is roped off, so it's hard to see the memorial tiles. When I took a group there in 2010 the Chief Yeoman Warder actually took us past the rope and we were allowed to go and lay flowers on Anne's tile. It was a moving moment and one I will never forget. Sadly, they have never let us repeat that experience.

Tudor Graffiti

One of my favourite places to visit at the Tower of London is the Beauchamp Tower, which is situated near the Chapel of St Peter ad Vincula and the glass memorial on Tower Green. What I love about it is its graffiti, or, to be more precise, its carvings. Its interior stone walls are covered with carvings made by prisoners; I am always overawed by just how detailed they are, as well as moved by their poignancy. Graffiti today is done with spray paint or permanent markers; this graffiti was carved into stone and is amazing. Well worth a visit.

Here are my favourite carvings:

Dudley Brothers 1553-4

The beautiful carving of the Dudley coat of arms (Figure 32) is thought to have been made by John Dudley, son of John Dudley, Duke of Northumberland. Dudley, his brothers and his father were imprisoned after the fall of Lady Jane Grey. The carving features the bear and ragged staff (the badge of the Earls of Warwick), the double-tailed lion rampant (the badge of the Dudley family), and a floral border with oak leaves and acorns for Robert Dudley (*quercus robur* is the Latin for English oak). It also features roses for Ambrose Dudley, honeysuckle for Henry Dudley (*lonicera henryi*) and Gilly Flower for Guildford Dudley.

Figure 32 - Carving attributed to John Dudley

Figure 33 - Stone carving of "Jane" in the Beauchamp Tower

Figure 34 - Carving by Thomas Abell in the Beauchamp Tower

Figure 35 - Anne Boleyn's falcon badge stone carving

The inscription reads:

"You that these beasts do wel behold and se, may deme with ease wherefore here made they be, with borders eke within [there may be found] 4 brothers names who list to search the ground."

It is a breathtakingly beautiful carving.

Jane 1553-4

The simple carving shown in Figure 33 is of the word "Jane" or "IANE", as it is written, with a simple rectangular border. It is unlikely that it was carved by Jane, because she was imprisoned "in a small house next to the royal apartments".[11] However, her husband, Guildford Dudley, and his brothers were imprisoned in the Beauchamp Tower, so it was probably carved by one of them. It is a very simple carving, but I find it very poignant.

Thomas Abell ca.1533-40

The carving of a bell with an "A" on it (Figure 34) and the name "Thomas" above was the work of Thomas Abell, who was imprisoned in 1533 and executed in July 1540. Abell had been Catherine of Aragon's chaplain and was the author of the 1532 document *An answere, That by no manner of law, it may be lawfull for the most noble King of England, King Henry the eight to be divorced from the queens grace, his lawfull and very wife*. He was imprisoned in December 1533 for spreading the prophecies of Elizabeth Barton, the Maid of Kent, and for encouraging Catherine "obstinately to persist in her wilful opinion against the same divorce and separation".

Anne Boleyn's Falcon Badge ca. 1536

This simple rendition of Anne Boleyn's falcon badge (Figure 35) is thought to have been carved by a Boleyn supporter at the fall of Anne and her brother in 1536. The falcon is missing its usual royal crown and sceptre, so the carving speaks clearly of the fall of Anne. It's not an easy carving to spot because it is not on the list of famous carvings, but it is below that of Thomas Miagh and to the left of No. 31 on the wall.

Thomas Miagh 1581

Above Anne Boleyn's falcon badge is an inscription by Thomas Miagh which reads:

"THOMAS MIAGH WHICH LETH HERE THAT FAYNE WOLD FROM HENS BE GON BY TORTURE STRAUNGE MI TROUTH WAS TRYED YET OF MY LIBERTY DENIED-THOMAS MIAGH"

Miagh was imprisoned in the Beauchamp Tower, and, if we are to believe his inscription, tortured for his links with Irish rebels.

Charles Bailly 1571

This rather wordy carving is dated 1571 and reads:

"Principium sapientie timor Domini. I.H.S. X.P.S. Be frend to one. Be ennemye to none. Anno D. 1571. 10. Sept.

"The most unhappy man in the world is he that is not pacient in adversities. For men are not killed with the adversities they have, but with ye impacience which they suffer. Tout vient apoient, quy peult attendre. Gli sospiri ne son testimoni veri dell' angoscia mia. aet. 29. Charles Bailly."

Bailly was the Bishop of Ross's servant and a member of Mary, Queen of Scots's household. He was implicated in the Ridolfi Plot against Elizabeth I when incriminating letters were found on him at Dover in April 1571. He was racked and imprisoned in the Tower of London, but was released sometime around 1573.

Figure 36 - The Court Gate at The Tower of London

Figure 37 - Traitors' Gate at the Tower of London

The Gates

The Court Gate, through which Anne entered at her coronation and when she was arrested, is a bit of a disappointment. It is found outside the Tower on the river-side. Instead of having a plaque telling of Anne's entrance into the Tower and her first public kiss with Henry, it is sadly neglected; when I visited it had rubbish bags piled up against it. Instead, visitors are shown Traitors' Gate and told that that is where Anne Boleyn entered.

When Anne's daughter, Elizabeth, was imprisoned in the Tower on 18th March 1554 after Wyatt's Rebellion, she didn't enter by Traitors' Gate either. It was low tide, so she was taken to Tower Wharf. David Starkey comments on how terrifying her walk from the wharf would have been, She would had to have walked past the Tower menagerie, past a line of guards and under the Bloody Tower where she may well have seen, across the court, the scaffold left over from the execution the previous month of Lady Jane Grey.[12] Although some books state that Elizabeth was imprisoned in the Bell Tower, she actually stayed in the royal palace, just like her mother before her. Elizabeth was released from the Tower on 19th May 1554, the 18th anniversary of her mother's execution.

A Royal Fortress

When you visit the Tower of London, you may think of it as simply a tourist attraction, but it's not. The Tower is still a royal fortress and the Yeoman Warders, or Yeoman of the Guard, are not everyday people dressed up in silly costumes. In fact, it's a requirement that they be former senior non-commissioned officers who have served in the armed forces with an honourable record for at least twenty-two years, and who have received the Long Service and Good Conduct medal. Yeoman Warders were royal bodyguards in the past and their commander in chief today is still Her Majesty the Queen.

Ceremony of the Keys

The Ceremony of the Keys takes place every night at the Tower of London and has been going on for around 700 years.

At 9.53pm, on the dot, the Chief Yeoman Warder, wearing his long red Tudor watchcoat and bonnet, makes his way out of the Byward Tower to Traitors' Gate to meet his escort, a member of the Tower of London Foot Guards. They lock the main gates of the Tower, and also the gates of the Middle Tower and Byward Tower, to secure the fortress for the night.

As they make their way back towards Traitors' Gate, they are stopped in Water Lane by a sentry who says, "Halt, who comes there?"

The Chief Yeoman Warder replies, "The keys."

"Whose Keys?'" asks the sentry.

"Queen Elizabeth's Keys." replies the Chief Yeoman Warder.

"Pass Queen Elizabeth's Keys, and all's well." replies the sentry.

The party then makes its way through the archway of the Bloody Tower and to the Broadwalk Steps, where the Tower Guard and escort present arms. The Chief Yeoman Warders steps forward, raises his bonnet and proclaims "God preserve Queen Elizabeth". "Amen", replies the Guard as the bell strikes ten o'clock. The Last Post is then played and the Chief Yeoman Warder takes the keys to the Queen's house.

The only known time in history when the ceremony has been interrupted was during the Second World War. During an air raid, incendiary bombs fell on the guardroom as the Chief Yeoman Warder and his escort were walking through the Bloody Tower archway. They were unhurt and simply dusted themselves off and carried on with their duty. They were simply late that night completing the ceremony and even wrote to King George VI apologising for the delay. The King did not mind!

Members of the public can apply for tickets to attend the ceremony at the Historic Royal Palaces website.

Notes and Sources

1   Ives, The Life and Death of Anne Boleyn, 175.
2   Weir, The Lady in the Tower: The Fall of Anne Boleyn.
3   Ross, "Winchester Castle."
4   Russell, "May 17th 1536 - Deaths on Tower Hill."
5   Bell, Notices of the Historic Persons Buried in the Chapel of St Peter Ad Vincula in the Tower of London, 21.
6   Ibid., 26.
7   Bell, Notices of the Historic Persons Buried in the Chapel of St Peter Ad Vincula in the Tower of London, 30.
8   Freeman-Mitford, Lord Redesdale, A Tragedy in Stone and Other Papers.
9   "Red Roses for Anne Boleyn."
10   "Tower Green."
11   de Lisle, The Sisters Who Would Be Queen, 114.
12   Starkey, Elizabeth:Apprenticeship, 143.

19. Thomas and Elizabeth Boleyn, Parents of Anne Boleyn

I recently read a comment on a Tudor history Facebook page which really got me thinking, as well as causing me to bang my head on my desk. The writer was of the opinion that Thomas Boleyn did not deserve to be buried in St Peter's Church in Hever; indeed, that he should have been buried in a field somewhere, in an unmarked grave, because of the "horrible things" he did to Anne and to George. I considered these to be incredibly harsh words, but it made me think that perhaps this was the general perception of Thomas Boleyn, father of Mary, Anne and George.

I decided to carry out a bit of an experiment on Facebook and Twitter to see what people thought of Thomas. Obviously, you have to bear in mind that Anne Boleyn Files followers are Tudor history lovers with some knowledge of the Boleyns rather than people who know nothing about the period. Even so, the general consensus was that Thomas Boleyn was an awful man who forced his daughters into their relationships with the King so that he could rise at court. There were a few comments giving him the benefit of the doubt, but the comments below summed up the general perception and got "liked" by other Facebook members:

"*Her father?! I don't like him at all. He seemed to only care about his position, his wealth, how much power he had. Did he care that 2 of his children were killed?! That one was disgraced?! I doubt it.*"

"*Overly ambitious, not the best Father for pretty daughters...Yes I know it was the way of court to sell off your daughters to the highest bidder...however I think he took it toooooo [sic] far.*"

"*I think he used his children for family advancement.*"

"*He was very greedy and wanted power.*"

"*Used his family to gain power. In the end, it destroyed his family.*"

"*He was definitely a clever character, but I do not like how he treated the situation with his daughter Anne, when she was executed. To save his own life, he just let her die without a fight.*"

Although his intelligence is recognised, the comments are rather damning, don't you think?

I thought I'd try the same experiment with his wife, Elizabeth Boleyn (née Howard), and here are a few of the comments left:

"*Don't know much about her...if she was a real mum I just can imagine the horror she went through.*"

"*I think she was an intelligent woman; she saw that her children needed a good standard of educating in a day that it wasn't seen fit to educate girls.*"

"*So little is known about her.*"

"*She must have loved her children dearly because Anne said something like 'my poor mother will die of sorrow' upon learning of her execution.*"

"*I feel for her. The execution of one child would be horrible enough, but having two of your children executed...I can't imagine the sorrow she went through.*"

"She isn't buried with her husband, so perhaps she never did speak to him again."

"Elizabeth seems like she was such a product of her times; very much the homemaker, handling things within the home."

"I don't think Elizabeth was without ambition either - after all, she was a Howard."

"I thought that Anne's mother had died when she was young and that Mrs Boleyn was her step-mother. I read that they were very close and had a loving relationship."

The comments about Elizabeth are much more sympathetic. People feel that Thomas was a cunning, manipulative, money grabbing man who prostituted his daughters and then abandoned Anne and George to their fate in 1536, and that Elizabeth Boleyn died of a broken heart and never forgave her husband. Great fiction, but is it really true?

Where do people get this kind of idea of the Boleyns from? Well, more often than not it is from *The Other Boleyn Girl* or *The Tudors*, so let's look at how this couple are presented by Philippa Gregory and Michael Hirst.

The Boleyns of *The Other Boleyn Girl*

In *The Other Boleyn Girl*, Thomas and Elizabeth always seem to be having family conferences with Elizabeth's brother, Thomas Howard, 3rd Duke of Norfolk. Norfolk is the man in charge, the one pulling the strings; and when he says "jump", everyone else says, "how high?". It is then up to Thomas and Elizabeth to put these plans into place and to tell Mary, Anne or George what they should do to ensure the family's rise in status and wealth. Their children are like puppets, and every action they take has to be good for the family or woe betide them.

The Boleyns of *The Other Boleyn Girl* appear happy to prostitute their daughters and to use them to climb the ladders of success and wealth. We see Thomas Boleyn being created Viscount Rochford when Mary becomes pregnant by the King; yet when the King appears to be looking for a new wife, Thomas comments that he won't pick Mary because "she's had her heyday". Everything is just business to him, and he doesn't think about his children's feelings. In the book, Thomas Boleyn is quite a strong, intelligent character, but in the movie he is spineless and is completely controlled by his brother-in-law. Elizabeth seems the stronger of the couple.

Elizabeth Is a cold, unfeeling character. When Anne confesses to secretly marrying Henry Percy and to consummating the marriage, her mother tells her to forget about it and to keep it to herself otherwise she'll be "whipped and sent to Hever". Elizabeth continues, saying, "I would rather see you dead at my feet than dishonoured....You make yourself hateful to us all." Not at all motherly and caring. She then forces Anne's sister, Mary, to forge a letter to Percy from Anne to break up the relationship, and comments that Anne and Mary need to be taught obedience. Elizabeth seems to lack all maternal feeling. When Mary misses her baby, Elizabeth just can't understand it. When Mary asks her if she missed her daughters when they were sent to France, Elizabeth Is surprised by the question and answers that she simply did the best she could for her daughters; in her opinion, there was no better place than the French court. Her life revolves around supporting her husband in his bid to help the family climb the social scale.

Although Thomas and Elizabeth were happy to reap the rewards when Mary and Anne were in favour with the King, they abandoned Anne and George when they were arrested, and Thomas advised Mary to "keep out of sight." He thought she was mad for wanting to help them and advised her against it.

As you can see, they weren't your dream parents. Money and status definitely came first, and their children were just a means to an end.

The Thomas Boleyn of The Tudors

Although *The Tudors* has, in many ways, followed Philippa Gregory's example and maligned Thomas Boleyn, I do prefer its portrayal of Thomas because he's a "somebody", not just his brother-in-law's puppet.

So, how is he portrayed in the series?

The good

- **Thomas is close to the King.** We see him playing chess with the King and reassuring Henry that Francis I is nowhere near as good looking as Henry: "Your majesty, no one has calves like you." We see the King entrusting him with important missions and embassies.

- **He's important and influential.** We see him interacting with the Dukes of Norfolk, Buckingham and Suffolk, and also Cardinal Wolsey and Thomas Cromwell. He is a powerful man even before the King starts courting Anne. For example, the Duke of Buckingham calls Thomas to him for support when he is plotting against the King. Ambassadors also seek him out because they know he has influence.

- **Thomas has a career.** He is an ambassador and is given offices and titles like Lord Privy Seal and Comptroller of the King's Household, during which latter position we see him uncovering Wolsey's corruption.

- **He's close to his children.** He is fraught when Anne has sweating sickness. He has tender moments with her, and shares jokes with George.

The bad

- **He is always plotting.** Thomas seems to always be in a dark corner somewhere plotting with his son, George, or with the Duke of Norfolk.

*Figure 38 - The tomb brass of Thomas Boleyn
at St. Peter's Church, Hever, Kent*

Figure 39 - St. Peter's Church, Hever, Kent

- **He acts as his daughters' pimp.** At the Field of Cloth of Gold, he tells Mary, knowing full well what it entails, that the King has noticed her and wants to see her. Later, he recalls Anne from France and tells her that the King is tiring of her sister – he wonders if she can think of a way to keep the King's interests more "prolonged"? At the Château Vert pageant, Thomas pays Master Cornish to position Anne where the King will notice her and when the King does fall for Anne, he uses her influence over the King to bring down Cardinal Wolsey.

- **Thomas is a murderer.** He and George pay Bishop Fisher's cook, Richard Roose, to poison the soup to get rid of the man they see as standing in Anne's way. Fisher survives but four of his guests die. Later, in the episode, Thomas attends Roose's interrogation to make sure that he doesn't break, and then he and George watch him get boiled to death for a crime which, in reality, they were responsible for.

- **He's ruthless.** When his daughter Mary turns up at court pregnant and tells Thomas and Anne that she has got married, he cuts off her allowance and says that she and her husband can rot in hell as far as he's concerned. After the King's jousting accident, instead of gathering with others to pray, he meets with Cromwell to make sure that everything is in place for Princess Elizabeth to become Queen and for him to be made Lord Protector.

- **He is responsible for Cardinal Wolsey's fall.**

- **He is cruel.** When Anne miscarries, rather than comforting her, he says "What did you do to kill the baby?" He also seems to enjoy telling Henry VIII's daughter, Mary, that her parents' marriage has been annulled and that she is now to be known as "Lady Mary" rather than as "Princess".

- **He's a heretic.** There is a rather strange scene where Chapuys, the imperial ambassador, asks Thomas to use his influence to bring England back "from the brink of catastrophe" for "the love of Christ and the Apostles." Thomas states that he doesn't believe that Christ had apostles and that, furthermore, the men were all liars and charlatans who pretended to speak in Christ's name and who built a church on their lies. Very strong words.

- **He's desperate.** After Anne's second miscarriage, he tells her that they must give up the idea of a French alliance and that she must make a great fuss of the imperial ambassador. Anne isn't really listening to him so he grabs her forcefully and says, "We've come this far, nobody's going to be allowed to destroy us!" Later, when he's interrogated after Anne's arrest, we see him trying to save himself, condemning the men who are alleged to have slept with his daughter and saying that there should only be one punishment for them. One of those men is his son!

- **He is self-serving.** Everything he does and that he compels Anne to do is for the good of the Boleyns, even if it costs others their lives. At their fall, he won't risk defending his children for fear of losing his own life. As George is executed and Anne sobs her heart out, Thomas sits stony-faced in his cell, reading.

The Real Thomas Boleyn

Contemporary sources, however, give us a very different picture of Thomas Boleyn, Earl of Wiltshire.

Family Background

Thomas was born around 1476 or 1477, probably at Blickling in Norfolk. He was the son of Sir William Boleyn of Blickling, a landowner, and of William's wife, Margaret Butler. Thomas's paternal grandfather was Sir Geoffrey Boleyn, a wealthy mercer who had worked his way up from Sheriff of London and Alderman of the City of London to Lord Mayor of London. It was Geoffrey

Boleyn who bought Hever Castle, in Kent, in 1462. Thomas's mother, Margaret Butler, was the second daughter and co-heiress of Thomas Butler, 7th Earl of Ormond. The Butlers were a wealthy family in Ireland and Margaret was descended from men who had been magnates, landowners and justiciars of Ireland. Thomas could trace his roots back to Edward I and ultimately to Eleanor of Aquitaine and Henry II.

Early Career Highlights

- **1497** - At around the age of twenty, Thomas had fought on the King's side against the rebels of the Cornish Rebellion. His father had also fought in these battles.

- **1501** - Thomas was present at the wedding of Prince Arthur and Catherine of Aragon

- **1503** - Thomas was chosen by Henry VII to accompany his eldest daughter, Margaret Tudor, to Scotland to marry James IV.

- **1509** - He had been appointed an esquire of the body before Henry VII's death and Henry VIII chose to keep him on. During Henry VIII's coronation celebrations in 1509, Thomas was created a Knight of the Bath. His wife, Elizabeth, served as one of the "baronesses" of the Queen's Chamber during the coronation of Henry VIII and Catherine of Aragon.

- **July 1509** - Thomas was appointed Keeper of the Foreign Exchange in Calais.

- **1509 and 1510** - Thomas served as sheriff of Norfolk and Suffolk.

- **January 1510** - Thomas participated in a revel in honour of the Queen and dressed up as one of Robin Hood's (the King's) men. On 23rd May he was involved in the knightly combat and jousts, and accepted a challenge from King's team.

- **1511** - Thomas was involved in the jousts to celebrate the birth of Prince Henry, Duke of Cornwall. He was also a chief mourner and one of the knight bearers at Prince Henry's funeral on the 27th February 1511.

- **1511** - Rewards and grants made to Thomas in 1511 included the keepership of the park of "Beskwode", Nottinghamshire; the manors of Borham and Powers in Essex; "Busshy" in Hertfordshire; Purbright in Surrey and Henden in Kent; and Culverts and Little Waltham in Essex. He was also appointed Sheriff of Kent.

- **1512** - Grants and appointments received by Thomas included:
  - Being granted, jointly with Henry Wyatt, the office of Constable and Keeper of the castle and gaol of Norwich, which was also reconfirmed to them in 1515
  - Being granted one half of the custody of the lands, wardship and marriage of John, son and heir of Sir George Hastings;
  - Being reconfirmed and granted in survivorship the manor of Wykmer in Norfolk with his wife Elizabeth.

- **1512-1513** - Thomas Boleyn was sent to the court of Margaret of Austria, along with John Young and Sir Robert Wingfield, to act as an envoy to her father, Maximilian I, Holy Roman Emperor. Their task was to secure an alliance between England and the Empire against France. Thomas Boleyn became so friendly with Margaret that they had a wager on how long the negotiations would take – Margaret bet Thomas that her father, the Emperor, would allow them to conclude their negotiations within ten days. If Thomas won the bet then Margaret would give him a "courser of Spain" and if Margaret won then Thomas would give her "a hobby".[1] Their close relationship led to Thomas securing a place for his daughter, Anne, at Margaret's court. A place in Margaret's court was highly sought after by royal and noble families in Europe so this showed just how much Margaret respected Thomas.

- **1514** - Grants were made to Thomas which included the life grant of the lordship of the manors of Saham Tony, Nekton, Panworth Hall, Cressingham, Parva, and the hundreds of Waylond and Grymmeshowe in Norfolk.[2] By this time, as William Dean[3] points out, Thomas Boleyn owned, or had been granted, the controlling interest in around twenty manors. He was also the keeper of various other estates as well as being the Keeper of the Exchange at Calais and the Foreign Exchange in all English ports.

- **1514** - Thomas secured places for both his daughters in the entourage of Mary Tudor, who was going to France to marry Louis XII.

- **1516** – He acted as a canopy bearer at the christening of Princess Mary, daughter of Henry VIII and Catherine of Aragon.

- **1517** – Thomas acted as Queen Margaret of Scotland's official carver for the forty days of her visit to England.

- **1518** – Thomas was by this time a member of the Privy Council. As such, he was involved in the negotiations for the Treaty of Universal Peace signed that October.

- **Late 1518/early1519** – Thomas was appointed as the English ambassador to the French court. He served there as Henry VIII's ambassador and as Cardinal Wolsey's agent. While in France, Thomas became good friends with the French royal family.

- **5th June, 1519** – Thomas sponsored Francis I's baby son, Henry, Duke of Orleans, in the name of Henry VIII.

- **1520** – On his return to England, he was appointed Comptroller of the Household.

- **1520** – Thomas attended the Field of Cloth of Gold, having been chosen as one of forty select members of government, nobility and the Church who were to ride with the King to his first meeting with Francis I. Thomas's wife, Elizabeth, was appointed to attend Queen Catherine.

- **May 1521** – Thomas was now the Treasurer of the Household and was also appointed to the special commissions of oyer and terminer[4] which tried Edward Stafford, Duke of Buckingham. He benefited from Buckingham's fall, being granted in survivorship the manor, honour and town of Tunbridge, the manors of Brasted and Penshurst, and the parks of Penshurst, Northleigh, and Northlands, in Kent. He had also recently been granted the manor of Fobbing in Essex and Fritwell in Oxfordshire. His manors now totalled around two dozen.

- **1521** – Thomas accompanied Cardinal Wolsey to meet Margaret of Austria under the pretext of mediating between France and the Empire, but actually to secure an alliance between England and the Empire.

Thomas Boleyn had a talent for languages and was said to be the best French speaker at court. It was this gift combined with his intelligence and ambition that led to him being appointed ambassador to the Low Countries, at the court of Margaret of Austria, in 1512. There, he quickly became good friends with Margaret. His talent for negotiating, which led him to conclude business in a mere ten days, led to him winning the bet with Margaret and earning himself her Spanish courser. Between 1519 and 1523, Thomas served as ambassador to the court of France. This saw him making arrangements for the meeting between Henry VIII and Francis I at the Field of Cloth of Gold in 1520 and the Calais conference of 1521. He also served as ambassador to the Spanish court at one point.

Now, I could go on with detail after detail of Thomas Boleyn's diplomatic duties and of his grants, but I just wanted to cover the period up to 1522, when it is thought that Mary Boleyn caught the King's eye. If you cast your eye over the above list and consider that Thomas Boleyn was Treasurer of the Household by 1522, had over 24 manors and was the man Henry VIII and Cardinal Wolsey trusted with diplomatic missions, then it really is hard to argue that he owed his rise in status and wealth merely to acting as a pimp for his daughters. William Dean, who wrote a detailed thesis on Thomas Boleyn, summed it up when he said, "One cannot, as some have done, simply attribute Boleyn's advancement to Henry's preferment of his daughters up to this point. Granted, a case may be made for this influence later, but Henry had no history of doing generous things for his mistresses, much less their parents. It is more likely that Henry recognised ability and past service and rewarded Boleyn for it."[5] I agree. Bessie Blount's family had not benefited from her relationship with the King and she had borne him a son, so how could Thomas Boleyn have expected to? He was already a powerful man by the time Mary slept with the King, his rise having been rapid and deserved. He was a key courtier, a trusted advisor and a skilled negotiator and diplomat. He worked hard for his rewards.

Later Career Highlights

- **1520s** - Rewards for his diplomacy came thick and fast in the 1520s and included lands which had once belonged to the fallen Duke of Buckingham. Thomas was made Treasurer of the Household in 1522, a Knight of the Garter in 1523 and Lord Rochford in 1525.

- **1527 – 1529** - More diplomatic missions were carried out in 1527 to France and then in 1529 to the Pope and Emperor regarding Henry's Great Matter, the annulment of his marriage to Catherine of Aragon.

- **1529** - Thomas was created Earl of Wiltshire and the Earl of Ormonde, and after Wolsey's fall in 1530, he became Lord Privy Seal.

- **1532** - Thomas was active in Parliament and was, predictably, one of the first men to declare that neither the Pope nor Prelate had the right to make laws. He canvassed heavily for the Statute in Restraint of Appeals, an act passed by Parliament in 1533. This law is considered by many historians to be the key legal foundation of the English Reformation.

• **1534** - In July 1534, he and Sir William Paulet were sent to Princess Mary to persuade her to renounce her title of Princess and acknowledge herself as illegitimate.

Renaissance Man and Reformer

Thomas Boleyn the Renaissance man and religious reformer has been forgotten by fiction and by some history books, yet he was an incredibly gifted person who was interested in the arts and the religious ideas sweeping into England from the Continent.

As well as being a gifted French speaker, Thomas obviously had a good grip of Latin because he owned a copy of Martial's *Epigrams*. He was a patron of humanism and corresponded with Erasmus, the famous Dutch humanist, scholar and theologian, commissioning several pieces from the latter between 1530 and 1534. In her book *Humanism in the Age of Henry VIII*, Maria Dowling writes about a humanist scholar, Gerard Phrysius, who was in the service of Thomas Boleyn between 1529 and 1533.[6] Thomas was also the patron of Thomas Cranmer, of John Baker, and of Robert Wakefield, who taught Hebrew at Cambridge.

Thomas was also a patron of reform and gave help to reformers when he could, something that his daughter also did when she was Queen. He kept in touch with French reformers, men like Clément Marot, the French poet, and he supported his godson, Thomas Tebold, in his travels around Europe in 1535 and 1536, spreading the news that Thomas was a patron of the New Learning and New Religion. Tebold then reported back to Thomas on the inquisition in Europe. Eustace Chapuys, the imperial ambassador, described Anne and Thomas Boleyn as "more Lutheran than Luther himself" which, although is not a correct description of their religious views, shows that they were enthusiastic about reform.

Thomas Boleyn was also "adept at courtly entertainments",[7] fighting with the King in a tournament in May 1510 at Greenwich Palace and then taking part in the Burgundian-style Westminster Tournament Challenge in February 1511 as an answerer. His name is listed as a participating knight on the second day of the tournament along with the likes of Thomas Howard, Henry Stafford and Charles Brandon.[8]

Thomas the Pimp?

As I said earlier, Thomas's early career highlights show that he had no need to manipulate his daughters into sleeping with the King; indeed, evidence suggests that Thomas Boleyn was actually unhappy about his daughters' relationships with the King. The fact that the King had to step in and ask Thomas to provide for his daughter, Mary, after she was widowed in 1528 suggests that the Boleyns had distanced themselves from Mary after her affair with the King, and there is also evidence that Thomas was initially against Henry VIII's plans to marry Anne. Chapuys wrote to the Emperor in February 1533:

"I must add that the said earl of Wiltshire has never declared himself up to this moment; on the contrary, he has hitherto, as the duke of Norfolk has frequently told me, tried to dissuade the King rather than otherwise from the marriage."[9]

Then, at the end of May 1533, just before Anne Boleyn's coronation, he wrote:

"Shortly after the Duke [Norfolk] began to excuse himself and say that he had not been either the originator or promoter of this second marriage, but, on the contrary, had always been opposed to it, and tried to dissuade the King therefrom. Had it not been for him and for the father of the Lady, who feigned to be attacked by frenzy to have

the better means of opposing it, the marriage would have been secretly contracted a year ago; and for this opposition (the Duke observed) the Lady had been exceedingly indignant with the one and the other."[10]

Chapuys was obviously convinced that Anne's father had opposed the marriage plans and that this had angered Anne.

As for Thomas being cunning, manipulative and cruel, the Duke of Norfolk actually described Thomas Boleyn as "very timid" and "not of a warlike disposition".[11] He must have had drive and ambition to be a successful courtier; but the manipulative, cruel and overbearing Thomas Boleyn definitely belongs in the realms of fiction.

The Fall of Anne Boleyn

In April 1536, Thomas Boleyn was appointed to the commission of oyer and terminer set up to try cases of treason. This led to him trying the men accused of committing adultery with his daughter, who was by then the Queen: namely Mark Smeaton, Henry Norris, Francis Weston and William Brereton. Although some sources - Alexander Aless, Chapuys, the Bishop of Faenza and Dr Ortiz - reported that Thomas sat in judgement too on George and Anne, this is not now thought to be the case as he is not mentioned in the Baga de Secretis, the record of the opening of the trial.

Thomas lost George and Anne to the executioner in May 1536. And although he survived physically, he fell from grace and was stripped of his office of Lord Privy Seal on 29th June 1536. He was also removed from the commission of the peace in Norfolk, although he was kept on this commission in Kent. However, Thomas was the ultimate survivor and after helping squash the rebels of the Pilgrimage of Grace in late 1536, he managed to climb his way back into the King's favour and was present at Prince Edward's baptism in October 1537. Eric Ives describes how he diligently went to Order of the Garter functions, even lending Thomas Cromwell his chain and best Garter badge at one point, and how he was back at court by January 1538.[12] In July 1538, three months after Elizabeth Boleyn's death, Henry Maunke wrote to Lady Lisle saying that he had "heard say that my lord of Wolshyre will marry lady Margaret Dowglas".[13] The marriage never took place, obviously, but Thomas Boleyn must have been high in favour for it to be rumoured that he was going to marry the King's niece.

I often read comments about how Thomas abandoned his children to their fates and did nothing to help them, but we don't actually know that. We know that various records from that period are missing, so it is impossible to say whether or not Thomas Boleyn wrote to Cromwell or the King.

The Death of Thomas Boleyn

Thomas Boleyn died on the 12th March 1539 at his home, Hever Castle, aged around sixty-two. His servant, Robert Cranwell, wrote to Cromwell the next day to inform him of his death:-

"My good lord and master is dead. He made the end of a good Christian man. Hever, 13 March."[14]

Thomas was laid to rest in a tomb in the family church of St Peter's in Hever, Kent. Visitors to the church today can pay their respects to Thomas and admire the incredibly detailed brass which shows him in the full robes and insignia of a Knight of the Garter, including the badge on his left breast and garter around the left knee. It is said to be one of the finest brasses in England and is beautiful. Near his tomb, set into the stone floor, is a simple brass cross marking the tomb of Thomas's infant son, Henry Boleyn.

Thomas Boleyn Portraiture

Thomas Boleyn's brass and a small drawing of him in profile in The Black Book of the Order of the Garter ca.1534 are the only surviving images of Thomas Boleyn. However, art historian

Roland Hui believes that a Hornebolte miniature of an unknown man from ca.1525 could well be Thomas Boleyn:

"As the unknown gentleman is not Charles Brandon, it was someone else drawn from the upper ranks of the King's court. The most feasible nobleman is Sir Thomas Boleyn, father of the future Queen Anne..."

The age fits, and we know that the Boleyns were linked to Hornebolte. Hui makes a convincing argument, but we won't know for sure unless more evidence is found.

Hui's theory can be read at: http://tudorfaces.blogspot. com/2011/10/two-new-faces-hornebolte-portraits-of.html

The Real Elizabeth Boleyn

Elizabeth Boleyn is a far more shadowy figure than her husband and very little is known about her. She was born around 1476 and was the daughter of Thomas Howard, the Earl of Surrey and later Duke of Norfolk, and his wife Elizabeth Tylney. Her brother was Thomas Howard, 3rd Duke of Norfolk, the man who presided over the trials of George and Anne Boleyn in 1536. The Howards were one of the premier families in England, having a long history of service to the monarch. Elizabeth's father had been attainted and stripped of his titles and lands after the Battle of Bosworth because he had fought on Richard III's side, but he managed to work his way back into favour and by 1497 had been restored as Earl of Surrey. In 1514, he was finally restored to the title of Duke of Norfolk.

Marriage and Children

Elizabeth married the up and coming Thomas Boleyn, son of another East Anglian family, in around 1499. We know from a letter written by Thomas Boleyn to Thomas Cromwell that, in the early years of their marriage Elizabeth gave birth on an annual basis.

Figure 40 - St. Marys Church, Lambeth
Resting place of Elizabeth Boleyn

We have evidence of five children – Anne, George and Mary, and then Thomas and Henry who died in infancy and who are buried at Hever and Penshurst - but there may have been others whose graves were lost. We know, for example, that there are further tombs in Hever church but that at some point the floor collapsed and these are now hidden. Intriguingly, Elizabeth's wikipedia page lists her as also having children called William, Margaret and Catherine (don't you just love Wikipedia?).

Elizabeth's Career

Traditionally, it is said that Elizabeth served as lady in waiting to Elizabeth of York, Catherine of Aragon and then her own daughter, but I have not found any evidence at all of her serving Elizabeth of York. Alison Weir challenges the idea that Elizabeth was one of Elizabeth of York's ladies, due to her series of pregnancies.[15] Weir also does not believe that Elizabeth served Catherine of Aragon, saying that there is no evidence to back this up and that Elizabeth may have been confused with Edward Boleyn's wife, Anne Tempest, who definitely did serve Catherine.[16] Elizabeth was, however, present at the Field of Cloth of Gold so may have been called on to serve the Queen at big state occasions, rather than on a permanent basis. We just don't know.

Elizabeth's Dubious Reputation

In her biography of Mary Boleyn, Alison Weir writes of the rumours that Elizabeth had an affair with the King, resulting in the birth of Anne Boleyn. If we were to believe these rumours, then it would mean, of course, that Henry VIII committed incest when he married and slept with Anne Boleyn. The sources Alison Weir[17] cites for the story are:

- **Friar William Peto** – On Easter Sunday 1532, Princess Mary's confessor, Friar William Peto, preached a rather controversial sermon in the King's presence at Greenwich's Franciscan chapel, in which he compared Henry VIII to Ahab and drew comparisons between Anne Boleyn and Jezebel. After the sermon, it is said that Peto spoke to the King and warned him that "it was being said that he had meddled with both Anne's sister and her mother."

- **Sir George Throckmorton** - According to Cardinal Pole, Throckmorton had heard the story from Peto. Throckmorton further recalled a conversation he had had with the King about Henry's troubled conscience over marrying his brother's wife: "I told your Grace I feared if ye did marry Queen Anne your conscience would be more troubled at length, for it is thought ye have meddled both with the mother and the sister. And your Grace said "Never with the mother."

- **Elizabeth Amadas** - Amadas was the wife of the royal goldsmith and a woman some believe to have been the King's mistress at one time. She asserted "that the King had kept both the mother and the daughter" and also alleged that "my lord of Wiltshire was bawd both to his wife and his two daughters."

- **Thomas Jackson, a Yorkshire chantry priest** – He claimed that Henry VIII had "kept the mother and afterwards the daughter."

- **John Hale, Vicar of Isleworth** - He said that "the King's Grace had meddled with the "Queen's mother."

- **The Catholic writers Nicholas Harpsfield, William Rastell and Nicholas Sander** - Harpsfield wrote that he "had credibly heard reported that the King knew the mother of Anne Boleyn." Lord Herbert wrote of Rastell asserting that Anne Boleyn was the fruit of an affair between Henry VIII and Elizabeth Boleyn. And Nicholas Sander gave quite a detailed account of the affair, which, according to him, took place while Thomas Boleyn was in France on an embassy.

- **Adam Blackwood** - Blackwood was a lawyer defending the reputation of Mary, Queen of Scots in 1587, shortly after her execution.

Alison Weir points out that although there are many sources for this alleged affair between Henry VIII and Elizabeth Boleyn, the King denied it. She also comments that all the sources for the affair are "hostile" and the claims of Rastell and Sander simply don't add up because Thomas Boleyn "was not sent as ambassador to France until 1519". Weir also says that "Henry was probably less than ten years old when Anne was conceived"[18] but that obviously depends on what you believe to be her birthdate. Henry VIII was indeed ten years old in 1501, but it is also claimed she was born in 1507, when he would have been sixteen.

Let's examine the sources and see just how credible they may be:

Friar William Peto

In *The Life and Death of Anne Boleyn*, Eric Ives writes of how Friar Peto preached a sermon on Easter Sunday 1532 "telling Henry to his face that he would end up like the Old Testament tyrant Ahab (though he left unspoken the implication that Anne Boleyn was Jezebel)."[19] Ives does not mention Peto talking to the King afterwards. However, I have looked up reports of this day in Letters and Papers, Alison Weir's reference, and also in the Spanish Calendar of State Papers. All I can find is a report from Chapuys stating that the sermon upset the King, and the following paragraph:

"And I hear that the King himself, happening to converse privately with the said friar after the sermon, heard from his lips what was not much to his taste, for the Provincial spoke openly to him about the royal marriage in contemplation, telling him in plain words that if he did not take care he would be in great danger of losing his kingdom, since all his subjects, high and low, were opposed to it."[20]

There is no mention of any scandalous relationships between the King and Elizabeth Boleyn or the King and Mary Boleyn. Even if there were to have been such comments, Peto was head of the Observant Friars and as such was in agreement with the likes of Warham and More. These latter men opposed the King's proposed annulment of his marriage to Catherine of Aragon, viewing Catherine as his true wife and Anne Boleyn as Jezebel.

Historian G.W. Bernard writes of how Peto had told the King that "it was said that he [the King] had meddled both with Anne Boleyn's sister, Mary Boleyn, and their mother";[21] he cites Nicholas Harpsfield as a reference. I searched through Harpsfield's book *A Treatise on the Pretended Divorce Between Henry VIII and Catharine of Aragon*; Harpsfield mentions Peto's sermon but not what Peto said to the King afterwards, although a few pages later he comments "Yea, I have credibly heard reported that the King knew the mother of the said Anne Bulleyne", meaning "knew" in a sexual way.[22] It all sounds like gossip to me, a salacious rumour put about to blacken Anne's name during the time of Henry's quest for the annulment of his first marriage.

Sir George Throckmorton

In *Letters and Papers*, in the records for 1537, there is a report concerning Sir George Throckmorton and Sir Thomas Dyngley. In it, we read of a conversation between Throckmorton and the King:

"About six or seven years ago [Throckmorton] conversed with Sir Thos. Dyngley in the garden at St. John's about the Parliament matters. Dyngley wondered that the Act of Appeals should pass so lightly, and Throgmorton said it was no wonder as few would displease my lord Privy Seal. Told Sir Thomas he had been sent for by the King after speaking about that Act, and that he saw his Grace's conscience was troubled about having married his brother's wife. "And I said to him that I told your Grace I feared if ye did marry Queen Anne your conscience would be more troubled at length, for it is thought ye have meddled both with the mother and the sister. And his Grace said 'Never with the mother'."[23]

In the same report, we hear that Throckmorton gleaned the information regarding Henry VIII and Elizabeth Boleyn from Friar Peto:

"Explains his conduct since the beginning of the Parliament of 21 Hen. VIII. Just before that Parliament friar Peto, who was in a tower in Lambeth over the gate, sent for him and showed him two sermons that he and another friar had made before the King at Greenwich, and reported a long conversation he had had with the King in the garden after the sermon. He said he had told the King that he could have no other wife while the Princess Dowager lived unless he could prove carnal knowledge between prince Arthur and her; which he said was impossible, as she, who knew best, had received

the Sacrament to the contrary, and she was so virtuous that her word deserved more credit than all the other proofs; that prince Arthur's saying that he had been in the midst of Spain was probably but a light word; and that the King could never marry Queen Anne as it was said he had meddled with the mother and the daughter. He moreover advised Throgmorton if he were in the Parliament house to stick to that matter, as he would save his soul."

So, Throckmorton is not a separate source for the scandal; he got his information from Friar Peto. Furthermore, G.W. Bernard believes that Throckmorton was just boasting to his friends and that he never spoke these words to the King.[24]

Elizabeth Amadas

In *Letters and Papers*, in the records for 1533, there is a collection of prophecies spoken by "Mistress Amadas". The eighth prophecy is:

"She rejoiced when the Tower was made white, for she said shortly after my lady Anne should be burned, for she is a harlot; that Master Nores was bawd between the King and her ; that the King had kept both the mother and the daughter, and that my lord of Wiltshire was bawd both to his wife and his two daughters."[25]

Now, I'm not sure that we can take that claim very seriously when it is amongst sixteen rather fanciful prophecies regarding Mouldwarp, dragons, blazing stars and the destruction of the King. Josephine Wilkinson points out that when Mrs Amadas was abandoned by her husband "she began to champion the causes of other discarded wives", like Catherine of Aragon. This would have naturally put her against Anne Boleyn and the Boleyn family.[26] Wilkinson also believes that Amadas may have had a fling with Henry VIII at some point, so this prophecy may also be a case of sour grapes. Whatever the motive behind her words, we cannot take Amadas's words as proof of a relationship between Elizabeth Boleyn and the King without also believing her other fanciful claims.

Thomas Jackson, Chantry Priest

In June 1535, William Fayrfax reported to Thomas Cromwell of an indictment against "Sir Thos. Jakson, priest":

"Deposition by John Lepar and Brian Banke before Wm. Fayrefax, sheriff, co. York, against Thos. Jackson, chantry priest of Chepax, for saying: 1. That the King lived in adultery [with Anne Boleyn] before his marriage, and still lives so. 2. That he kept the mother and afterwards the daughter, "and now he hath married her whom he kept afore, and her mother also."[27]

I suspect that this priest, a Catholic who was obviously opposed to the King's marriage to Anne Boleyn, was simply spreading gossip which blackened the royal couple's names.

John Hale, Vicar of Isleworth

In 1535, John Hale, Vicar of Isleworth was reported as saying "the King's grace had meddling [sic] with the Queen's mother."[28] Further objections against Hale included that he had "called the King the 'Molywarppe' that Merlin prophesied of, that turned all up, and that the King was accursed of God's own mouth, and that the marriage between the King and Queen was unlawful."[29] The fact that he referred to the King as "Mouldwarp" suggests to me that he was simply repeating the prophecies of Elizabeth Amadas. In his own account to the council, Hale states that "the fellow of Bristow showed, both to me and others of Syon, the prophecies of Marlyon; for, by my truth, Master Skydmore showed me also the same, with whom I had several conversations concerning the King's marriage and other behaviours of his bodily lust." He is simply repeating hearsay. Hale also said "Moreover, Mr. Skydmore dyd show to me yongge Master Care, saying that he was our suffren Lord the Kynge's son by our suffren Lady the Qwyen's syster, whom the Qwyen's grace myght not suffer to be yn the Cowrte"; more hearsay concerning the paternity of Mary Boleyn's son, Henry Carey.

Harpsfield, Rastell and Sander

When reading the claims of these men regarding Henry VIII and Anne Boleyn, we have to take into account who the men were. Nicholas Harpsfield was a Catholic priest who was friends with Thomas More and his family. He wrote a biography of More, which he dedicated to his patron, William Roper, More's son-in-law. He also wrote *A Treatise on the Pretended Divorce between Henry VIII and Catharine of Aragon*. He was against Henry VIII's annulment and was a supporter of Catherine of Aragon.

William Rastell was a printer, judge and Catholic who was related to Sir Thomas More. He wrote a now lost "Life" of his uncle and saw Anne Boleyn as a Salome type,[30] who put on a special banquet for Henry VIII to persuade him to execute More and Bishop Fisher.

Nicholas Sander was a Catholic recusant writing about Anne Boleyn while he was in exile during her daughter Elizabeth I's reign. He wrote:

"ANNE BOLEYN was the daughter of Sir Thomas Boleyn's wife; I say of his wife, because she could not have been the daughter of Sir Thomas, for she was born during his absence of two years in France on the king's affairs. Henry VIII. sent him apparently on an honourable mission in order to conceal his own criminal conduct; but when Thomas Boleyn, on his return at the end of two years, saw that a child had been born in his house, he resolved, eager to punish the sin, to prosecute his wife before the delegates of the archbishop of Canterbury, and obtain a separation from her. His wife informs the king, who sends the marquis of Dorset with an order to Thomas Boleyn to refrain from prosecuting his wife, to forgive her, and be reconciled to her. Sir Thomas Boleyn saw that he must not provoke

the king's wrath, nevertheless he did not yield obedience to his orders before he learned from his wife that it was the king who had tempted her to sin, and that the child Anne was the daughter of no other than Henry VIII."[31]

Sander goes on to describe Anne Boleyn as "rather tall of stature, with black hair, and an oval face of a sallow complexion, as if troubled with jaundice. She had a projecting tooth under the upper lip, and on her right hand six fingers. There was a large wen under her chin, and therefore to hide its ugliness she wore a high dress covering her throat." He then writes of her being banished to France at the age of fifteen after having sexual relationships with her father's butler and chaplain. No other source describes Anne Boleyn in such a way; and she was in France serving Queen Claude when she was fifteen so the story about her scandalous behaviour at Hever is pure fiction. How, then, can we set much store by Sander's claim that Anne was Henry VIII's daughter? Sander was simply blackening the name of Anne Boleyn, the mother of the Protestant Queen Elizabeth I who was the reason for him being in exile.

Adam Blackwood

Adam Blackwood was "a Scot, a Catholic, a lawyer and a poet"[32] who wrote *Martyre de la royne d'Escosse* (The martyrdom of the Queen of Scotland) or *The History of Mary Queen of Scots* in 1587, a defence of the Queen's virtues and an attack on Elizabeth I. Blackwood wrote his book shortly after Sander wrote his, and he repeated Sanders' story about Anne Boleyn being Henry VIII's daughter. Blackwood also collected and contributed to a collection of poems known as *de Jezebelis*[33] which painted Elizabeth as Jezebel and perpetuated the myth that she was the result of an incestuous relationship between Henry VIII and Anne Boleyn, father and daughter. Blackwood's work was simply propaganda aimed at defending Mary Queen of Scots's reputation and slandering the woman he viewed as her murderess.

Other Sources

I found another source for the myth: *The Life and Death of the Renowned John Fisher, Bishop of Rochester*. The writer is stated as Thomas Bailey (1655), although the real author is said to be Dr Richard Hall, writing in the reign of Elizabeth I. In this book, Bailey writes of Cardinal Wolsey investigating a possible pre-contract between Henry Percy and Anne Boleyn and of Wolsey calling for the Countess of Wiltshire, Elizabeth Boleyn, to see what she had to say about this. According to Bailey, Elizabeth Boleyn "better liked of the marriage of her daughter with the said Lord Percy, than if the King should marry her" and Wolsey, guessing the reason for this, sent her to the King. Elizabeth Boleyn then, according to Bailey, said to the King:

"Sir, for the reverence of God, take heed what you do in marrying my daughter; for if you record your conscience well, she is your own daughter as well as mine."[34]

The King didn't care and told Elizabeth that he would marry her regardless of who her father was.

Of course, we have to remember that Bailey/Hall was writing a sympathetic account of the life of John Fisher, a man who was executed for refusing to accept Henry VIII as the supreme head of the church and also for his support of Catherine of Aragon. Fisher had advised Catherine during the annulment proceedings and had spoken up in her defence at the Legatine Court.

My Thoughts

It's difficult to sort truth from fiction, fact from legend, nearly five hundred years later, but the only sources we have for the alleged affair between Elizabeth Boleyn and Henry VIII are suspect in my opinion because they:

- Are hostile to the Boleyns and to Henry VIII's annulment
- Have an agenda; a reason why they are attacking Anne

Boleyn, Henry VIII or Elizabeth I

- Seem to be based on the same rumour stemming from Friar Peto

These sources are not separate, all backing each other up; and I don't believe there is any evidence that Elizabeth Boleyn did indeed have an affair with Henry VIII, never mind have a child by him. As Alison Weir states, Thomas Boleyn was not in France when Anne Boleyn was conceived or born. He went to the Low Countries on an embassy in 1512 and to France in 1519. He was in England in 1501 and 1507 and surely would have noticed if his wife had got pregnant by the King. Also, would the paranoid Henry VIII, who worried about his marriage to Catherine of Aragon being contrary to God's law because she was his brother's widow, really marry his own daughter? I think not.

I'm sure that if there was any truth in these rumours then the rumours would have been used to stop Henry annulling his marriage to Catherine so that he could marry Anne; Chapuys would have gleefully passed such news on to Charles V. I just cannot see the opposition ignoring such ammunition.

In her book on Mary Boleyn, Alison Weir ponders whether these rumours spread and were believed "because of Elizabeth Howard's dubious reputation" and whether she "had gained some ill fame for straying from the connubial couch".[35] Weir even wonders if "the fact that all her offspring became notorious in one way or another for sexuality might suggest that she herself had set them a poor example by her loose morals and by betraying her marriage vows." Weir supports this theory with the poetry of John Skelton, who compared Elizabeth to the beautiful Cressida, a woman who pledged undying love to Troilus but then betrayed him with Diomedes. Weir writes that by the 14th century, Cressida's name "had become synonymous with female inconstancy" and that a Tudor audience would "have instantly grasped the double entendre." Weir does admit that Skelton may simply have been praising Elizabeth's looks, "but if so, he had chosen a strange and compromising comparison, when there were plenty of others to be drawn." I don't agree with Weir's theory. Here are Skelton's words:

> "To My Lady Elisabethe
> To be your remembrancer, Madam, I am bownd:
> Lyke to Aryna maydenly of porte,
> Of vertew and konyng the wel and parfight grownd,
> Whome Dame Nature, as wele I may reporte,
> Hath freshely enbewtid withe many a goodely sorte
> Of womanly feturis: whos florisshinge tender age
> Is lusty to loke on, plesant, demure and sage.
>
> Goodely Creisseyda, fairar than Polycene,
> For to envyve Pandarus appetite:
> Troylus, I trow, if that he had yow sene,
> In yow he wold have set his hole delight:
> Of alle your bewte I suffice not to wright,
> Bot as I sayde your florisshynge tender age
> Is lusty to loke on, plesant, demure and sage."[36]

This allegorical poem was written in praise of the ladies of the Countess of Surrey at Sheriff Hutton Castle, who made Skelton a garland of silks, golds and pearls in a pageant around 1495. It praised not only Elizabeth Howard, but also the Countess and other ladies such as Jane Hasset, Isabell Pennel, Geretrude Statham and Isbell Knyght (Skelton's spellings). Although it was not printed until 1523, I cannot see Skelton changing a poem complimenting these ladies to one of satire. I think it should just be taken as praise of Elizabeth's beauty, without "a sting to its tail". To read it as evidence of a dubious reputation and infidelity is a huge leap, in my opinion.

Elizabeth and Anne

I receive emails on a fairly regular basis asking me for my views on the idea that Anne Boleyn had a stepmother. The email writers refer to novels which give Anne a stepmother, for example

Jean Plaidy's *Lady in the Tower* which has Elizabeth Boleyn dying before Anne goes to France and Anne talking affectionately of her stepmother. My correspondents want to know if this is true. Now, those may be novels but this myth actually has its roots in history books. Agnes Strickland, the Victorian author, seems to have been the first to write about Anne having a stepmother. In *Lives of the Queens of England*, Strickland writes:

"The first misfortune that befel Anne was the loss of her mother, Lady Boleyn, who died in the year 1512, of puerperal fever... Sir Thomas Boleyn married again; at what period of his life we have no record, but it is certain that Anne's step-mother was a Norfolk woman of humble origin."[37]

This "fact" is repeated in Hester W. Chapman's 1974 biography of Anne Boleyn,[38] so it is likely that Chapman used Strickland as her source and novelists have then used Strickland or Chapman. Joanna Denny also writes, "it is said that Thomas remarried, giving his children a stepmother, a new Lady Boleyn", although she does comment that there are "conflicting dates" given for Elizabeth's date of death.[39] Strickland cites her sources for Elizabeth's death in 1512 and for Thomas Boleyn's second marriage as *Thoms Traditions, Camden Society* and *Howard memorials by Mr Howard of Corby*, so I looked them up and found *Annecdotes and Traditions illustrative of Early English History and Literature* edited by William J. Thoms on Google Books. In that book, I found Strickland's reference, which is a note by Thoms on an anecdote told by Sir Nicholas L'Estrange about Elizabeth I. L'Estrange's anecdote is:

"One begg'd of Queene Elizabeth, and pretended kindred and alliance, but there was no such relation. "Friend," says she, "grant it be so, do'st thinke I am bound to keepe all my kindred? Why that's the way to make me a beggar." L'Estranye, No. 124. Mr. Derham."[40]

Thoms notes that "Queen Elizabeth had numerous maternal relations, and many of them among the inferior gentry particularly in Norfolk, an inconvenience which arose from her father having selected for his second consort a subject of no very elevated extraction, whilst the blood of the Boleynes was widely diffused by the intermarriages of numerous junior branches."

As Philip Sergeant points out in his *The Life of Anne Boleyn*,[41] Strickland seems to have misread Thoms' note. He is talking about Queen Elizabeth's father's second marriage, i.e. Henry VIII's marriage to Anne Boleyn, NOT Thomas Boleyn's second marriage.

I was unable to obtain a copy of *Indication of Memorials, Monuments, Paintings and Engravings of Persons of the Howard Family* by Henry Howard, but Philip Sergeant discusses the record on Elizabeth Boleyn in his book. In this privately printed memorial of the Howard family, Howard apparently records Elizabeth Howard, wife of Thomas Boleyn, as dying of puerperal fever on 14th December 1512 and being buried at Lambeth. Sergeant searched for a funeral certificate but was unable to find one. However, he notes that J. Nichols's *History of the Parish of Lambeth* (1786) stated that there used to be a brass plate at St Mary's Church, Lambeth (now a garden museum), which was inscribed "Here lyeth the Lady Elizabeth Howard, some time Countess of Wiltshire". I've got a copy of this book, which is actually published by Nichols but written by Thomas Allen, and I cannot find any mention of Elizabeth's brass. I did, however, find mention of the brass plate in John Aubrey's *The Natural History and Antiquities of the County of Surrey*. No date of death was mentioned, but we know for certain that Lady Wiltshire, Thomas Boleyn's wife, was buried in the Howard aisle of St Mary's Church, Lambeth on 7th April 1538. This information can be found in a letter written by John Hussey to Lady Lisle on 9th April 1538:

"My lady Wiltshire was buried at Lamehithe on the 7th... She was conveyed from a house beside Baynard's Castle by barge to Lambeth with torches burning and four baneys (banners?) set out of all quarters of the barge, which was covered with black and a white cross."[42]

This Lady Wiltshire must have been a Howard woman to be interred with other Howard women in the Howard aisle of the church, rather than being some other "Norfolk woman of humble origin". She must surely have been Elizabeth Boleyn (nee Howard).

So why the confusion?

Sergeant couldn't understand the confusion; nor could he find another Elizabeth Howard who died in 1512. However, there is a Howard woman who died in December 1512; namely, Elizabeth's sister, Muriel Howard, wife of Sir Thomas Knyvett. Muriel died during or shortly after childbirth, in December 1512, and was buried at Lambeth. Her will was proved on 12 January 1513.[43] [44] [45] This must be the Howard woman that Henry Howard was referring to in his memorials on the family; the two sisters have been conflated.

Unfortunately, once a "fact" is written in a book, or these days in a blog post or online somewhere, it quickly spreads. Elizabeth Boleyn's mythical early death is in many novels, so people will continue to believe that Anne Boleyn had a stepmother.

Elizabeth appears to have had a close relationship with her daughter Anne, acting as a chaperone when Henry was courting her. We know from Chapuys that Elizabeth accompanied Anne and the King to view York Place in October 1529 after Wolsey had fallen from favour:

"The downfall of the Cardinal is complete. He is dismissed from the Council, deprived of the Chancellorship, and constrained to make an inventory of his goods in his own hand, that nothing may be forgotten. It is said that he has acknowledged his faults, and presented all his effects to the King. Yesterday the King returned to Greenwich by water secretly, in order to see them, and found them much greater than he expected. He took with him "sa mye" (his darling—Anne Boleyn), her mother, and a gentleman of his chamber (Norris?)"[46]

And Eric Ives writes that in 1530, "Anne Boleyn's one refuge was Wolsey's former palace of York Place, soon to be known as Whitehall... Anne and her mother could lodge in the chamber under the cardinal's library."[47] In those frustrating days of waiting, Anne's mother seems to have been there for her daughter, and Anne appreciated it. Around 1531 Anne Boleyn wrote a letter to her good friend, Lady Bridget Wingfield, telling Lady Wingfield, "And assuredly, next mine own mother I know no woman alive that I love better",[48] showing that she loved her mother dearly.

Elizabeth attended her pregnant daughter at her coronation in 1533, riding in one of the carriages in the procession. I'm sure that Elizabeth would have enjoyed this day of triumph after years of struggle.

Anne's love for her mother is again shown in words she spoke to Sir William Kingston at her arrival at the Tower after her arrest on the 2nd May 1536:

"O, my mother, [thou wilt die with] sorow."[49]

Now, it is not known whether Anne was simply worried that her mother would be heartbroken at the news of what had happened or whether she was concerned because her mother was already in ill health, but we do know that Elizabeth had recently been ill. On 14th April 1536, Thomas Warley wrote to Lady Lisle commenting that Elizabeth was suffering from a bad cough:

"Today the countess of Wiltshire asked me when I heard from your Ladyship, and thanked you heartily for the hosen. She is sore diseased with the cough, which grieves her sore."[50]

This may have just been a simple cough, but it could also have been something more serious, something which led to Elizabeth's death in April 1538. On 7th April 1538, Warley wrote to Lady Lisle reporting Elizabeth's death:

"My lady of Wiltshire died on Wednesday last beside Baynard's castle."[51]

And two days later, John Hussee wrote to Lady Lisle of Elizabeth's funeral:

"My lady Wiltshire was buried at Lamehithe [Lambeth] on the 7th... She was conveyed from a house beside Baynard's Castle by barge to Lambeth with torches burning and four baneys (banners?) set out of all quarters of the barge, which was covered with black and a white cross."[52]

Sir John Russell, Lord Comptroller, was the chief male mourner and Elizabeth's half-sister, Katherine Howard, Lady Daubenay, was the chief female mourner.

Elizabeth's Resting Place

In May 2013, I visited Elizabeth Boleyn's resting place. St Mary's Church, Lambeth, is no longer a place of worship; it is now the Garden Museum. This is a bit of a disappointment for Tudor history fans because the Howard Chapel, where Elizabeth and other Howard family members were laid to rest, is now a café. However, we have to thank our lucky stars; if the Garden Museum had not been set up in 1977 to preserve the tomb of famous botanist and gardener John Tradescant (ca.1570 – 1638), the church would have been demolished. OK, so the Howard Chapel has a counter and tables, and people sit there eating salads and drinking coffee, but the tombs have been preserved under the wooden floor. The museum has not messed with the structure of the building and no tombs have been desecrated; that had already happened during the rebuilding work in Victorian times.

It is frustrating that we can't see Elizabeth's tomb but she is there, somewhere under that floor.

Some people wonder if Elizabeth's burial at Lambeth, rather than at Hever, is evidence of a breakdown in her marriage after the execution of her son and daughter, but I feel that this is reading far too much into it. Elizabeth was a Howard woman and it appears to have been traditional for Howard women to be buried at Lambeth in the Howard Chapel. Norfolk House, where Catherine Howard spent part of her upbringing and the London home of the Howard family, was just down the road, and Elizabeth died in London. Just what she was doing at the home of the Abbot of Reading is a mystery, but perhaps she was taken ill nearby and then died there. Her husband had been at court since January 1538, so it appears that she had accompanied him to London.[53] Whatever the truth of the matter, there is no evidence that Elizabeth and Thomas Boleyn had marital problems.

The History of St Mary's Church, Lambeth

We know from the Domesday Book that there has been a church on the site since before the Norman Conquest, but the oldest part of St Mary's as we know it today is the tower, which was built ca. 1378. In the 18th century, the only part of the medieval church still standing was the tower, but the church had been rebuilt from Henry VII's reign on. The Howard Chapel was built around 1522. Unfortunately, the main structure of the church was pulled down in 1851 and the church was restored, or rather rebuilt, opening again in February 1852.

One brass that still survives at Lambeth is that of Lady Katherine Howard, who died in 1535 and who "is depicted wearing pedimental head-dress and a long mantle which bears the arms of Howard with the Flodden augmentation. At her feet is a squirrel holding a nut."[54] John Aubrey recorded the inscription which accompanied her brass:

"Here lyeth Katherine Howard,
one of the Sisters and Heires of John
Broughton, Esq, Son and Heire of John Broughton, Esq,
and late Wife of the Lord Willm. Howard,
one of the Sonnes of the Right High and Mighty
Prince Lord Thomas, late Duke of
Norfolke, High Treasurer and Earl
Marshal of England; which Lord William and Lady
Catherine left Issue between them,
lawfully begotten, Agnes Howard, the only
Daughter and Heir; which said Lady Catherine
deceased the xxiii. Day of Aprill
Anno Dni. MCCCCCxxxv. Whose Soule Jesu pardon."[55]

Lambeth

If you're in London visiting Westminster Abbey and the Houses of Parliament, do take the time to walk across the bridge over the Thames to Lambeth. The Garden Museum is right next door to Lambeth Palace, which is a good photo opportunity, and it is free to visit the café. Also, just down the road from the museum is the Novotel London Waterloo Hotel, which stands on the former site of Norfolk House at 113 Lambeth Road. Norfolk House was once the London home of the Dukes of Norfolk, Elizabeth's family, coming into their possession when Elizabeth FitzAlan, wife of Thomas Mowbray, Duke of Norfolk, inherited it from her brother, Thomas FitzAlan. Agnes Tilney, wife of Thomas Howard, 2nd Duke of Norfolk, resided at Norfolk House where she brought up a household of ladies, including her step-granddaughter Catherine Howard. It was at Norfolk House, and at the Dowager Duchess' other home, Chesworth House near Horsham, that Catherine was said to have had relationships with her music tutor Henry Manox and with Francis Dereham. The Dowager Duchess lost Norfolk House when she was imprisoned after the fall of Catherine Howard in 1541, but in 1543 it was granted to her stepson,

Thomas Howard, 3rd Duke of Norfolk, who used it as his London residence until he was imprisoned in December 1546. When he was released by Mary I in 1553, he eventually regained possession of Norfolk House. After Norfolk's death in 1554 his grandson, Thomas Howard, 4th Duke of Norfolk, sold the house to Richard Garthe and John Dyster. The house then went through a number of owners, including Margaret Parker (wife of Archbishop Matthew Parker) and her sons, Matthew and John, Archbishop Whitgift, Sir George Paule and John Dawson who bought it in 1618. In a 1951 survey of London, I found the following information on Norfolk House and what it consisted of in the early 17th century:

> *"Sir George Paule bought the house from Whitgift's son in 1608 and lived there until his death in 1635. From the details contained in this sale some idea can be gained of the size of Norfolk House and the disposition of the buildings. There was a great gate from 'the King's highway leading from Lambeth Town to St. George's Fields' (i.e. Lambeth Road) leading into a paved yard. On the west was the Duke's chapel which, by 1590, had been partitioned to make a hall, buttery and parlour, and a number of small rooms; on the east were the kitchen offices with 'a greate chamber' on the first floor, a gallery, oratory and several closets and the hall opening on to the garden on the south. The total width of the garden was 125 feet, and it is a reasonable assumption that the street frontage was approximately the same."[56]*

I had trouble finding out what happened to Norfolk House after 1618 so I contacted Marilyn Roberts, an historian working on a book about the Howards and Norfolk House.[57] Marilyn explained that in 1680, potter James Barston set up a business producing tin-glazed earthenware, now called "Lambeth Delftware", on the site of Norfolk House and that the site eventually became the Doulton factory in Lambeth. It was in the late 17th century that Old Paradise Street (formerly Paradise Street and then Paradise Row) was formed, and it was at this time that the house was split from its gardens. The 1951 survey gives the following information about

Old Paradise Street:

> "This street was formed in the late 17th century on land which had formerly belonged to Norfolk House. Nos. 2–18 formed part of the endowment left by Archbishop Tenison to the school for girls founded by him in High Street. In the 18th century they were let by the school trustees on long lease to Richard Summersell, who held the offices of bailiff of the manors of Kennington, Vauxhall, Lambeth and Walworth, surveyor of the Parish Roads and surveyor of Thrale's Brewery. His daughter, Elizabeth Pillfold, widow of Alexander Pillfold, surrendered the lease when land was required to enlarge the burial ground."[58]

Marilyn explained that from the late 17th century, "The house itself was being altered and chopped about to suit new purposes and disappeared and decayed by stages rather than being pulled down in its entirety, as far as I can tell, and was demolished by the 1780's, apart from part of an outside wall that had been incorporated into a building on the Norfolk Row side." She also mentioned the site being used as a distillery at one point; I found a mention in the 1951 survey of Hodges' Distillery, a gin distillery. It appears that the distillery stood on the site in the early to mid 19th century. After that, an Ordnance Survey Map of 1872 shows a candle factory being on the site and Marilyn explained to me that this factory "so badly and deeply contaminated the former site of Norfolk House that the archaeologists' findings in the 1980s, prior to the Novotel being built, were very sparse and disappointing." How sad that Norfolk House is now lost to us.

∞∞∞∞∞∞∞∞∞∞∞∞∞∞∞∞∞∞∞∞∞∞

Notes and Sources

1   Warnicke, "Anne Boleyn's Childhood and Adolescence."

2   "Status Details for Hundred," para. The Hundred is a division of the Ancient County, also known as a Leet (East Anglia), a Ward (Cumberland, Durham and Northumberland), and Wapentake (Counties of York). It held administrative and judical functions, although the level of administrative responsibilities held by each of these units differed. Its origins are unclear, but possibly derive from the geographical area containing a hundred "families" or households. By the late 16th Century hundreds were comprised of parishes (formerly Medieval Vills).

3   Dean, "Sir Thomas Boleyn: The Courtier Diplomat (1477-1539)," 48.

4   "Oyer and Terminer," sec. a commission authorizing a British judge to hear and determine a criminal case at the assizes. Middle English, part translation of Anglo–French oyer et terminer, literally, to hear and determine.

5   Dean, "Sir Thomas Boleyn: The Courtier Diplomat (1477-1539)," 101.

6   Dowling, Humanism in the Age of Henry VIII, 145.

7   Ives, The Life and Death of Anne Boleyn, 10.

8   "Letters and Papers, Foreign and Domestic, Henry VIII, Volume 1: 1509-1514," n. 698.

9   "Calendar of State Papers, Spain, Volume 4: Part 2," n. 1048.

10 Ibid., n. 1077.

11 "Calendar of State Papers, Spain, Volume 4: Part 1, Henry VIII, 1529-1530," n. 255.

12 Ives, The Life and Death of Anne Boleyn, 353.

13 "Letters and Papers, Foreign and Domestic, Henry VIII, Volume 13 Part 1 - January-July 1538," n. 1419.

14 "Letters and Papers, Foreign and Domestic, Henry VIII, Volume 14 Part 1: January-July 1539," n. 511.

15 Weir, Mary Boleyn: The Great and Infamous Whore, 12.

16 Ibid., 29.

17 Ibid., 30–33.

18 Ibid., 33.

19 Ives, The Life and Death of Anne Boleyn, 154.

20 "Calendar of State Papers, Spain, Volume 4: Part 2," n. 934.

21 Bernard, The King's Reformation, 152.

22 Harpsfield, A Treatise on the Pretended Divorce Between Henry VIII and Catharine of Aragon, 236.

23   "Letters and Papers, Foreign and Domestic, Henry VIII, Volume 12 Part 2: June-December 1537," n. 952.

24   Bernard, The King's Reformation, 211.

25   "Letters and Papers, Foreign and Domestic, Henry VIII, Volume 6 - 1533," n. 923.

26   Wilkinson, Mary Boleyn: The True Story of Henry VIII's Mistress, 134.

27   "Letters and Papers, Foreign and Domestic, Henry VIII, Volume 8," n. 862.

28   Ibid., n. 565.

29   Ibid., n. 567.

30   Ives, The Life and Death of Anne Boleyn, 47.

31   Sander, Rise and Growth of the Anglican Schism, 23–25.

32   Lewis, The Trial of Mary Queen of Scots: A Brief History with Documents, 120.

33   Wormald, Mary, Queen of Scots: Pride, Passion and a Kingdom Lost, 13.

34   Bailey and Hill, Richard, The Life and Death of the Renowned John Fisher, Bishop of Rochester, Who Was Beheaded on Tower Hill, the 22nd of June 1535, 62–63.

35   Weir, Mary Boleyn: The Great and Infamous Whore, 34.

36   Skelton, The Book of the Laurel.

37   Strickland, Lives of the Queens of England, 2:178.

38   Chapman, Anne Boleyn, 19.

39   Denny, Anne Boleyn: A New Life of England's Tragic Queen, 29.

40   Thoms, Annecdotes and Traditions Illustrative of Early English History and Literature, 16.

41   Sergeant, The Life of Anne Boleyn, sec. Appendix C.

42   "Letters and Papers, Foreign and Domestic, Henry VIII, Volume 13 Part 1 - January-July 1538," n. 717.

43   Gunn, "Knyvet, Sir Thomas (c.1485–1512)."

44   Emerson, "Muriel Howard."

45   "Muriel Howard."

46   "Letters and Papers, Foreign and Domestic, Henry VIII, Volume 4: 1524-1530," n. 6026.

47   Ives, The Life and Death of Anne Boleyn, 146.

48   "Letters and Papers, Foreign and Domestic, Henry VIII, Volume 5: 1531-1532," n. 12.

49   "Letters and Papers, Foreign and Domestic, Henry VIII, Volume 10 - January-June 1536," n. 793.

50   Ibid., n. 669.

51   "Letters and Papers, Foreign and Domestic, Henry VIII, Volume 13 Part 1 - January-July 1538," n. 696.

52   Ibid., n. 717.

53   St Clare Byrne, "The Lisle Letters, Volume 5," n. 1086. John Husee to Lord
     Lisle, 3 January 1538: "My Lord of Wiltshire is again now in the Court
     and very well entertained."
54   "Survey of London: Volume 23: Lambeth: South Bank and Vauxhall."
55   Aubrey, The Natural History and Antiquities of the County of Surrey:
     Begun in the Year 1673, V:232.
56   "Survey of London: Volume 23: Lambeth: South Bank and Vauxhall,"
     chap. 28: Norfolk House and Old Paradise Street.
57   Roberts, "Trouble in Paradise."
58   "Survey of London: Volume 23: Lambeth: South Bank and Vauxhall,"
     chap. 28: Norfolk House and Old Paradise Street.

20. George Boleyn, Lord Rochford – Fiction versus Evidence

In the opening credits of Season One of the TV series *The Tudors*, Jonathan Rhys Meyers says: "You think you know a story but you only know how it ends, to get to the heart of the story you have to go back to the beginning."[1] Many people think they know who George was, but are they right?

The Boleyns are a famous, perhaps even infamous, family, but the real Boleyns have been lost to us. They're surrounded by myths and scandal. To get to the truth about them, we have to dig deep and get past the preconceived ideas, labels and stereotypes. Anne Boleyn has been rehabilitated by the work of historians like the late Eric Ives. Even though there are still some people who believe that she was guilty of adultery and incest, or that she was a witch and a whore, the majority of people now question those perceptions of her and believe that she was framed. Other members of the Boleyn family, however, have not fared so well and many of the myths that surround them and the fictional representations of them are taken as fact. Even some historians simply accept these depictions. I, however, have been brought up to question everything.

In this chapter I'm going to focus on George Boleyn, and examine how he has been portrayed by fiction and by some historians, in comparison to what we know about the real George.

The George Boleyn of The Other Boleyn Girl

Philippa Gregory's *The Other Boleyn Girl*,[2][3] as both novel and movie, is many people's first proper introduction to George Boleyn and his wife, Jane (née Parker), and I know from the many emails I've received that what people think they know about George comes from this novel. They may have heard of Anne Boleyn in history at school, but not of George and Jane. With the exception of Mary, Gregory's depiction of the Boleyns is not a flattering one, but George is a likeable character, although perhaps lacking backbone.

In both the novel and the movie, George is a cheerful, popular courtier who is trusted by Henry VIII. The King invites him to his private chapel for mass and uses George to usher Mary Boleyn, George's sister, to and from his bedchamber while he's having his affair with her. George is even popular with Queen Catherine of Aragon, who calls him her "little star Boleyn". He is not so happy and trusted at home, though. George is very unhappily married to the "poisonous", "vilely jealous" Jane Parker. His wife is "a monster" and they are described as "a silent ill-matched couple". Instead of spending time with Jane, he chooses to see his sisters, Mary and Anne. His sisters confide in him and he's the one who comforts Anne when her betrothal to Henry Percy is broken up. What could be a normal close sibling friendship is twisted, however, by Philippa Gregory into a very inappropriate relationship between brother and sisters. In the novel, he knocks at the door while Mary and Anne are bathing and Anne invites him in. He goes over and combs her hair, a very intimate act when his sister is half-naked . Then there's a scene with Mary when he kisses her "deeply on the mouth" and asks her to kiss him again like she kisses her lover, the King. In a later scene with Anne, he kisses her and strokes her bare shoulder and neck – it is far from a brotherly kiss.

But the George of *The Other Boleyn Girl* is not just sexually interested in his sisters; he is also attracted to men. Mary mentions hearing "some running joke about a young page who had been besotted with George" and George tells his sisters how Jane, his wife, offered to get him a maid and then a boy so that she could watch them together. George explains that he's "sickened by women", but "a boy is so clean and so clear..." He then confesses to Mary that he is in love with a man, Francis Weston. When Mary knocks at George's chamber one day, she hears "scuffling" from inside and when George finally answers, she sees Weston straightening his doublet. There is no mistaking what she has seen.

And then, of course, there is the thing that everybody remembers about the novel: the incest bit. In the novel, George is quite capable of incest with Anne. He has already acted inappropriately with both of his sisters, acting more like a lover than brother, so when Anne is feeling the pressure to provide the King with a son, she turns to George for help. Anne confides in Mary that she "went on a journey to the very gates of hell" to conceive and when Mary tells George that Anne felt the baby move, he suddenly looks guilty, flashing the look that Mary recognises from their childhood when he'd done something bad. Mary knows that George was Anne's "companion of her journey to the gates of hell to conceive this child for England" and when she questions him about it, he explains that it was all done "for love". He then embraces Anne like a lover. There is no misunderstanding this scene. It makes clear that Anne and George have slept together and that Anne's baby was fathered by George.

George of The Tudors

The Tudors series is another portrayal which has affected many people's perception of George. In the series, we have the loving brother who listens to Anne reading out Henry VIII's love letters and then teases her. Anne confides in him, especially when she's worried about Queen Catherine and Princess Mary. He's her ally, the person she can turn to when she's feeling the pressure from her father and the frustration of her situation. He's her best friend.

One aspect of George that was missing from The Other Boleyn Girl was George the Reformer, the man with evangelical beliefs which were in opposition to the established church at the time. Although this part of his character is not emphasised in the series, we do see him discussing convocation with Archbishop Cranmer and Thomas Cromwell. Also, Cromwell shows George the printing press and talks about how he's going to use it to spread the message of Reform.

Unfortunately, we then have George the murderer. We see George and his father, the ambitious and manipulative Thomas Boleyn, paying Bishop Fisher's cook, Richard Rouse, to murder the bishop. John Fisher is a thorn in the Boleyns' side because of his opposition to the King's supremacy and the annulment of the marriage of Henry VIII and Catherine of Aragon. The Boleyns provide Rouse with poison. He uses this to doctor the soup served to Fisher and other bishops who stand against the King's plans. Four men die as a result, but Bishop Fisher and Thomas More survive. When Rouse is apprehended for the crime, Thomas Boleyn threatens to harm Rouse's family if he betrays the Boleyns. When Rouse is boiled to death for his crime, Thomas and George watch. It is a deeply unsettling scene and shows that the Boleyns will stop at nothing in their quest for power. The George of The Tudors is a powerful man but he uses his power to his advantage, and not to do good. We see him threatening Eleanor Luke, the King's mistress, to get her to leave court because Anne finds Eleanor's relationship with the King troublesome, and he and his father are always in the thick of things.

The George of The Tudors also has a very unhappy marriage. He is forced into marrying Jane Parker as a consequence of his family's ambition, and does not take the marriage at all seriously.

He fools around at the wedding and makes fun of Jane when talking to his friends. On their wedding night, he brutally rapes her and on another occasion, when she questions him about where he's been, he throws her down on the bed. He despises her and treats her like something he's scraped off his shoe. Although, in one episode, he seems quite excited about finding two women in his bed, this George, like Philippa Gregory's George, prefers men. He has a sexual relationship with court musician Mark Smeaton.

Then we have George the coward. When Anne falls from power in May 1536 and George is arrested too, he pleads ignorance, telling Thomas Cromwell, "Whatever my sister has done, it's not with me or mine." He and Anne may have been best friends, but he won't risk his life by defending her. He doesn't save himself though. He is found guilty of high treason and, rather than dying with courage and dignity like his sister, he goes to the scaffold a blubbering wreck.

Now before anyone argues that *The Other Boleyn Girl* and *The Tudors* cannot be taken seriously because they're fiction, let's consider the following. In the Question and Answer section of *The Other Boleyn Girl*, Philippa Gregory is asked if George really did sleep with Anne. Her answer has confused many readers. Gregory states that Anne was found guilty of incest with George; that Jane Boleyn, George's wife, gave evidence against the siblings; and that if Anne had thought that Henry was impotent and was looking for someone to get her pregnant, then "George would have been the obvious choice." Regarding George's sexuality, Gregory explains that historian Retha Warnicke theorised that the men who were close to Anne were "a homosexual group" and that it was George's homosexuality that he "apologises for on the scaffold." So there we have Philippa Gregory stating quite clearly that although her novel is fiction, Anne and George may well have been capable of incest and that George was definitely homosexual because he confessed to it on the scaffold.

Alison Weir and Retha Warnicke

Someone once commented on the Anne Boleyn Files website[4] that the idea that George is bisexual or gay only stems from fiction, thus should not be taken seriously. But that's not true. What about the work of Alison Weir and Retha Warnicke, both respected and reputable historians? It is Warnicke's work that Philippa Gregory references in *The Other Boleyn Girl* and which Alison Weir cites in her work.

In her book *The Rise and Fall of Anne Boleyn*, Retha Warnicke explains that Anne Boleyn was surrounded by a group of men who were known libertines, saying that "libertines were expected to move in a progression from adultery and fornication to buggery and bestiality".[5] She then writes of George Boleyn's execution speech, commenting, "That Rochford refrained from specifying his crimes is consistent with the suggestion that he was guilty of sexual acts, including buggery, which were considered unnatural"[6] and goes on to suggest that Mark Smeaton was the courtier most likely to be George's lover because George loaned Smeaton a book attacking the institution of marriage.

Alison Weir also paints a pretty dark picture of George Boleyn. She writes that the poetry of George Cavendish, Wolsey's former gentleman usher, "strongly implies that Rochford omitted even to stop at rape" and that Cavendish's use of "bestial" must refer to "buggery".[7] Weir also believes that George's execution speech and his "description of his sinfulness" went beyond the usual acceptance of one's fate due to original sin, and suggests "he had indulged in what were then regarded as unnatural sexual practices."[8]

The Evidence

The evidence used by Gregory, Weir and Warnicke to back up their depictions of George include:

- The Charges against George listed in the Middlesex

indictment

- George Cavendish's "Metrical Visions"
- George's execution speech

The Indictment

Here is the part of the indictment used against Anne and George:

"Also that the Queen, 2 Nov. 27 Hen. VIII [1535] and several times before and after, at Westminster, procured and incited her own natural brother, George Boleyn, lord Rochford, gentleman of the privy chamber, to violate her, alluring him with her tongue in the said George's mouth, and the said George's tongue in hers, and also with kisses, presents and jewels, whereby he, despising the commands of God, and all other human laws, 5 Nov. 27 Henry VIII [1535], violated and carnally knew the said Queen, his own sister, at Westminster, which he also did on divers other days before and after, at the same place, sometimes by his own procurement and sometimes by the Queen's."[9]

As Eric Ives points out in *The Life and Death of Anne Boleyn*, the dates of the indictments simply don't make sense. In many cases, Anne was not actually in the locations it was alleged she had been, let alone, committing such offences there.[10] In this instance, Anne was actually in Windsor with her husband, the King, on both the 2nd and 5th November, and not at Westminster with George. Of course, the Crown was careful in adding the phrase "and several times before and after"; by including a catch-all phrase like that, they didn't need to be accurate.

Metrical Visions

Then we have George Cavendish's "Metrical Visions", in which he gives his account of George Boleyn's execution speech:

> "My life not chaste, my lyvyng bestyall;
> I forced wydowes, maydens I did deflower.
> All was oon to me, I spared none at all.
> My appetite was all women to devoure.
> My study was both day and hower.
> My onleafull lechery how I might it fulfill.
> Sparing no woman to have on hyr my will."[11]

Despite the old English, we can make out that Cavendish was of the opinion that George was "bestial" and that the latter was also deemed to be promiscuous and lustful. Warnicke and Weir have both read the word "bestial" and the phrase "unlawful lechery" as referring to George's homosexuality. However, Clare Cherry, who has been researching George Boleyn for nearly a decade, points out that Cavendish "has Thomas Culpepper [Catherine Howard's alleged lover] warning his fellow courtiers of their bestiality, and in his verses regarding Henry VIII he also talks of Henry's unlawful lechery."[12] Here is Cavendish's verse on Henry VIII:

> "My lusts too frequent, and have by them experience,
> Seeking but my lust of unlawful lechery,
> Whereof the slander remains still in me;
> So that my willful and shameful trespass
> Does all my majesty and nobleness deface."

Since Cavendish uses the same phrases here to refer to Henry VIII and his courtiers (who have not been cited as being homosexual), it is clear that Cavendish is talking about adultery, not homosexuality, when he employs this turn of phrase.

Another Cavendish verse which Alison Weir uses to back up her theory regarding George's sexuality is:

> "Alas! To declare my life in every effect,
> Shame restrains me the plains to confess,
> Least the abomination would all the world infect:
> It is so vile, so detestable in words to express,
> For which by the law, condemned I am doubtless."[13]

Warnicke believes that the "abomination" that George can't even put into words to confess is "buggery". She writes, "As he had stoutly denied charges of incest, the likelihood is that he was referring to other sexual practices then regarded as perversions"[14], but, as Clare Cherry points out, "if you read the whole verse, it says he is too ashamed to confess the crime for which he was condemned. He was condemned for incest with his sister, not for buggery, and it is incest with his sister which he never confessed to, neither in court nor on the scaffold."[15]

George's Execution Speech

George preached a bit of a sermon at his execution, what Eric Ives describes as "the language of Zion",[16] urging those witnessing his death to "stick to the truth and follow it", and not to make the mistakes that he had. However, one particular part of his speech has been used by Warnicke and Weir as evidence of George's homosexuality:

"And I beseech you all, in his holy name, to pray unto God for me, for I have deserved to die if I had twenty (or a thousand) lives, yea even to die with more shame and dishonour than hath ever been heard of before. For I am a wretched sinner, who has grievously and often time offended; nay in truth, I know not of any more perverse sinner than I have been up till now. Nevertheless, I mean not openly now to relate what my many sins may have been, since it were no pleasure for you hear them, nor yet me to rehearse, for God knoweth them all."[17]

As I said earlier, Weir believes that George's description of his sin went beyond the usual execution confessions of original sin and that he must have been referring to "unnatural sexual practices". Warnicke is of the opinion that because George emphasised just how bad his sins were but did not specify what they were, this suggests that he committed "unnatural"[18] sexual acts, which included buggery. However, people convicted of a crime "did not doubt that they deserved to die"[19] and felt that it was a punishment from God for their sinful lives, even if they were innocent of the crime of which they were convicted. The belief in original sin was very strong and I think that Weir is reading far too much into George's words, particularly as the latter was using his execution speech as an opportunity for evangelism.

We cannot actually call "Metrical Visions" and the execution speech two different pieces of evidence because Cavendish's poetry is based, loosely, on George's execution speech; it is Cavendish's own interpretation of the speech put into verse. We also have to take into account that Cavendish's rendition of George Boleyn's speech is just one version of George's last words. Furthermore, it differs considerably to the accounts in *The Spanish Chronicle*, *The Chronicle of Calais* and *Letters and Papers*, as well as in an anonymous Portuguese account, none of which use the words "bestial" or "unlawful lechery". George Cavenish was writing poetry and he was also not a Boleyn fan, so his words really should be taken with a pinch of salt.

Another piece of evidence which Warnicke uses to back up her theory regarding George Boleyn's sexuality is his ownership of a manuscript which contained a translation by Jean Lefèvre of Mathieu of Boulogne's 13th century satirical poem *Liber lamentationum Matheoluli* ("The Lamentations of Matheolus"). The poem is an attack on women written by a man betrayed by one. In the poem, Mathieu likens women to basilisks, "a chimaera with horns and a tail" and " the mother of all calamities", and writes how "all evil and all madness stem from her". The manuscript, which can now be found in the British Library, is inscribed, "Thys boke ys myn, George Boleyn. 1526". Near the end of the volume

Figure 41 - Tower Hill Scaffold Memorial, London

is inscribed, "Amoy m marc S", showing that the book had also belonged to Mark Smeaton, one of the men executed alongside George Boleyn. Warnicke writes that "it is extraordinary that a manuscript, attacking the institution of marriage, should belong within the period of one decade to two of the five men executed for illicit sexual relations with the queen", particularly as such manuscripts would have been expensive. She concludes, therefore, that Smeaton "was the one most likely to have been Rochord's intimate friend"; it is clear what she means by "intimate".[20] I find it a huge leap of imagination, however, to draw the conclusion that George and Smeaton were lovers based upon George passing a manuscript on to Smeaton, even if that manuscript was an attack on women and marriage. In my own research into "The Lamentations of Matheolus", I have found that the text was widely circulated amongst scholars in Europe and "quickly became one of the most seminal examples of medieval antifeminist and antimatrimonial discourse".[21] It has been suggested that Chaucer knew of this poem, and drew on it heavily for "The Wife of Bath's Prologue",[22] and that Christine de Pizan was inspired to refute it in her "Cité de Dames".[23] George Boleyn was keen on French literature and it is likely that this satire was simply part of a wider collection of popular works in French. He may simply have passed it on to Mark because it was popular at the time, or perhaps as a joke if Mark was becoming involved with a woman. We don't know the facts and therefore cannot make a judgement.

If there had been rumours of homosexuality surrounding any of the men then they would certainly have come up in their trials in 1536. Moreover, Eustace Chapuys, the imperial ambassador, would have gleefully shared these rumours with Charles V. Three years prior to the Boleyn family's fall, Parliament had passed "an Acte for the punysshement of the vice of Buggerie" making the "abominable vice of buggery committed with mankind or beast" a capital crime punishable by hanging(1533-4, 25 Hen. 8 c.6), yet none of the men were charged with buggery. Norris, Weston, Smeaton and Brereton were charged with treason and adultery and George was charged with treason, adultery and incest; no mention of buggery. George, as a zealous evangelical, would have been mortified by the idea of buggery, let alone the practising of it. The homosexuality theory really cannot be taken seriously and belongs to the realms of fiction and fantasy, where it should stay. It was never used to blacken the Boleyn name in the sixteenth century, when it was illegal, and it should not be given any credence today.

The Real George Boleyn

So who was the real George Boleyn? What do we know about him?

Well, we do know that he was a fervent religious reformer. After their deaths, a number of heretical evangelical books were found amongst George and Anne's belongings and we know that George completed two beautiful presentation manuscripts of evangelical literature for Anne, both based on the work of the evangelical scholar, Jacques Lefèvre d'Etaples. These were *The Ecclesiaste* and *Epistres et Evangiles des cinquante et deux semaines de l'an*, or "Epistles and Gospels for the 52 weeks of the Year", a collection of Epistles and Gospel readings for the year followed by a short homily. *Epistles* was based on the principle that the Gospel should be accessible to the laity, the general people, and *The Ecclesiaste* was the Book of Ecclesiastes with a commentary by German evangelical Johannes Brenz. The commentary was derived from Martin Luther's writings and emphasised the pre-eminence of the Bible over the traditions and sacraments of the established church. George translated the commentary into English for Anne but kept the French the same.

Historian James Carley also believes that George may have persuaded Anne to show a copy of Simon Fish's *Supplication for the Beggars* to the King.[24] This was an evangelical and revolutionary sixteen page pamphlet attacking the Catholic Church and accusing it of many crimes. Simon Fish contested the existence of purgatory and the sale of indulgences, and also accused the Church of holding half of England's wealth, something which would have keenly interested Henry VIII.

George's execution speech is also evidence of his religious views. George spoke of how he was "a setter forth of the Word of God", that he was "a great reader and a mighty debater of the Word of God" and stated that if he had followed the Word of God he would not "be in the piteous condition wherein I now stand". He drew his speech to a close by saying "Wherefore I do beseech you all, for the love of our Lord God, that ye do at all seasons, hold by the truth, and speak it, and embrace it, for beyond all peradventure, better profiteth he who readeth not and yet does well, than he who readeth much and yet liveth in sin." Evangelicals put God's Word first over the rituals of the Church, and George's scaffold speech shows just how important the Bible was to him and how it should be to others - words fit for a Sunday sermon.

George was also a renowned poet. He loved music and poetry and although we think of Henry Howard, the Earl of Surrey, and Thomas Wyatt as the poets of that age, we know that George Boleyn was actually just as talented. Raphael Holinshed, the chronicler, wrote that George "wrote divers sings and sonnets";[25] George Cavendish described how nature had endowed him with "gifts of natural qualities" and that "Dame Eloquence" had also taught him "the art in meter and verse, to make pleasant ditties".[26] Playwright Jon Bale wrote of his "rythmos elegantissimos".[27] George's only biographer, Edmond Bapst, wrote of George and Henry Howard, Earl of Surrey, bringing the Renaissance to England with their beautiful poetry;[28] and in 1575 Richard Smith included George's name in a list of poets which included the likes of Chaucer, Surrey and Wyatt. Clare Cherry also points out that when imprisoned, in the Tower in May 1536, Anne Boleyn heard that the men had to make their own beds. She suggested that they make their pallets as they made their ballads, but said that only her Lord Rochford had the skill to do so. She had to be reminded that Thomas Wyatt, who was also in the Tower, was equally skilled at verse.

So if George Boleyn was such a renowned poet, where on earth is this poetry? Well, either destroyed or attributed to someone else are the likely answers. After all, George died a convicted traitor and a man who allegedly committed incest with his sister, the Queen. A reader of the 16th century *"Tottel's Miscellany"*, a collection of poems from the era, including those by Wyatt and Surrey, may well be reading the works of George Boleyn without even realising it. John Harington, John Bale and Horace Walpole all attribute one particular poem to George, although Tottel assigns it to Wyatt. It is called *The Lover Complayneth the Unkindnes of his Love* and the first verse goes:-

"My Lute awake, perform the last
Labour that thou and I shall waste.
And end that I have now begun!
And when this song is sung and rest,
My Lute be still, for I have done!"

As well as being a poet, George was also a royal favourite. In *The Tudors* series, George is actually conspicuous by his absence in Season One; in this series, the King spends all his leisure time with Charles Brandon, Sir William Compton and Anthony Knyvert. However, George was a gentleman of the privy chamber until Cardinal Wolsey weeded him out in 1526 via the Eltham Ordnance. Even before Anne came on the scene, George was receiving grants, offices and land. For example, he was awarded the keepership of Penshurst in 1522, after the fall of Stafford, the Duke of Buckingham, and in 1524 he was given Grimston Manor in Norfolk. George's name is also mentioned frequently in the Privy Purse Expenses, showing that he played dice, bowls and cards with the King and also accompanied him hunting. He was clearly a close friend of the King.

Then we have George the diplomat. Like his father before him, he was an important diplomat and carried out many missions to France on behalf of the King, including those in December 1529, March 1533, Summer 1533, April 1534, July 1534 and May 1535. Those are all recorded in *Letters and Papers*. He was also very influential in Parliament. It is noted that his attendance rate was higher than many others, possibly because of his reformist persuasions and his desire to push Reform.

Of course, we'll never know who the real George Boleyn was. Although I can argue here against the theories of Warnicke, Weir and Gregory, because there is a lack of evidence to support them, we just cannot know for sure what George was like. Evidence has been twisted to fit theories, fiction has taken over and the majority of the public probably believe that what they see or read in *The Tudors* and *The Other Boleyn Girl* is fact-based. George Boleyn the poet, reformer and diplomat just isn't remembered.

George Boleyn was executed on 17th May 1536 on Tower Hill and was laid to rest in the chancel area of the Chapel of St Peter ad Vincula, Tower of London.

◇◇

Notes and Sources

1   Hirst, "The Tudors."
2   Gregory, The Other Boleyn Girl.
3   Chadwick, The Other Boleyn Girl.
4   "The Anne Boleyn Files."
5   Warnicke, The Rise and Fall of Anne Boleyn: Family Politics at the Court of Henry VIII, 4.
6   Ibid., 218.
7   Weir, The Lady in the Tower: The Fall of Anne Boleyn, 100.
8   Ibid., 243.
9   "Letters and Papers, Foreign and Domestic, Henry VIII, Volume 10 - January-June 1536," n. 876.
10   Ives, The Life and Death of Anne Boleyn, 344.
11   Cavendish, The Life of Cardinal Wolsey, Volume 2, 2:22.
12   Cherry, "George Boleyn's Sexuality."
13   Cavendish, The Life of Cardinal Wolsey, Volume 2, 2:22.
14   Weir, The Lady in the Tower: The Fall of Anne Boleyn, 101.
15   Cherry, "George Boleyn's Sexuality."
16   Ives, The Life and Death of Anne Boleyn, 278.
17   Gruffudd, "Gruffudd's Chronicle."
18   Warnicke, The Rise and Fall of Anne Boleyn: Family Politics at the Court of Henry VIII, 218.
19   de Lisle, The Sisters Who Would Be Queen, 49.
20   Warnicke, The Rise and Fall of Anne Boleyn: Family Politics at the Court of Henry VIII, 218–219.
21   Gray, Gender, Rhetoric, and Print Culture in French Renaissance Writing, 17–18.
22   Thundy, "Matheolus, Chaucer, and the Wife of Bath."
23   Percival, Chaucer's Legendary Good Women, 106.
24   Carley, The Books of King Henry VIII and His Wives, 131.
25   Holinshed, Holinshed's Chronicles of England, Scotland, and Ireland, 6:1613.
26   Cavendish, The Life of Cardinal Wolsey, Volume 2, 2:20.

27 Walpole, A Catalogue of the Royal and Noble Authors of England: With Lists of Their Works, 64.

28 Bapst, Deux Gentilshommes-Poetes de La Cour de Henry VIII.

21.Jane Boleyn (née Parker) – History's Scapegoat

I once saw a Tumblr "confession" which said "Jane Parker deserved her execution more than any woman Henry VIII put to the block". Many people seem to agree with that sentiment. She's seen as the devil incarnate, a jealous and spiteful woman who was implicated in the deaths of her husband and two queens. Not a week goes by when I don't read a comment online suggesting that Jane Boleyn got "what was coming to her" when she was executed in February 1542, that it was karma and that she got her just desserts. But where does this view come from?

Well, let's take a look first at the Jane Boleyn of popular culture: Philippa Gregory's *The Other Boleyn Girl* and *The Boleyn Inheritance*, and *The Tudors* TV series.

Jane of The Other Boleyn Girl

As I said in my chapter on George, Jane is referred to as a "monster" and Gregory writes of her "avaricious desire for scandal".[1] George and his sisters hate her and the way she snoops around. The name "nosy parker" fits her well because she listens at doors and looks through keyholes. She is drawn to gossip "like a buzzard to carrion", and is always the first to know things and pass them on to others. The Jane of Gregory's novels is also the woman who betrays her husband and her sister-in-law by giving evidence against them in May 1536. The "despised" wife gets her own back on the Boleyns who made fun of her.

In *The Boleyn Inheritance*,[2] which tells Jane's story after the fall of the Boleyns, she brings down another queen. She is used by the plotting Duke of Norfolk, who wants Jane to gather evidence against Anne of Cleves, Henry VIII's new queen. The Duke reminds Jane how she has played the traitor before and so she signs a statement regarding Anne of Cleves. In the false statement, she tells that, although she and the other ladies advised Anne on sexual matters, Anne didn't want to know; it appears to be all Anne's fault that the King could not consummate their marriage.

Jane is a liar. She gave evidence at George and Anne's trial to save the "Boleyn inheritance" (the lands, titles and wealth that George and Anne had built up), she betrays Anne of Cleves and then, when Catherine Howard falls, Jane feigns madness to try and save herself from execution.

Jane is also portrayed as a jealous and lustful woman. She tells of how "jealousy and lust brought me so low that it was my pleasure, a wicked sinful pleasure, to feel his touch on me and think of him touching her", and she talks about how she got a kick out of imagining George with his sister, Anne. This part of her character leads to her being the chief instigator of the affair between Catherine Howard and Thomas Culpeper. It is Jane who tells Culpeper that Catherine wants him, and who offers to let him into Catherine's privy chamber to talk to her while she chaperones them. When the couple do meet, Jane is a voyeur. She watches them make love and is "aroused with stolen lust."

There really is nothing to like about Jane's character in Gregory's books and it is little wonder that those who read them feel that she got her comeuppance when she was beheaded in February 1542.

Jane of The Tudors

The Jane of *The Tudors* series is very similar to Philippa Gregory's Jane, but because Jane is a victim of George's cruelty, the viewer can be more forgiving of her betraying the Boleyns and giving false evidence. Her statement is portrayed as an act of revenge against a wicked husband.

Later in the series, we also see Jane acting as the go-between between Catherine Howard and Culpeper. She arranges meetings between them, acts as a look out and encourages their affair. Culpeper accuses her of acting like a madam in a brothel, and it's quite an apt description. Jane is also Culpeper's lover. Although Culpeper is attracted to Catherine, he sleeps with Jane first after getting her rather tipsy on wine and then seems to use Jane as a way of getting to Catherine. Jane doesn't seem particularly bothered by this because she can derive sexual pleasure from watching Catherine and Culpeper through the keyhole.

When word comes out about Catherine's affair with Culpeper, Jane is imprisoned in the Tower of London and there she goes insane. Gregory's Jane feigns madness, but the Jane of *The Tudors* really is mad; we see her smearing excrement on the walls and completely losing it.

The Jane Boleyn of Non-fiction

But it's not just fiction in which Jane is portrayed badly. In the "Author's Notes" section of *The Boleyn Inheritance*, Philippa Gregory explains that her Jane Boleyn was "drawn from history" and that "few novelists would dare to invent such a horror as she seems to have been." She goes on to say that Jane's "jealousy and a determination to preserve her inheritance" led to her giving evidence against George and Anne, and that her evidence against Anne of Cleves could have led to Anne being beheaded. Gregory also states that Jane encouraged Catherine and Culpeper "fully understanding the fatal danger to the young queen." A horror indeed, if we are to believe Gregory.

In *The Lady in the Tower: The Fall of Anne Boleyn*, Alison Weir writes how "most sources agree that the only evidence for incest would rest upon the testimony of Jane Parker, Lady Rochford."[3] Weir cites the corroborating sources as:

- Edward, Lord Herbert of Cherbury - The 17th century biographer who described Jane "as the 'particular instrument' in the ruin of her husband and his sister",[4] basing his account on contemporary evidence: namely Anthony Anthony's lost journal.

- Eustace Chapuys, the imperial ambassador.

- An anonymous Portuguese account.

- The writings of Lancelot de Carles, secretary to the French ambassador.

- Jane's execution confession.

Weir goes on to describe Jane's jealousy of the close relationship between George and Anne, the unhappiness of her marriage to George, the possibility that George had "subjected Jane to sexual practices that outraged her"[5] and her resentfulness towards Anne over her banishment from court after she plotted with Anne to remove a lady from court, a lady who had caught the King's eye. These reasons, along with her father Lord Morley's sympathy with the Lady Mary, could, Weir theorises, have led to Jane's betrayal of the Boleyns.

Lacey Baldwin Smith, Catherine Howard's biographer, says of Jane: "the lady was a pathological meddler, with most of the instincts of a procuress who achieves a vicarious pleasure from arranging assignations"[6] and C.Coote said "the infamous lady Rochford... justly deserved her fate for the concern which she had in bringing Anne Boleyn, as well as her own husband, to the block."[7] Perhaps the general public can be forgiven for judging Jane harshly, I suppose, when historians do too.

The Evidence

But did Jane Boleyn actually betray George and Anne?

No, I don't believe so; and I am not alone in thinking this way. Historian Julia Fox argues against this fallacy in her book on Jane, calling Jane "a scapegoat", and Fox's husband, historian John Guy, in a review of Alison Weir's *The Lady in the Tower*, points out the following problems with the sources Alison Weir uses to build her case against Jane.[8] He states:

- That Lord Herbert of Cherbury was not quoting from the lost chronicle of Anthony Anthony, as Weir states, but actually quoting from his very own book.

- That Chapuys never named Jane as the witness against George and Anne

- That the Portuguese source also did not name Jane, it simply said "that person"

- That Lancelot de Carles was talking about Lady Worcester, not Jane Boleyn

- That Jane's execution confession did not exist, it was a forgery and the work of Gregorio Leti, a man known for making up stories and inventing sources

As for an unhappy marriage; well, a childless marriage is not necessarily an unhappy one. When we combine the points that John Guy makes with the fact that we have no evidence that Jane and George's marriage was unhappy, or that George was homosexual or bisexual, then we have to question these depictions of Jane. There is also no evidence that she was jealous, that she spied through keyholes, that she plotted with the Duke of Norfolk or that she slept with Thomas Culpeper; all of those claims are pure fantasy and belong only in fiction. Just as Anne and George have been maligned by fiction and history, Jane has been made into a monster and a scapegoat; "the bawd", "the infamous Lady Rochford"; and it just isn't fair or correct.

The Real Jane Boleyn

It is thought that Jane was born around 1505. Her father was Henry Parker, Lord Morley, a man who had been brought up in the household of Lady Margaret Beaufort, Henry VII's mother. Jane's mother was Alice St John, daughter of Sir John St John, a prosperous and respected landowner. We know that Jane was present at the Field of Cloth of Gold in 1520, we know that she played Constancy in the 1522 Chateau Vert masquerade and we know that a jointure was signed on the 4th October 1524, so it is thought that she married George Boleyn in late 1524 or early 1525. By this time, George Boleyn was a "flourishing, prosperous courtier"[9] so Jane was an important woman. Although it was unlikely that it was a love match, there is no reason to think that the marriage was unhappy or that George didn't want to marry her. Contrary to popular opinion, young men and women were not forced into marriage. A couple was only supposed to become betrothed, and then married, if they liked each other. This 'like' was supposed to turn into love as the couple got to know each other better.

In April 1533, Jane and George were granted the wardship of twelve year-old Edmund Sheffield, son and heir of the late Sir Robert Sheffield and his wife Jane Stanley, daughter of George Stanley, 9th Baron Strange. It was a lucrative grant because the couple would benefit from administering Edmund's inheritance (lands in Nottinghamshire and Lincolnshire) during his minority.[10] [11] Jane used some of her wealth to act as a patroness of education by supporting scholar William Foster in his studies at King's College, Cambridge.[12]

Jane attended Anne Boleyn at her coronation in 1533 and she appears to have been close to Anne. Anne turned to Jane for help in 1534 when she wanted to get rid of a rival who had caught Henry's eye. This resulted in Jane being exiled from court for a time when the plan was discovered, but there is no evidence that this caused any trouble in the women's relationship. Anne felt close enough to Jane to confide in her about Henry's erratic sexual prowess, something that Jane then told George about. Anne must have trusted Jane to talk about such an intimate subject, and one that involved the King. The evidence, therefore, points to Jane being close to both Anne and George, rather than to her being an outsider and feeling jealous of the siblings' close relationship.

When George Boleyn was arrested in May 1536, far from abandoning her husband to his fate Jane sent a message to Sir William Kingston, Constable of the Tower of London. Although this message was damaged in the Ashburnam House fire of 1731, which affected the Cottonian Library, we know that she sent it to Kingston to give her husband, asking after George and promising him that she would "humbly [make] suit unto the king's highness for him."[13] We also know that George was grateful and that he replied saying that he wanted to "give her thanks".

Although some writers and historians portray Jane as being the star witness for the Crown in 1536, the evidence does not support this theory. Eustace Chapuys clearly states that there were no witnesses at the trials of George and Anne, and, as Julia Fox points out, "He had no reason to lie, every reason to gloat, if Anne's own sister-in-law had actually spoken out against her."[14] George Boleyn is recorded as saying "On the evidence of only one woman you are willing to believe this great evil of me, and on the basis of her allegations you are deciding my judgement."[15] Since the Crown's main piece of evidence was the Countess of Worcester's conversation with her brother regarding the Queen's inappropriate relationship with George, surely this was the "one woman" to whom George was referring? He could also have been referring to the letters of the late Lady Wingfield which were recorded by Judge John Spelman as disclosing evidence of Anne's "bawdery and lechery".[16] If George had been referring to Jane then wouldn't he have said "my wife" rather than "one woman"?

Jane's name is also not mentioned in Thomas Cromwell's reports on the case against Anne and the men, or in other contemporaneous reports. As I said earlier, the account of Jane's scaffold confession was a forgery and merchant Otwell Johnson, who was present at Jane's execution, mentioned no such confession in his account. It appears that all Jane was guilty of in 1536 was talking to George about Henry's sexual problems and telling the truth when she was interrogated.

Jane survived the falls of her husband and sister-in-law, but life was not easy for her and she ended up having to beg Cromwell for help. It was he who intervened to get her jointure money from Thomas Boleyn. Jane went on to serve three more queens: Jane Seymour, Anne of Cleves and Catherine Howard, and it was, of course, her service to Catherine Howard that led to Jane being executed in February 1542. It appears that Jane foolishly helped Catherine Howard have secret assignations with Thomas Culpeper, a gentleman of Henry VIII's privy chamber. We have no way of knowing the full story of Jane's involvement in Catherine's relationship with Culpeper. It could be that she was simply carrying out the Queen's orders or it could be that she was being manipulated by Thomas Culpeper. I discussed the matter with Julia Fox, Jane's biographer, who believes that Jane was persuaded to help the couple once and then was on a slippery slope because she'd already committed misprision of treason. Having already incriminated herself, it got harder and harder to back out so, instead, she just carried on and ended up digging her own grave. Jane was on her own; she had no-one to turn to for help and advice – no husband and no Thomas Cromwell to act as a go-between with her and the King. What she did was reckless and foolish, but I cannot see how her actions prove that she was "a pathological meddler" or a "procuress".

We need to question and challenge the accepted depictions of Jane Boleyn, just as we have done with Anne Boleyn. We will never know the full truth about her, but there is no need to twist the evidence or fill in the blanks by making Jane out to be a monster. If Catherine Howard's story provokes sympathy, then surely her lady deserves some of it too.

Jane Boleyn, Lady Rochford, was executed on 13th February 1542 with Queen Catherine Howard within the Tower of London confines. She was laid to rest in the chancel area of the Chapel of St Peter ad Vincula, at the Tower, alongside her mistress the Queen.

Notes and Sources

1   Gregory, The Other Boleyn Girl.
2   Gregory, The Boleyn Inheritance.
3   Weir, The Lady in the Tower: The Fall of Anne Boleyn, 77.
4   Herbert, The Life and Raigne of King Henry the Eighth., 474.
5   Weir, The Lady in the Tower: The Fall of Anne Boleyn, 144.
6   Baldwin Smith, Catherine Howard, 154.
7   Coote, The History of England, from the Earliest Dawn of Record to the Peace of MDCCLXXXIII.
8   Guy, "The Lady in the Tower: The Fall of Anne Boleyn by Alison Weir - Sunday Times Review."
9   Fox, Jane Boleyn: The Infamous Lady Rochford.
10   "Letters and Papers, Foreign and Domestic, Henry VIII, Volume 6 - 1533," n. 419.8.
11   Fox, Jane Boleyn: The Infamous Lady Rochford, 115.
12   Ibid., 120.
13   "Letters and Papers, Foreign and Domestic, Henry VIII, Volume 10 - January-June 1536," n. 798.
14   Fox, "Jane Boleyn: The Infamous Lady Rochford - A Guest Post."
15   Ives, The Life and Death of Anne Boleyn, 331.
16   ed. Baker, The Reports of Sir John Spelman, 71.

22.   Mary Boleyn –
One Big Boleyn Myth

Let me tell you a story…

Mary Boleyn was a classic English rose, taking after her mother's side of the family, whose innocence was wrecked by her father and sister. Not only was she used and abused by the French king, Francis I, and his cronies, she was pimped out to the English king and shown how to satisfy him by her sister, Anne. She was but a pawn in her family's hands.

After bearing the King two illegitimate children and losing her husband, William Carey, to sweating sickness, Mary finally found true love only to be banished from court by her spiteful sister, who was now queen and married to Mary's former love, Henry VIII. So cruel and ambitious was Mary's sister that she even stole Mary's son from her. Mary chose true love over ambition and was thus saved from the awful events of May 1536. Her forgiving nature and angelic disposition, however, led to her visiting the King and pleading for Anne's life. Unfortunately, Anne was not pardoned and was executed. However, Mary was able to steal Elizabeth from court and take her away from all the corruption there.

It's a fairy tale with glaring holes and blatant inaccuracies in it, but that's the version of Mary that some people believe in and it's the version of Mary promoted by books like Karen Harper's *The Last Boleyn*, Philippa Gregory's *The Other Boleyn Girl* and Hilary Mantel's *Wolf Hall*. But what do we actually know about Anne Boleyn's sister?

Not a lot.

Mary Boleyn came up in a conversation I was having with the late historian Eric Ives. Ives commented that what we knew about Mary Boleyn "could be written on the back of a postcard with room to spare", and he is right. Despite the fact that two biographies have been written about her, that she is the subject of countless online articles and the heroine of at least two novels, Mary Is a puzzle. The biographies are full of theories about her and the facts are lacking; that's just the way it is. What we think we know about her is probably based on fiction or theory, rather than on hard fact. What we don't know about her could fill a book; what we do know would fit on that postcard mentioned by Eric Ives.

So, what are the cold hard facts about Mary Boleyn?

- Mary was born in the late 15th/early 16th century. We don't even know her birthdate.

- She was the daughter of Thomas Boleyn and Elizabeth Howard, sister of Queen Anne Boleyn and niece of the Duke of Norfolk. She had brothers named George, Thomas and Henry.

- She served Mary Tudor in France in 1514 and was back in England by 4th February 1520, when she married William Carey, a member of the King's household. The King was present at the ceremony.[1]

- Mary had some kind of relationship with Henry VIII in the 1520s. It is not known how long it lasted.

- She played Kindness in the Chateau Vert pageant of March 1522.[2]

- Mary was pregnant at least three times and had two surviving children, Catherine and Henry Carey.

- Her first husband, William Carey, died of sweating sickness on 22nd June 1528 and her sister, who was at that time involved with Henry VIII, was granted wardship of Henry Carey, Mary's son, in July 1528.[3] Mary was a widow and this agreement helped to provide her son with an education. Anne neither adopted nor stole Mary's son; she simply provided for him.

- Henry VIII intervened with Thomas Boleyn on Mary's behalf, prompting him to make provision for her at the end of June 1528.[4] In December 1528, Henry assigned Mary an annuity of £100 (£32,000), which had once been paid to her husband.[5]

- Mary was at court at New Year 1532 and 1534. In 1532,[6] "Mary Rocheford" gave Henry VIII a shirt with a blackwork collar and he gave her a piece of gilt plate. Her name also appears on the lists of New Year's gifts for 1534. The list for 1533 is missing.

- Mary accompanied the King and Anne Boleyn on their trip to meet Francis I in Calais in October 1532.[7]

- Mary served Anne in 1533 and attended her at her coronation.[8]

- She married William Stafford in secret in 1534 and turned up at court pregnant in September 1534.[9] This was when she was banished from court for marrying without Anne's permission and when her allowance was cut off by Thomas Boleyn. She was forced to write to Thomas Cromwell for financial help.

- Her marriage to Stafford was a love match. In her letter to Cromwell, she wrote "I loved him as well as he did me... I had rather beg my bread with him than to be the greatest queen in Christendom."[10]

- Her husband, William Stafford, was one of the men chosen to meet Anne of Cleves at Calais in 1539,[11] and her daughter, Catherine Carey, was appointed as one of Anne of Cleves' ladies in November 1539.[12]

- Mary received her inheritance from her father and grandmother in 1543.[13]

- She died on the 19th July 1543, but it is not known where she was laid to rest. Alison Weir[14] dates her death as the 19th July 1543 though Josephine Wilkinson chooses the 30th July[15] and David Loades[16] chooses to simply write "July 1543". Alison Weir cites John Horace Round, the 19th century historian and genealogist, as her source for the 19th July date of death; his account reads, "According to an inquisition taken at Mary's death (19th July, 1543)...",[17] so it appears that he based the date on her inquisition post mortem.

- Her children were favourites of Elizabeth I. Catherine Carey served Elizabeth I as one of her ladies of the bedchamber and the offices of Henry Carey, 1st Baron Hunsdon, included Privy councillor and Lord Chamberlain of the Household.

We don't know what she looked like, what her personality was like, who the father of her children was, the nature of her relationships with Francis I and Henry VIII (or even if she slept with Francis), her whereabouts at various times of her life, her relationship with her family... Mary Is, in fact, the perfect blank canvas for an historical novelist. Her life and story, as we know it, is, in short, one big myth.

Notes and Sources

1   "Letters and Papers, Foreign and Domestic, Henry VIII, Volume 3: 1519-1523," 1539, The King's Book of Payments, 1519.
2   Hall, Hall's Chronicle, 630.
3   "Letters and Papers, Foreign and Domestic, Henry VIII, Volume 5: 1531-1532," n. 11.

4   "Letters and Papers, Foreign and Domestic, Henry VIII, Volume 4: 1524-1530," n. 4410.

5   "Letters and Papers, Foreign and Domestic, Henry VIII, Volume 5: 1531-1532," 306.

6   Ibid., n. 686.

7   Ibid., n. 1484.

8   Wilkinson, Mary Boleyn: The True Story of Henry VIII's Mistress, 137.

9   "Letters and Papers, Foreign and Domestic, Henry VIII, Volume 7," n. 1554.

10   Ibid., n. 1655.

11   "Letters and Papers, Foreign and Domestic, Henry VIII, Volume 14 Part 2: August-December 1539," n. 572.

12   Ibid.

13   "Letters and Papers, Foreign and Domestic, Henry VIII, Volume 18 Part 1: January-July 1543," n. 623.

14   Weir, Mary Boleyn: The Great and Infamous Whore.

15   Wilkinson, Mary Boleyn: The True Story of Henry VIII's Mistress.

16   Loades, The Boleyns: The Rise and Fall of a Tudor Family.

17   Round, The Early Life of Anne Boleyn: A Critical Essay.

23.   The Boleyns and Religion

In running The Anne Boleyn Files, I regularly encounter confusion regarding Anne Boleyn's faith and that of her family. People want to label her "Protestant" or "Catholic", but she doesn't seem to fit either label neatly. Even historians are divided on the subject.

Those who label Anne "Protestant" back up their arguments with sources like martyrologist John Foxe and the writings of Eustace Chapuys, who was imperial ambassador while Anne Boleyn was Queen. Foxe was writing during Elizabeth I's Protestant reign and he presented Anne Boleyn as a Protestant martyr. He praised her for her modesty, goodness, charity, and her "fervent desire" for "setting forth of sincere religion." He believed that her execution was caused by "secret practising of the papists", "wily papists" who whispered in the King's ear.[1] Chapuys referred to the Boleyns as "more Lutheran than Luther himself",[2] and spoke of how, when he met with George Boleyn in April 1536, Chapuys avoided "all occasions of entering into Lutheran discussions, from which he [George] could not refrain".[3] Of course, in Chapuys' view, anyone who was not a conservative Catholic was probably a Lutheran. When Chapuys heard about the plot against Anne in 1536, he wrote to the Emperor saying that it was "a remedy for the heretical doctrines and practices of the concubine – the principal cause of the spread of Lutheranism in this country."[4]

Historians Eric Ives,[5] James Carley[6] and Maria Dowling[7] don't see Anne as a fully-fledged Protestant or Lutheran, but as an evangelical, a woman with a personal faith who believed in justification by faith, in relief of the poor, in the dissemination of the Bible in the vernacular, and in the reform of the Church. I agree and I would also say the same of Anne's father and brother, Thomas and George Boleyn. Historian G. W. Bernard, however, challenges the views of Foxe, Chapuys, Ives and Dowling, arguing that "there is nothing that clinches the case for Anne as evangelical or proto-protestant."[8] He concludes that Anne was actually a conventional Catholic and that "dabbling with the new sects may for both Rochford and Anne have been more a matter of politics and radical chic than a matter of religious conviction." Carley, Dowling and Ives argue that George Boleyn's translation of two reformist manuscripts for Anne show that the siblings were evangelicals, but Bernard dismisses this view, saying that the privy purse expenses show that George had a busy social life, winning money from various people at shuffleboard, shooting, cards etc. He adds that "Rochford's interests were more those of a courtier-nobleman than of a scholar" and that "there is no evidence of Rochford's literary activities." In other words, George was a fun-loving guy far too busy for reading, writing and religion.

Alison Weir regards Anne and her father, Thomas Boleyn, as "orthodox Catholics" but feels that George Boleyn's collection of books show that he was "quite near to becoming a Lutheran." She concludes that "the Boleyns were zealous for the cause of reform within the Catholic Church."[9] David Loades sees it slightly differently. In his view, Thomas Boleyn was a religious conservative who fell out with Anne and George over their "evangelical programme".[10] So, even the historians cannot agree on the Boleyns' faith.

I was lucky enough to discuss the Boleyns and their faith with

Eric Ives. He felt that the labels "Protestant" and "Catholic" just cannot be used for people in the 1530s because it was too early in the English Reformation for people to have formed set religious ideas. It was a time of immense upheaval in the Church, due to the break with Rome, and a time when new religious ideas and teachings were coming over from the Continent. There were also various types of reform, ideas from very different scholars and teachers. Anne Boleyn had spent around seven years in France and thus was influenced by French reform, not German reform. In this sense, her beliefs would not fit our usual understanding of "Protestant". However, it also doesn't mean that she was a conventional Catholic. I feel that "evangelical" would be the best label.

In my research on the Boleyns, I've realised that you cannot look at or write about the family without considering their religious beliefs. Whatever you think about the cause of the coup against Anne, her family and supporters in 1536, religion was a factor, as is shown by the gleeful dispatches of Chapuys. Of course, it is not accurate to describe the coup as simply a battle between the religious reformers and the Catholic Conservatives, but there was that part to it. Anne Boleyn, Cranmer and Cromwell all had an influence on the King during Anne's time as Queen, and Henry's relationship with her had led to him breaking with Rome. He may well have broken with Rome at some point anyway; but his relationship with Anne was the catalyst, and the reformist literature Anne shared with him helped him to justify his actions in a theological way.

Religion was also immensely important in Tudor times. It was important to everyone – the laws of the land were based on it; you lived your life according to the Church calendar and participated in religious rituals. It defined who you were and what you did, and the new religion was even more personal in that it was about you having a personal relationship with God. Religion and the Boleyns are also inseparable when you think about the influence Anne had as queen. Not only did she have the ear of her husband, Henry VIII, but she was able to act on petitioners' requests and had influence on policy, on ecclesiastical appointments and on those around her. Her father and brother were also very influential men and George played an active role in Parliament.

As there are so many different points of view out there regarding the religious views of the Boleyns, we have to make our own minds up and we can only make an informed decision if we investigate it. Because the Boleyns died so early on in the English Reformation, it is hard to say what they really thought, what faith they held, and what was in their hearts. However, we can find clues and piece them together to give us some kind of picture. Clues include:

- What was said about them by their contemporaries
- Their actions
- The books they owned
- The things they said
- Reformers they had links with

Thomas Boleyn

Let us first consider Thomas Boleyn, head of the Boleyn family and a man who Joanna Denny[11] sees as an advocate of the New Religion but who David Loades sees as a conservative Catholic. What clues do we have about him? Well, we know that he was a Francophile and a real Renaissance man with a deep interest in Christian humanism. He commissioned religious works from Erasmus, showing his interest in religion, and he had links with French Reformers. Eric Ives mentions Thomas Boleyn's links with Thomas Tebold, so I did a bit of digging into this relationship to find out who Tebold was.

In an index of Kent wills,[12] Tebold is listed as a vicar, scholar and godson of Thomas Boleyn. Eric Ives writes, "There is even a possibility that the Boleyns sought, or maintained, private links with reformers abroad. In 1535 and 1536 Master Thomas Tebold, later known as one of Cromwell's continental agents, was travelling in Europe, supported by the earl of Wiltshire with some assistance from Cranmer."[13] Tebold reported on the current state of religious persecutions in France, after the Affair of the Placards in Paris, and was "spreading the idea that Thomas Boleyn was a promising patron of works - theological and other..." Tebold also sent Thomas Boleyn an epistle by French Reformer, Clément Marot, who had been forced to flee France due to his religious views. In one letter, Tebold says that he hopes to hear from Boleyn via "Reygnard Wolf, bookseller, of St Pauls Churchyard, London, who will be here in two days".[14] So I also did some digging into Reginald (or Reyner/ Reygnard) Wolf.

Wolf was born in Gelderland in the Netherlands but settled in Strasbourg, where he learned printing and where he set up connections in the printing trade. He knew Simon Grynaeus, the German reformer, and it appears that Wolf got to know Thomas Cranmer through him. Wolf settled in England around 1533 and worked as a bookseller in London. In his article on Wolfe, Andrew Pettegree writes of how Wolf travelled annually to the Frankfurt am Main book mart, which allowed him to work as an agent for the English government. For example, in 1536 he conveyed a message from the Swiss reformer Heinrich Bullinger to Cranmer and in 1539 he carried messages from Henry VIII to Christopher Mount, an agent in Germany. In 1536, Anne Boleyn supported him in becoming a freeman of the City of London's Stationer's Company and in 1542 he printed his first work in London. In 1543, he set up his printing press in St Paul's Churchyard. The press could be identified by the sign of the Brazen Serpent, a device used by Strasbourg printer Conrad Neobarius. Wolf went on to publish works by Archbishops Cranmer and Parker, the antiquarian John Leland and a 1544 account by Edward Seymour of the expedition into Scotland. Andrew Pettegree writes of how he cemented "ties with the reformist political elite".[15]

Going back to Thomas Tebold, there are four letters written by him in Letters and Papers: one to Thomas Cranmer and three to Thomas Boleyn. Having read Tebold's letters and having found out about Wolf, I just cannot see how Thomas Boleyn can be described as a conservative Catholic or as disagreeing with Anne and George's reformist beliefs. On the contrary, I feel that he was actually their influence. I can't see how Tebold would risk sending Thomas Boleyn a work by Marot or writing to him about the religious situation for reformers on the Continent if Thomas Boleyn was not a fellow reformer. It doesn't make sense.

Anne Boleyn

As far as books are concerned, Eric Ives writes of how we know about the existence of nine books related to Anne and George Boleyn. He says "Seven are religious and six of those are reformist in character; the one exception is an early and somewhat inferior Book of Hours. Five are editions of the Bible or parts of it (including a Tyndale New Testament)... Anne's own books, therefore, demonstrate reformist sympathies and particularly enthusiasm for the Bible." Anne and George would never have risked owning books viewed as heretical if they were not interested in reading them and learning from them.

As well as having a copy of Tyndale's English Bible, which she kept available to her household, Anne owned five French reformist books:-

- *La Saincte Bible en Francoys* (Antwerp 1534). – This was the first French translation of the Bible and was produced by the French theologian and humanist Jacques Lefèvre d'Etaples.
- *The Pistellis and Gospelles for the LII Sondayes in the Yere*, by Lefèvre d'Etaples (Paris, ca.1525) – Ives describes this as a part copy, part English translation of Lefevre's *Epistres and Evangiles des cinquante et deux semaines de l'an* or "Epistles and Gospels for the 52 weeks of the year". A book of Bible

readings to take the reader or preacher through the year.

- *Le livre des psaulmes* - A book of Psalms thought to have been translated into French by Louis de Berquin who was burned at the stake after being accused of heresy by the Sorbonne. "Berquin would have been a second Luther, had he found in Francis I. a second Elector," said Theodore Beza, the French theologian who was a disciple of John Calvin.

- *L'Ecclesiaste*, or The Ecclesiaste, (Alençon, 1530) which Ives describes as a "hybrid version of a Lefèvre publication, his translation of a commentary by Johannes Brenz.

- *Le pasteur évangélique* (Le Sermon du Bon Pasteur) – by Clément Marot, the famous French Reformer.

Two of Anne Boleyn's reformist books were presented to her by her brother, George, who had actually translated them. The first is *Les Epistres et Evangiles* which James Carley thinks "was very likely a New Year's Gift, composed and executed in the autumn of 1532 as a tribute to Anne's elevation as marquess." It consisted of the dates of the liturgical calendar followed by the Epistle or Gospel in French and was derived from a book written by Jacques Lefèvre d'Étaples. Carley explains that *Les Epistres et Evangiles* is important as a codification of the evangelical doctrine established at Meaux in the 1520s, based on a principle of making the Gospel accessible to the laity and an emphasis of the centrality of Christ above the tradition of the Church." It was condemned by the Sorbonne because of "its possible Lutheran overtones". Meaux was the diocese of Bishop Guillaume Briçonnet, who was committed to reforming his diocese, and who invited a number of evangelical humanists to work in the bishopric to help implement his reform program. This group of humanists became known as the "Circle of Meaux", and included Josse van Clichtove, Guillaume Farel, Jacques Lefèvre d'Étaples, Martial Mazurier, Gérard Roussel, and François Vatable. The members of the Meaux circle were of different talents, but they generally emphasized the study of the Bible and a return to the theology of the early Church. Briçonnet was an evangelical and a humanist, and actually condemned Martin Luther. George's book was based on the second edition of Lefèvre's book published by Simon Du Bois in 1530-1532.

The second book presented to Anne by George was *The Ecclesiaste*, written between 1533-36 when Anne was queen. The commentaries were in English and the text derived from Lefèvre's *L'Ecclesiaste* printed by Simon Du Bois at Alençon ca.1531. Carley explains: "Translated by Lefèvre, the commentary derives from Johannes Brenz... Brenz was evangelical in his orientation; by nature his enterprise emphasizes the pre-eminence of the Bible itself over the traditions and sacraments of the Church."[16] Johannes Brenz was a German theologian and reformer whose Bible commentaries received praise from Martin Luther, a man by whom he was influenced. Brenz was investigated in 1522 for teaching Lutheran ideas; in 1525 he wrote *Syngramma Suevicum* which attacked his former teacher, reformer Oecolampadius, and defended the doctrine of the real presence of Christ's body and blood in the Lord's Supper.

We know that George translated these books for Anne because he wrote a dedication to her in the first one, saying that it was from her "moost lovyng and fryndely brother". He also wrote that he undertook the translation at her request: "by your commandement". The second book was definitely prepared by the same person. Eric Ives notes the "obvious similarities" in the penmanship, the fact that the text is in French but the exhortation in English, and the use in both manuscripts of blue for editorial matter. Ives even wonders if George had them produced by Flemish trained craftsmen in a studio under Anne's patronage.

In his execution speech, George described himself as "a settar forthe of the word of God"; these manuscripts are definite examples of him promoting reform and spreading God's message.

Another book related to Anne Boleyn is the Hever Castle Book of Hours. It is in that book that we can see not only Anne's signature but also the inscription "le temps viendra": "the time will come", under an illumination of the Last Judgement. These words are an abbreviation of the proverb "a day will come that shall pay for all", a precis of part of *The Ecclesiaste*, which says "the judgement of God shall be general and universal where as all things shall be discovered and nothing shall abide hidden, whether it be good or evil."[17] The fact that Anne wrote this inscription in her own Book of Hours shows that these words had real meaning to Anne and were something that she was pondering deeply.

As I said earlier, the Boleyn siblings' book collection consisted of works by French reformers. Two of those reformers are Clément Marot and Jacques Lefèvre d'Étaples, so here are some facts about them:

Clément Marot

- Marot was the famous 16th century French poet who put into verse the Biblical Psalms that were to be sung all over France and become the well-known Huguenot Psalter.
- His father was court poet to Anne of Brittany
- Marguerite of Angouleme/Navarre was his sponsor. She appointed him valet de chambre, court poet, and her secretary.
- In 1526, he was imprisoned for religious infraction at Châtelet while Marguerite was in Spain negotiating the release of Francis I. Francis had Marot released on his return.
- Marot's religious views caused him to be charged with heresy in 1529 and sent to prison. He was released by Francis I, who then chose him as his court poet
- In 1534, when the French King turned against reform, Marot was in danger both because of his attacks on the conservative religious views of the Sorbonne and for his reformist convictions. His home was raided, and forbidden

tracts and a translated copy of the Bible were found. These were hanging offences, but Marot had fled to Marguerite's court at Nérac, a known shelter for those with reformist beliefs. Marguerite was also under suspicion, so she sent him to Italy to the court of her cousin Renée of Ferrara. However, Renée's husband was a Catholic so Marot couldn't stay there long; he soon moved to Venice, a city known for tolerance.

- In 1539, he offered François I the manuscript of the first thirty Psalms. They were set to music by using famous or secular tunes and were tremendously successful, both at the court and all over France.

- In 1542, Marot was forced to take refuge in Geneva with Calvin

Lefèvre d'Étaples

- Jacques Lefèvre d'Étaples was a French theologian and humanist and is viewed as a precursor of the Protestant movement in France. He saw himself as a Catholic seeking to reform the Church within, rather than as someone trying to separate from it.

- His 1517 work *de Maria Magdalena et triduo Christi disceptatio*, which argued that Mary the sister of Lazarus, Mary Magdalene, and the penitent woman who anointed Christ's feet were different people, provoked violent controversy and was condemned by the Sorbonne and Bishop John Fisher.

- In 1520, he moved from Paris to Meaux, where he was appointed vicar-general to Bishop Briconnet in 1523 and where he also published his French version of the New Testament.

- His works were often viewed as heretical, but he was protected by Francis I and Marguerite of Angoulême.

- He was a prolific Bible translator and emphasized the literal sense of Scripture over the medieval fourfold approach, which emphasized the allegorical interpretation. Ives writes of "the spiritual revivalism and non-schismatic reform of Jacques Lefèvre d'Étaples."

- His approach to reform, reforming the church from within, seems to have had a real impact on Anne's beliefs and way of thinking.

Marguerite of Angoulême

One person that Lefèvre and Marot have in common is Marguerite of Angoulême, Queen Consort of Navarre and sister of Francis I. She was a famous Renaissance figure and is known for her patronage of the arts and her strong religious views. Marguerite wrote *Le Miroir l'âme pécheresse* ("The Mirror of the Sinful Soul"). Coincidentally, this is the same poem which Anne Boleyn's daughter, Elizabeth, translated as a gift for her stepmother, Catherine Parr. This poem is a mystical verse which combines evangelical reformist ideas with Marguerite's idea of her relationship with God as a familial one: God as her brother, father or lover.

Simon Du Bois was the printer of Lefèvre's books, which were later translated by George Boleyn. Du Bois was a protégé of Margaret d'Angoulême. James Carley comments that "during her brief period of ascendancy, Anne's name was often associated with that of Margaret [Marguerite] of Angoulême" :

- In 1532, Henry VIII hoped that Marguerite would come to Calais to meet Anne

- In 1534, George Boleyn took a message to Marguerite concerning Henry's cancelled meeting with Francis

- In 1535, Anne sent a message to Marguerite stating that "her greatest wish, next to having a son, was to see you again."

- Nicholas Bourbon and Clément Marot were both protégés of Marguerite and were also linked to Anne Boleyn. Anne

Figure 42 - Clement Marot

Figure 43 - Jaques Lefèvre d'Etaples

helped Bourbon flee from France and employed him as a tutor for her ward, Henry Carey; she also read works by Marot. Carley points out, too, that in Anne's copy of *Le Pasteur Evangélique,* Marot "specifically linked Henry and Francis, Anne and Margaret."

Carley believes, and I agree with him, that Anne's links with books printed by Du Bois, whose patron was Marguerite, and with French evangelicals, both point to Marguerite being "an intellectual model for Anne during the 1530s." We cannot say for certain that Anne spent significant time with Marguerite in France, but it's possible; she clearly had an impact on Anne.

Anne Boleyn's Actions

Anne Boleyn's own actions provide evidence of her evangelical faith:

- Anne had links with known reformers - Edward Fox, Hugh Latimer, William Barlow, Nicholas Shaxton, Edward Crome, Thomas Garrett and William Betts are just some of the reformers who gained positions due to Anne's help and patronage.

- One of Anne's silkwomen was the wife of mercer Stephen Vaughan, an evangelical agent of Thomas Cromwell. Cromwell used Vaughan to negotiate with Bible translator William Tyndale in Antwerp. Another silkwoman, Jane Wilkinson, helped William Latymer, Anne Boleyn's chaplain, import religious works for Anne.[18]

- Anne rescued Nicholas Bourbon from trouble in France and was also petitioned for help by those in trouble for possessing heretical books. Bourbon praised and thanked Anne for her help in his verses: "A poor man, I lie shut in this dark prison: There is no one who would be able or would dare to bring help: Only you,

Oh, Queen: you, Oh noble nymph both can and will dare:
As one whom the King and God Himself loves."[19]

- William Latymer recorded Anne helping a French woman, Mrs Marye, who was forced to flee to England because of her reformist faith. According to Latymer, the woman said that she had "gayned more by her banishment then she coulde have hoped for at home emongest her deare frendes and naturall countrye men of Fraunce."[20]

- Anne's support of poor relief. Maria Dowling points out that "Poor relief was both a humanist and a Lollard preoccupation, and Anne was, according to all her panegyrists, outstandingly generous to the poor."[21] This quality was emphasised in *The Ecclesiaste*.

- Dissemination of the Bible. Anne believed that the Bible should be available to everyone to read in English and supported the translation and trade of such Bibles. She kept an English Bible open in her apartments and encouraged her ladies to read it. She also gave each of her maids a book of devotions to hang on their girdles "for their constant use and meditation."[22] William Latymer recorded that Anne told her chaplains "I have carefully chosen you to be the lanterns and light of my court" to teach her household "above all things to embrace the wholesome doctrine and infallible knowledge of Christ's gospel."

- Her refusal of Tristram Revell's book. Revell's version of Lambertus' *Farrago Rerum Theologicarum* was presented to Anne by Revell through William Latymer in 1536, but Anne refused it. The book denied transubstantiation, salvation through good deeds and prayers for the dead, and it is not known whether Anne refused it because she didn't agree with it or because it was too risky for her to endorse it. Eric Ives writes that her refusal to accept the dedication of Revell's book shows that "she had no time for radicals"; but she had also just miscarried a son, so it may have been a case of bad timing.

- John Skip's Sermon. On Passion Sunday 1536, Anne Boleyn's almoner, John Skip, preached a rather controversial sermon in front of the King. Skip's theme was "Quis ex vobis arguet me de peccato?", or "Which of you can convict me of sin?", and was an attack on the King's council and the advice the council was giving the King. It was, however, not a reformist sermon. In preaching about the abuses of ancient and traditional ceremonies, Skip said that it was right to get rid of the abuses of the ceremonies but that it would be a "greite pyte" if the ceremonies themselves were taken away:

"As for theis litle ceremonys of the churiches (he sayde) I am suire their is none of you that wold haue them takon awey and no marvell therof for they cost you litle and litle ye shall gayne by the takyng awey of them."

Skip was defending the ceremonies of the church and attacking its abuses. He wanted superstition to go away and pure religion to replace it. The sermon was also an attack on the decision to secularize monastic endowments instead of diverting them to reforming purposes, something which Anne had argued with Thomas Cromwell about.

- Anne's link to Hans Holbein the Younger's painting "The Ambassadors". The painting is packed with symbolism about religious division and the hope of reunion. It is linked to Anne because she was Holbein's patron at the time and because the date shown on the pillar dial in the painting was 11th April 1533. This was both Good Friday and the day that the royal court were informed that Anne was queen. Eric Ives wonders if we can guess from the themes of the painting that Anne had sympathy with "the reunionist position".[23]

George Boleyn

We also have many clues as to George Boleyn's evangelical beliefs:

- Books. The books that I've listed under Anne's name previously were books that belonged to both siblings.

- George's translations of Lefèvre's books. He obviously had copies of the printed books from which his translations were derived, and spent a significant amount of time working on the translations.

- His execution speech. In his scaffold speech on 17th May 1536, George described himself as a "setter forth of the word of God", which implied that the two books he translated for Anne were not the only religious works he had completed. Ives describes his speech as "the language of Zion"; it was just as if George was preaching a sermon to the crowd. He said "And yet, my masters all, I have one thing for to say to you, men do come and say that I have been a setter forth of the word of God, and one that have favoured the Gospel of Christ; and because I would not that God's word should be slandered by me, I say unto you all, that if I had followed God's word in deed as I did read it and set it forth to my power, I had not come to this. I did read the Gospel of Christ, but I did not follow it; if I had, I had been a living man among you: therefore I pray you, masters all, for God's sake stick to the truth and follow it, for one good follower is worth three readers, as God knoweth."

- Historian James Carley believes that George may have been responsible for Anne sharing with the King a copy of Simon Fish's *Supplication for the Beggars*. This was an evangelical and revolutionary 16-page pamphlet attacking the Catholic Church and accusing it of many crimes. Simon Fish contested the existence of purgatory and the sale of indulgences and also accused the Church of holding half of England's wealth.

- George's evangelism – As I stated earlier, Chapuys spoke of how, when he met with George Boleyn in April 1536, he avoided "all occasions of entering into Lutheran discussions, from which he [George] could not refrain". It seems that George took every opportunity to evangelize.

The Other Boleyns

Elizabeth Boleyn's faith is a mystery; but obviously, she was married to a man with reformist views and acted as chaperone to Anne when she was courting Henry and promoting reform. We just cannot say, though, because we have no evidence of her beliefs.

Mary Boleyn, too, is a mystery. Her second husband, William Stafford, and his second wife, Dorothy Stafford, went into exile in Geneva during the Catholic Mary I's reign and the reformer John Calvin stood as godfather for their youngest son, John. In her book on Mary Boleyn, Alison Weir wonders if Stafford's involvement in the fall of Catherine Howard – by giving information about Dereham – was due to him having reformist views, that he perhaps "collaborated with the reformists at court in bringing down the Catholic Howards." Since Mary Boleyn's marriage to him in 1534 was a love match, they may have both been interested in reform. Mary Boleyn's daughter, Catherine Carey, was married to Sir Francis Knollys, a man who had links with Protestant men, and the couple went into exile in Mary I's reign. Mary's son, Henry Carey, was tutored by the French reformer Nicholas Bourbon so it is likely that that had an effect on him. He also had an active political career under Elizabeth I so would have been outwardly "Protestant" whatever his inner beliefs. His daughter, Margaret, married Sir Edward Hoby, a man known for publishing Protestant works in the reign of James I. Of course, Mary's second husband, son and daughter being reformers does not necessarily mean that Mary shared their beliefs, but she was certainly exposed to them.

Anne Boleyn's Religious Stance

Anne Boleyn does not fit the label of Protestant as we use it today, but that does not mean that she was a conservative Catholic. She was neither a radical, a Lutheran nor a Calvinist, but she was an evangelical and her idea of reform was French in its 'flavour'. Eric Ives concludes that "Her attitude would be characteristic of all shades of English evangelical reform for at least a decade more: real spiritual experience, yes; the priority of faith, yes; access to the Bible, yes; reform of abuses and superstition, yes; but heretical views on the miracle of the altar, no." England was on the verge of a true reformation and Anne died before it really took off. When you consider that the Council of Trent was still trying to define Catholicism and Protestantism as late as the 1560s, it is impossible to label Thomas, Anne and George, who died in the 1530s. If you really have to label them, then the correct label would be "Evangelical".

Notes and Sources

1   Foxe, The Acts and Monuments of the Christian Church, 6:321.
2   "Letters and Papers, Foreign and Domestic, Henry VIII, Volume 5: 1531-1532," n. 148.
3   "Letters and Papers, Foreign and Domestic, Henry VIII, Volume 10 - January-June 1536," n. 699.
4   "Calendar of State Papers, Spain, Volume 5 Part 2: 1536-1538," n. 43.
5   Ives, The Life and Death of Anne Boleyn.
6   Carley, The Books of King Henry VIII and His Wives.
7   Dowling, "Anne Boleyn and Reform."
8   Bernard, Anne Boleyn, chap. 7.
9   Weir, Mary Boleyn: The Great and Infamous Whore, 208.
10   Loades, The Boleyns: The Rise and Fall of a Tudor Family, 130.
11   Denny, Anne Boleyn: A New Life of England's Tragic Queen.
12   "Index of Kent Wills."
13   Ives, The Life and Death of Anne Boleyn, 263.
14   "Letters and Papers, Foreign and Domestic, Henry VIII, Volume 4: 1524-1530," n. 6304.
15   Pettegree, "Wolfe, Reyner (d. in or before 1574)."
16   Carley, The Books of King Henry VIII and His Wives.

17   Ives, The Life and Death of Anne Boleyn, 277.

18   Dowling, Humanism in the Age of Henry VIII, 241.

19   Ives, "A Frenchman at the Court of Anne Boleyn."

20   Dowling, "William Latymer's Cronickille of Anne Bulleyne," 56.

21   Dowling, "Anne Boleyn and Reform."

22   Cavendish, The Life of Cardinal Wolsey, Volume 2, 2:201.

23   Ives, "Anne Boleyn and the Early Reformation in England."

Further Reading

Thank you for reading this book. You can of course read more on Anne Boleyn at www.TheAnneBoleynFiles.com and in The Anne Boleyn Collection, but here are some books I highly recommend:

- **The Life and Death of Anne Boleyn**, Eric Ives
- **The Lady in the Tower**, Alison Weir
- **Six Wives: The Queens of Henry VIII**, David Starkey
- **The Anne Boleyn Papers** (published previously as Anne Boleyn in Her Own Words and the Words of Those Who Knew Her), Elizabeth Norton
- **The Fall of Anne Boleyn: A Countdown**, Claire Ridgway
- **Jane Boleyn: The Infamous Lady Rochford**, Julia Fox
- **The Reformation Experience**, Eric Ives
- **In the Footsteps of Anne Boleyn**, Sarah Morris and Natalie Grueninger
- **Henry VIII**, J. J. Scarisbrick

Do check out the Resources page of *TheAnneBoleynFiles.com* and the Extras page of *www.TheAnneBoleynCollection.com* for more book recommendations and links to sources.

Illustrations

Bibliography

A

Amt, Emilie. The *Accession of Henry II in England: Royal Government Restored, 1149-1159*. Boydell Press, 1993.

"Anne Boleyn, Six Wives Info." *Six Wives Info*, http://www.sixwives.info/anne-boleyn.htm

Archaeologia: Or Miscellaneous Tracts Relating to Antiquity. Vol. III. London, 1775.

Ascoli, Georges. *La Grande-Bretagne Devant L'opinion Française Depuis La Guerre de Cent Ans Jusqu'à La Fin Du XVIe Siècle*. Paris, 1927.

Aubrey, John. *The Natural History and Antiquities of the County of Surrey: Begun in the Year 1673*. Vol. V. London: E Curll, 1719.

B

Bailey, Thomas, and Hill, Richard. *The Life and Death of the Renowned John Fisher, Bishop of Rochester, Who Was Beheaded on Tower Hill, the 22nd of June 1535*. London, 1655.

Baker, J A. *The Reports of Sir John Spelman*. Selden Society, 1977.

Baldwin Smith, Lacey. *Catherine Howard*. Amberley, 2009.

Bapst, Edmond. *Deux Gentilshommes-Poetes de La Cour de Henry VIII*. Paris, 1891.

Baron de Reiffenberg. *Chronique Métrique de Chastellain et de Molinet: Avec Des Notices Sur Ces Auteurs et Des Remarques Sur Le Texte Corrigé*. Bruxelles: J. M. Lacrosse, 1836.

Bell, Doyne C. *Notices of the Historic Persons Buried in the Chapel of St Peter Ad Vincula in the Tower of London*, 1877.

Bernard, G.W. *Anne Boleyn: Fatal Attractions*. Yale University Press, 2011.

Bernard, G.W. *The King's Reformation*. Yale University Press, 2007.

Bevan, Richard. *"Anne Boleyn and the Downfall of Her Family."* *BBC History*, http://www.bbc.co.uk/history/british/tudors/anne_boleyn_01.shtml

Blomefield, Francis. *An Essay Towards a Topographical History of the County of Norfolk*. Vol. 3. London, 1805.

Borman, Tracy. *Elizabeth's Women: The Hidden Story of the Virgin Queen*. Vintage, 2010.

Brenan, Gerald, and Edward Philips Statham. *The House of Howard*. London: Hutchinson, 1907.

Brodeau, Julien. *La Vie de Maistre Charles Du-Moulin Advocat Au Parlement de Paris*. Paris: Jean Guinard, 1654.

Bruce, J (ed.), and T T (ed.) Perowne. *Correspondence of Matthew Parker*. Parker Society, 1853.

Bruce, Marie Louise. *Anne Boleyn*. Collins, 1972.

Bullen, Frank. *"Anne Boleyn A Norfolk Girl?"* Rootsweb, Ancestry. com, March 2008. http://archiver.rootsweb.ancestry.com/th/read/norfolk/2008-03/1206716205

Burke, John. *A General and Heraldic Dictionary of the Peerage and Baronetage of the British Empire. Vol. 2*. H. Colburn and R. Bentley, 1832.

C

"Calendar of Carew Manuscripts, 1515-1574." Longmans, Green, and co., 1867.

"Calendar of State Papers, Spain", 13 Volumes. London. 1862 - 1954

"Calendar of State Papers, Spain: Further Supplement to Volumes 1 and 2", ed. G. Mattingly. London 1940

"Calendar of State Papers Foreign, Elizabeth", 23 Volumes, London. 1863 - 1950

"Calendar of State Papers and Manuscripts, Venice", 39 Volumes. London

Camden, William. *Annales Rerum Anglicarum et Hibernicarum Regnante Elizabetha.* 1615,

Camden, William. *Annales Rerum Anglicarum et Hibernicarum, Regnante Elizabetha Ad Annum Salutis M.D. LXXXIX,* 1615.

Carley, James P. *The Books of King Henry VIII and His Wives.* British Library, 2005.

Carte, Thomas. *An History of the Life of James Duke of Ormonde.* Vol. 1. London: 1736,

Carte, Thomas. *The Life of James, Duke of Ormond.* The University Press, 1851.

Cavendish, George. *The Life of Cardinal Wolsey.* 2nd ed. London: Samuel Weller Singer, 1827.

Cavendish, George. *The Life of Cardinal Wolsey, Volume 2.* Vol. 2. Samuel Weller Singer, 1825.

Chadwick, Justin. *The Other Boleyn Girl,* 2008.

Chapman, Hester W. *Anne Boleyn.* Jonathan Cape, 1974.

Chapuys, Eustace. *"Letter to Charles V, 31 December 1530,"* P.C. 226, i. fol. 109. Vienna Archives.

Cherry, Clare. "George Boleyn's Sexuality." *The Anne Boleyn Files,* April 13, 2012. http://www.theanneboleynfiles.com/george-boleyns-sexuality/.

Cholakian, Rouben, and Mary Skemp, eds. *Marguerite (Queen, Consort of Henry II, King of Navarre): Selected Writings (Bilingual Edition).* The University of Chicago Press, 2008.

Clifford, Henry. *The Life of Jane Dormer, Duchess of Feria.* London: Burns and Oates, 1887.

Coote, C. *The History of England, from the Earliest Dawn of Record to the Peace of MDCCLXXXIII.* 9 vols., 1791.

Correspondance de L'empereur Maximilien Ier et de Marguerite d'Autriche, Sa Fille, Gouvernante de Pays-Bas, de 1507 à 1519. Vol. 2. Jules Renouard, 1839.

Cressy, David. *Birth, Marriage, and Death: Ritual, Religion, and the Life-Cycle in Tudor and Stuart England.* Oxford University Press, 1999.

Curtis, Edmun. *"Calendar of Ormond Deeds, Volume IV: 1509-1547,"* 43 1932.

D

Dean, William H. *"Sir Thomas Boleyn: The Courtier Diplomat (1477-1539)."* West Virginia University, 1987.

Debrett, John. *Debrett's Peerage of England, Scotland, and Ireland.* Revised, Corrected and Continued by G. W. Collen. Vol. II, Scotland and Ireland. London: William Pickering, 1840.

De Lisle, Leanda. *The Sisters Who Would Be Queen.* Ballantine Books, 2009.

Denny, Joanna. *Anne Boleyn: A New Life of England's Tragic Queen.* Piatkus, 2005.

Dewhurst, Sir John. "The Alleged Miscarriages of Catherine of Aragon and Anne Boleyn." *Medical History* 28 (January 1984): 49–56.

Dowling, Maria. "Anne Boleyn and Reform." *Journal of Ecclesiastical History* 35, no. No. 1 (January 1984).

Dowling, ed. Maria. "William Latymer's Cronickille of Anne Bulleyne." *Camden Miscellany XXX* 39 (1990): 23–65.

Dowling, Maria. "Anne Boleyn and Reform." *Journal of Ecclesiastical History* 35, no. No. 1 (January 1984).

Dowling, Maria. *Humanism in the Age of Henry VIII.* Routledge, 1986.

Duchess of Cleveland. *The Battle Abbey Roll with Some Account of the Norman Lineages in Three Volumes. Vol. 1.* London: J. Murray, 1889.

E

Edwards, John. *Mary I: England's Catholic Queen.* Yale University Press, 2011.

Elton, G.R. *England Under the Tudors.* Routledge, 1991.

Emerson, Kate. "Muriel Howard." *A Who's Who of Tudor Women*, http://www.kateemersonhistoricals.com/TudorWomenHi-Hu.htm

F

Flaccus, Marcus Verrius, and Sextus Pompeius Festus. *M. Verrii Flacci Quae Extant: Et Sexti Pompeii Festi De Verborum Significatione.* Vol. XX, 1826.

Fox, Julia. *Jane Boleyn: The Infamous Lady Rochford.* Phoenix, 2007.

Fox, Julia. "Jane Boleyn: The Infamous Lady Rochford - A Guest Post." *The Anne Boleyn Files*, June 3, 2011.

Fox (Foxe), John. *Fox's Book of Martyrs: Acts and Monuments of the Church in Three Volumes.* Vol. II. London: George Virtue, 1851.

Foxe, John. *The Acts and Monuments of the Christian Church*. Vol. 6. Ex-classics Project, 2009, http://www.exclassics.com

Frame, Robin. *"Butler, James, First Earl of Ormond (c. 1305-1338)."* Oxford Dictionary of National Biography. Oxford University Press, 2004.

Freeman-Mitford, Lord Redesdale, Algernon Bertram. *A Tragedy in Stone and Other Papers*. London: John Lane, 1913.

Friedmann, Paul. *Anne Boleyn, A Chapter of English History, 1527-1536*. London: Macmillan, 1884.

Froude, James Anthony. *History of England from the Fall of Wolsey to the Defeat of the Spanish Armada*. Vol. 11: Reign of Elizabeth Part V,

G

Garrett Fawcett, Millicent. Five Famous French Women, 1905.

Gray, Floyd. *Gender, Rhetoric, and Print Culture in French Renaissance Writing*. Cambridge University Press, 2000.

Gregory, Philippa. *The Boleyn Inheritance*. Pocket Books, 2006.

Gregory, Philippa. *The Other Boleyn Girl*. Touchstone, 2001.

Gruffudd, Elis. "Gruffudd's Chronicle," The National Library of Wales.

Gunn, S .J. "Knyvet, Sir Thomas (c.1485–1512)." *Oxford Dictionary of National Biography*. Oxford University Press, 2004.

Guy, John. "The Lady in the Tower: The Fall of Anne Boleyn by Alison Weir - Sunday Times Review." *The Sunday Times*, November 1, 2009.

H

Hall, Edward. *Hall's Chronicle*. London: J Johnson, 1809.

Herbert, Edward. *The Life and Raigne of King Henry the Eighth*. London, 1649.

Harpsfield, Nicholas. *A Treatise on the Pretended Divorce Between Henry VIII and Catharine of Aragon*. Camden Society, 1878.

Hirst, Michale. "The Tudors." Showtime, 2010 2007.

Holinshed, Raphael. *Holinshed's Chronicles of England, Scotland, and Ireland*. Vol. 6. London: J Johnson, 1808.

Hore, Herbert J., and Rev. James Graves. *The Social State of the Southern and Eastern Counties of Ireland in the 16th Century*. Dublin: The University Press, 1870.

Hume, Martin Andrew Sharp. *Chronicle of King Henry VIII. of England: Being a Contemporary Record of Some of the Principal Events of the Reigns of Henry VIII. and Edward VI.* Written in Spanish by an Unknown Hand. G. Bell and sons, 1889.

I

"Index of Kent Wills," http://vulpeculox.net/history/willst.htm
Ives, Eric. "A Frenchman at the Court of Anne Boleyn." *History Today* 48, no. 8 (1998).
Ives, Eric. "Anne Boleyn and the Early Reformation in England." *The Historical Journal* 37, no. 2 (1994): 389–400.
Ives, Eric. "Anne Boleyn on Trial Again." *Journal of Ecclesiastical History* 62, no. 4 (October 2011).
Ives, Eric. "The Fall of Anne Boleyn Reconsidered." *English Historical Review* (1992).
Ives, Eric. *The Life and Death of Anne Boleyn*. New edition. Wiley-Blackwell, 2004.

K

Kramer, Kyra Cornelius. *Blood Will Tell: A Medical Explanation of the Tyranny of Henry VIII*. Ash Wood Press, 2012.

L

Léchaudé-d'Anisy, Amédée-Louis, and Hippolyte-Jean-Jacques-René marquis de Sainte-Marie. Recherches Sur Le Domesday, *Ou Liber Censualis d'Angleterre. Tome Premier.* Caen: C M Lesaulnier, 1842.
Lindberg, Carter, ed. "Jacques Lefèvre d'Étaples by Guy Bedouelle." In *The Reformation Theologians: An Introduction to Theology in the Early Modern Period*. Wiley-Blackwell, 2001.
"Letters and Papers, Foreign and Domestic, Henry VIII", ed. J.S.Brewer, J.Gairdner and R.H. Brodie, 21 Vols. London. 1862 - 1932
Lewis, Jane Elizabeth. *The Trial of Mary Queen of Scots: A Brief History with Documents*. Bedford, 1998.
Loades, David. *The Boleyns: The Rise and Fall of a Tudor Family*. Amberley, 2011.
Loke, William. *"Account of Materials Furnished for the Use of Anne Boleyn and Princess Elizabeth 1535-36,"* http://babel.

hathitrust.org/cgi/pt?view=image;size=100;id=nnc1.cu041 47324;page=root;seq=3;num=1

Lofts, Norah. *Anne Boleyn*. Orbis Publishing, 1979.

M

Madams, Phillipa. *"Carnis Molem,"* December 2, 2012.

McIntosh, J.L. "From Heads of Household to Heads of State: The Preaccession Households of Mary and Elizabeth Tudor 1516-1558." English Historical Review CXXVI, no. 518: 151–153.

Micraelius, Johannes. *Lexicon Philosophicum Terminorum Philosophis Usitatorum*, 1661.

"Miscarriage Statitsics." *Tommy's*, http://www.tommys.org/page. aspx?pid=383

Mantel, Hilary. "Anne Boleyn: Witch, Bitch, Temptress, Feminist." *The Guardian*, May 11, 2012.

"Molar Pregnancy," http://www.nhs.uk/conditions/Molar-pregnancy/Pages/Introduction.aspx

"Muriel Howard," http://histfam.familysearch.org/getperson. php?personID=I17044&tree=Nixon

N

Nicholas, Thomas. *Annals & Antiquities of the Counties & County Families of Wales. Vol. 2*. London: Longmans, Green, and co., 1872.

Norton, Elizabeth. *The Boleyn Women*. Amberley, 2013.

O

"Odd Food and Drink Facts." *Unexplainable.net*, http://www. unexplainable.net/info-theories/odd_food_and_drink_ facts_i.php

"Oxford Dictionary of National Biography." Oxford University Press no. 2004 (n.d.).

"Oyer and Terminer." *Merriam-Webster*, http://www.merriam-webster.com/dictionary/oyer%20and%20terminer

P

Paget, Hugh. *"The Youth of Anne Boleyn."* Bulletin of the Institute of Historical Research no. LIV (1981).

Percival, Florence. *Chaucer's Legendary Good Women*. Cambridge University Press, 1998.

Pettegree, Andrew. "Wolfe, Reyner (d. in or before 1574)." *Oxford Dictionary of National Biography*. Oxford University Press, 2004.

Pierre de Bourdeille, seigneur de Brantôme. *Illustrious Dames of the Court of the Valois Kings,* The Lamb Publishing Co., 1912

Pollen, J.H. *"Dr. Niholas Sander."* English Historical Review VI, no. XXI (1891): 36–47.

"Pregnancy Loss." *March of Dimes*, http://www.marchofdimes. com/loss/miscarriage.aspx

R

"Red Roses for Anne Boleyn." *Green Fingers.com*, http://www. greenfingers.com/articledisplay.asp?id=627

"Rhesus Disease." *NHS Choices*, http://www.nhs.uk/Conditions/ Rhesus-disease/Pages/Introduction.aspx

Ridgway, Claire. *"Anne Boleyn Myths Coming Soon."* The Anne Boleyn Files, January 11, 2013. http://www. theanneboleynfiles.com/anne-boleyn-myths-coming-soon/

Ridgway, Claire. *The Anne Boleyn Collection*. MadeGlobal Publishing, 2012.

Roberts, Marilyn. *"Trouble in Paradise,"* http://www.queens- haven.co.uk/anne-mowbray-trouble-in-paradise.htm

Rose, Elliot. Cases of Conscience: Alternatives Open to Recusants and Puritans Under Elizabeth I and James I. Cambridge University Press, 1975.

Ross, David. "Winchester Castle." *Britain Express*, http://www. britainexpress.com/counties/hampshire/winchester/castle. htm

Round, John Horace. *The Early Life of Anne Boleyn: A Critical Essay*, 1886.

Russell, Gareth. "May 17th 1536 - Deaths on Tower Hill." *Confessions of a Ci-devant*, May 18, 2010. http:// garethrussellcidevant.blogspot.com.es/2010/05/may-17th- 1536-deaths-on-tower-hill.html

Russell, Gareth. "The Age of Anne Boleyn." *Confessions of a Ci- devant*, April 6, 2010. http://garethrussellcidevant.blogspot. com.es/2010/04/age-of-anne-boleyn.html

S

Sander, Nicholas. *De Origine Ac Progressu Schismatis Anglicani*, 1585.

Sander, Nicholas. *New Advent Catholic Encyclopedia*, http:// www.newadvent.org/cathen/13435d.htm

Sander, Nicholas. *Rise and Growth of the Anglican Schism*. Burns and Oates, 1877.

Scarisbrick, J.J. *Henry VIII*. Methuen, 1968.

Schofield, John. *The Rise and Fall of Thomas Cromwell: Henry VIII's Most Faithful Servant*. The History Press, 2008.

Sergeant, Philip W. *The Life of Anne Boleyn*. London: Hutchinson, 1923.

Sharp, Jane. *The Midwives Book: Or the Whole Art of Midwifry Discovered*. Edited by Elaine Hobby. Oxford University Press, 1999.

Shaw, William A. *The Knights of England: A Complete Record from the Earliest Time to the Present Day of the Knights of All the Orders of Chivalry in England, Scotland, and Ireland*. Vol. 1, 1906.

Sim, Alison. *The Tudor Housewife*. The History Press, 2010.

Skelton, John. *The Book of the Laurel*. University of Delaware Press, 1990.

St Clare Byrne, Muriel, ed. *"The Lisle Letters, Volume 5."* The University of Chicago Press, 1981.

Starkey, David. *Elizabeth: Apprenticeship*. Vintage Books, 2001.

Starkey, David. *Six Wives: The Queens of Henry VIII*. Vintage, 2004.

"Status Details for Hundred." *A Vision of Britain through Time*, http://www.visionofbritain.org.uk/types/status_page. jsp?unit_status=Hundred

Stewart, Hannah. "The Relief of the Poor Bill, 1535." *The Thomas Cromwell Experience*, http://masterthomascromwell. wordpress.com/2011/07/27/the-relief-of-the-poor-bill-1535/

Strickland, Agnes. *Lives of the Queens of England*. Vol. 2, 1864.

"Survey of London: Volume 23: Lambeth: South Bank and Vauxhall," http://www.british-history.ac.uk/report. aspx?compid=47057

T

The Anne Boleyn Files, http://www.theanneboleynfiles.com/

The Maner of the Tryumphe of Caleys and Bulleyn and The Noble Tryumphaunt Coronacyon of Quene Anne, Wyfe Unto the Most Noble Kynge Henry VIII. Wynkyn de Worde, 1533.

The Manuscripts of J. Eliot Hodgkin. Vol. Fifteenth Report: Appendix, Part II. Historical Manuscript Commission, 1897.

The Norman People and Their Existing Descendants in the British Dominions and the United States of America. London: H.S. King & Co., 1874.

"The Prayer Book of Claude de France." *The Morgan Library and Museum*, http://www.themorgan.org/exhibitions/claude.asp

Thoms, William J., ed. *Annecdotes and Traditions Illustrative of Early English History and Literature*, 1839.

Thrupp, Sylvia L. *The Merchant Class of Medieval London 1300-1500.* University of Michigan Press, 1989.

Thundy, Zacharias P. "Matheolus, Chaucer, and the Wife of Bath." In *Chaucerian Problems and Perspectives: Essays Presented to Paul E. Beichner, CSC*, 24–58. University of Notre Dame Press, 1979.

"Tour d'Anne Boleyn." *Topic Topos*, http://fr.topic-topos.com/tour-danne-boleyn-briis-sous-forges.

"Tower Green." *Historic Royal Palaces*, http://www.hrp.org.uk/TowerOfLondon/stories/towergreen

U

Urban, Sylvanus. "*The Family of Boleyn.*" The Gentleman's Magazine XXXII, no. August 1849.

W

Warnicke, Retha M. "Anne Boleyn's Childhood and Adolescence." *The Historical Journal* 28, no. No. 4 (December 1985).

Warnicke, Retha M. "Sexual Heresy at the Court of Henry VIII." *The Historical Journal* 30, no. 2 (June 1987).

Warnicke, Retha M. *The Rise and Fall of Anne Boleyn: Family Politics at the Court of Henry VIII.* Cambridge University Press, 1989.

Walpole, Horace. *A Catalogue of the Royal and Noble Authors of England: With Lists of Their Works.* London: J. Mundell & Co., 1796.

Weir, Alison. *Henry VIII: The King and His Court.* Ballantine Books, 2010.

Weir, Alison. *Mary Boleyn: The Great and Infamous Whore.* Random House, 2011.

Weir, Alison. *The Lady in the Tower: The Fall of Anne Boleyn.* Jonathan Cape, 2009.

Weir, Alison. *The Six Wives of Henry VIII.* London: Bodley Head, 1991.

Weis, Frederick Lewis, Walter Lee Sheppard, William Ryland Beall, and Kaleen E Beall. *Ancestral Roots Of Certain American Colonists Who Came To America Before 1700 Lineages from Alfred the Great Charlemagne Malcolm of Scotland Robert the Strong and Other Historical Individuals.* Genealogical Publishing Co, 2004.

Weisner, Merry E. *Women and Gender in Early Modern Europe.* Cambridge University Press, 2000.

Wellman, Kathleen. *Queens and Mistresses of Renaissance France.* Yale University Press, 2013.

Wilkinson, Josephine. *Mary Boleyn: The True Story of Henry VIII's Mistress.* Amberley, 2010.

Wilkinson, Josephine. *The Early Loves of Anne Boleyn.* Amberley, 2009.

W. L. E. Parsons, Rev. Canon. "Some Notes on the Boleyn Family." *Norfolk Archaeology or Miscellaneous Tracts Relating to the Antiquities of the County of Norfolk*, Norfolk and Norwich Archaeological Society XXV (1935): 386–407.

Wormald, Jenny. *Mary, Queen of Scots: Pride, Passion and a Kingdom Lost.* Tauris Parke Paperbacks, 2001.

Wriothesley, Charles. *A Chronicle of England During the Reigns of the Tudors, from A.D. 1485 to 1559.* 1875th ed. Camden Society

Y

Youings, Joyce A. *Sixteenth Century England.* Penguin, 1984
Younghusband, George. *The Tower from Within*, 1919.

Z

Zupanec, Sylwia. *The Daring Truth About Anne Boleyn: Cutting Through the Myth.* CreateSpace Independent Publishing, 2012.

Index

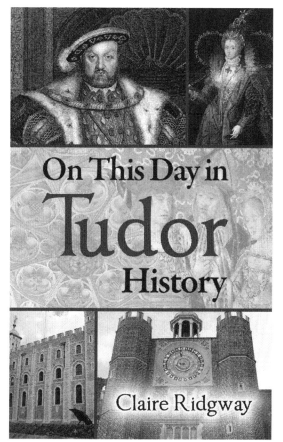

ISBN: 978-84-943721-9-3

On This Day in Tudor History gives a day-by-day look at events from the Tudor era, from 1st January to 31st December, including births, deaths, baptisms, marriages, battles, arrests, executions and more.

This must-have book for Tudor history lovers is perfect for:

- Dipping into daily over your morning coffee
- Using in the classroom
- Trivia nights and quizzes
- Finding out what happened on your birthday or special day
- Wowing friends and family with your Tudor history knowledge
- Researching the Tudor period

Written by best-selling Tudor history author Claire Ridgway, **On This Day in Tudor History** contains a wealth of information about your favourite Tudor monarchs, their subjects and the times they lived in.

Did you know: on 17th January 1569 Agnes Bowker gave birth to a cat?

An 'on this day in history' book presented in an easy-to-use diary format.

The real truth about the Tudors...

THE
ANNE BOLEYN
COLLECTION

CLAIRE RIDGWAY

ISBN: 978-84-944574-4-9

"I've been a history buff all my life, both as a reader and as a writer. I thought I knew about Anne and her Boleyn family, Henry VIII and his court, but this book fills in so many blanks for me that I will read it more than once...This is a book for the legion of Tudor fiction readers, who want to know the stories behind the myths, the truth behind the legend... Absolutely fascinating read." - **Jeane Westin, Author of His Last Letter**

"The Anne Boleyn Collection" brings together the most popular articles from top Tudor website The Anne Boleyn Files. Articles which have provoked discussion and debate. Articles that people have found fascinating.

Written in Claire's easy-going style, but with an emphasis on good history and sound research, these articles are perfect reading for Tudor history lovers everywhere.

- Should Anne Boleyn be pardoned and reburied as Queen?
- Anne Boleyn and "The Other Boleyn Girl".
- Did Anne Boleyn dig her own grave?
- The Six Wives' stereotypes - are they right?
- Did Anne Boleyn commit incest with her brother?

Discover the REAL truth about the Tudors

The real truth about the Tudors...

THE FALL OF
ANNE BOLEYN
A Countdown

CLAIRE RIDGWAY

ISBN: 978-84-94457-43-2

During the spring of 1536 in Tudor England, events conspire to bring down Anne Boleyn, the Queen of England. The coup against the Queen results in the brutal executions of six innocent people - Anne Boleyn herself, her brother, and four courtiers - and the rise of a new Queen.

Drawing on sixteenth century letters, eye witness accounts and chronicles, Claire Ridgway leads the reader through the sequence of chilling events one day at a time, telling the true story of Anne Boleyn's fall. **The Fall of Anne Boleyn: A Countdown** is presented in a diary format, allowing readers to dip in, look up a particular date, or read from start to finish. Special features include mini biographies of those involved, a timeline of events and full referencing.

- Why was Anne Boleyn executed?
- Who was responsible for Anne Boleyn's fall?
- Was Anne Boleyn's execution a foregone conclusion and was she framed?

Claire Ridgway, creator of The Anne Boleyn Files website and best-selling author of **The Anne Boleyn Collection**, continues her mission to share the real truth about Anne Boleyn.

MadeGlobal Publishing

Non-fiction History

- Tudor Places of Great Britain - **Claire Ridgway**
- On This Day in Tudor History - **Claire Ridgway**
- Illustrated Kings and Queens of England - **Claire Ridgway**
- A History of the English Monarchy - **Gareth Russell**
- Jasper Tudor - **Debra Bayani**
- The Fall of Anne Boleyn - **Claire Ridgway**
- George Boleyn: Tudor Poet, Courtier & Diplomat
  - **Ridgway & Cherry**
- The Anne Boleyn Collection - **Claire Ridgway**
- The Anne Boleyn Collection II - **Claire Ridgway**
- Two Gentleman Poets at the Court of Henry VIII
  - **Edmond Bapst**
- A Mountain Road - **Douglas Weddell Thompson**

"History in a Nutshell" Series

- Sweating Sickness in a Nutshell - **Claire Ridgway**
- Mary Boleyn in a Nutshell - **Sarah Bryson**
- Thomas Cranmer in a Nutshell - **Beth von Staats**
- Henry VIII's Health in a Nutshell - **Kyra Kramer**
- Catherine Carey in a Nutshell - **Adrienne Dillard**

Historical Fiction

- Between Two Kings: A Novel of Anne Boleyn
  - **Olivia Longueville**
- Phoenix Rising - **Hunter S. Jones**
- Cor Rotto - **Adrienne Dillard**
- The Claimant - **Simon Anderson**
- The Truth of the Line - **Melanie V. Taylor**

Please leave a review

If you enjoyed this book, *please* leave a review with the book seller where you purchased it. There is no better way to thank the author and it really does make a huge difference! *Thank you in advance.*